MONETARY GROWTH: TRENDS, IMPACTS AND POLICIES

MONETARY GROWTH: TRENDS, IMPACTS AND POLICIES

WILLIAM N. SQUIRES
AND
CHARLES P. BURDOCK
EDITORS

Nova Science Publishers, Inc.
New York

For permission to use material from this book please contact us:
Telephone 631-231-7269; Fax 631-231-8175
Web Site: http://www.novapublishers.com

Library of Congress Cataloging-in-Publication Data

Squires, William N.
Monetary growth : trends, impacts and policies / William N. Squires and Charles P. Burdock.
p. cm.
Includes index.
ISBN 978-1-60692-305-4 (hbk.)
1. Monetary policy. 2. Fiscal policy. I. Burdock, Charles P. II. Title.
HG230.3.S69 2009
339.5--dc22

2009014727

Published by Nova Science Publishers, Inc. ✦ New York

CONTENTS

PREFACE

This book presents important research in the field of monetary growth and how changes in monetary growth relate to changes in real output growth, nominal output growth and inflation.

A brief summary of monetary and fiscal policies in the European Monetary Union and empirical evidence of the interactions between monetary and fiscal policies is presented. There is also an analysis of monetary and education policies in the Uzawa-Lucas model. A study done in Korea is presented using a state-place model where expectations about the money growth rate depend on macroeconomic variables and their distributions.

Although technical analysis is used by practitioners as method of risk reduction, a theoretical and empirical discussion shows that this is not always right. Other topics in this book include the effects of inflation variability and the inflation level on the default risk of the private sector, a discussion about inflationary monetary policy as a successful tool for eliminating cumulative depressions and the possible ways monetary policy could effect economic growth process.

Chapter 1 examines the monetary policies adopted in the Euro Area, the United States and the UK by their respective Central Banks and tries to depict similarities and differences in their policy actions. In addition, the study investigates the reasons for the different monetary manoeuvres and analyses the links between the growth in monetary aggregates and inflation. The research is motivated by the recent and ongoing debates on the relevance of monetary aggregates in conducting monetary policies. Different from the monetary policy strategies adopted by the U.S. Federal Reserve and several other central banks, which do not give any particular role to monetary aggregates, the European Central Bank has preserved a central role for money in its two-pillar strategy. This chapter therefore contributes to the understanding of the importance of monetary aggregates dynamics for monetary policy choices. Finally, the relationship between inflation, monetary growth and exchange rate dynamics is briefly explored.

The European Monetary Union (EMU) creation has opened a new source of studies about interactions between monetary and fiscal policies. It has been especially interesting the study of fiscal policy influences in the credibility of European monetary policy because budget deficits could affect the achievement of the main monetary policy goal: price stability. It has also been attention-grabbing the study of fiscal policy as stabilisation means when country-specific shocks occur in this new political framework.

Central bankers consider fiscal discipline and coordination as a prerequisite for a successful monetary union. Fiscal discipline idea was included in the Delors Report (1989), the Treaty on European Union (1992) and the Stability and Growth Pact (SGP) (1997). Some fiscal limits have been imposed and, since December (1999) Helsinki Council, the Euro-area fiscal policies coordination has been increased. A part of the literature has criticized those constrains and doubt about the efficacy of fiscal policy when individual shocks could occur.

Chapter 2 presents a brief summary of monetary and fiscal policies implementation in the EMU. It also collects a survey of the literature about interactions between monetary and fiscal policies in the context of EMU. Finally, some empirical evidence of these interactions is analysed. This evidence supports the idea that European policy mix has been well performed, but some doubts have appeared in the new crisis panorama, especially on public finances sustainability.

The relationship between nominal and real macroeconomic variables is traditionally illustrated by the expectational Phillips curve. Empirically, there is evidence that short run changes in employment and output result from unanticipated changes in the stock of money and inflation. The problem is that expectations about the growth rates of money stock and prices are not observed. Previous literature estimates them using static models with a limited number of lagged variables. The possibility of omitting important factors or lags in these models is substantial. Furthermore, these models focus on mean expected growth rates and fail to explicitly account for the impact of the potential imprecision in these expectations. Chapter 3 uses a state-space model where expectations about the money growth rate depend on the long history of macroeconomic variables and their distributions. Priors about the growth rate are updated using a Kalman filter method. Historic quarterly data on the Korean economy is used to infer the one-period-ahead expected growth rates in money stock, price level and price of oil, and to estimate the relationship between the unanticipated growth in money stock and growth of national output. The study controls for the determinants of aggregate supply and demand, money stock and inflation. The results show that a one-percent shock to Korea's money stock increases national demand by 0.02%. The study also confirms validity of the expectational Phillips curve between shocks to unemployment and the unexpected inflation rate.

Traditionally different factors and variables have been considered in the economic growth models. Following Solow's model, economists considered physical capital and technology during 1950s-1980s as the main forces that promote economic growth. With the introduction of endogenous growth models, new forms of capital were introduced in the production function; human capital, public capital income distribution and more recently social capital.

The improvement of statistical information has favored the introduction of different kind of variables in the economic growth models. However, monetary policy has not been sufficiently analyzed in this literature. Except in the case of a few approaches, it is considered that monetary policy affects economic growth indirectly through other variables that directly have any influence on growth, for instnace, inflation. The main goal of Short Communication A is to show the way monetary policy could have effects on economic growth process, considering some approaches, such as Tobin, Levhari and Patinkin, Schumpeter and Kaleckian models.

As explained in Short Communication B, discount rate requests by the 12 district Federal Reserve Banks are highly reliable indicators of subsequent FOMC federal funds target rate decisions. In recent years, the correlation between the two has been approximately 90 percent. Because discount rate requests are submitted prior to FOMC meetings, monetary policy appears to flow from the district level to Washington rather than vice versa, or from the bottom up rather than top-down.

In Short Communication C, the authors analyze the effects of monetary and education policies in the Uzawa-Lucas model without externality and with a general cash-in-advance constraint. The authors present the analytical solution. In the setup with the cash-in-advance constraint on consumption purchases only, money is super neutral and the monetary policy has no effect on the behavior of the economy. When also a fraction of investment into physical capital must be bought using cash, inflation has negative growth effects in the short run, but not in the long run. The authors study in detail the transition of the economy from a high inflation equilibrium towards a low inflation equilibrium. They find that a monetary intervention produces an overshooting in the inflation rate. If the disinflation is performed via an education policy, inflation rate converges smoothly towards its new balanced growth path value. A combination of both policies enables to avoid transition and may induce a direct switch from high to low inflation balanced growth path.

Short Communication D analyzes the stability of the exchange rate with an irrational bubble. The fundamentalists pricing foreign exchange hold rational expectations. Monetary policy is affected by the bubble and in turn affects the fundamental exchange rate as well as speculation. When monetary policy experiences random changes the bubble and exchange rate are metastable. This means the bubble and exchange rate remain in one equilibrium for a long time and then abruptly break away to a new equilibrium. Large bubbles can be eliminated by a specific random policy for money growth.

Short Communication E studies the effects of inflation variability and the inflation level on the default risk of the private sector. Two alternative measures of default risk premia are used, one derived from bond market data and the other consisting of bank lending spreads. I find evidence of a robust positive effect of the inflation level on default risk. This positive impact appears to be considerably higher when default risk premia are measured on the basis of bond returns data. In contrast, the evidence about the effect of inflation variability on default risk is mixed. Inflation variability appears to raise my bank-based measure default risk when the former variable is defined as the standard error over a one-year horizon, but fails to do so when defined over a two-year horizon. Moreover, inflation variability does not seem to significantly affect default risk when the latter is defined in terms of bond-based alternative measure. Other results appear to depend on the definition of default risk used. For the bank-based measure, the default risk is found to be very persistent and rise with higher realisations of money supply growth. In the case of the bond-based measure, the default risk is particularly affected by external variables, in particular going down as a result of higher world interest rates.

While the academic world is still discussing if charting works or if it is more or less something like "Voodoo finance", the practical orientated world has been using technical analysis for decades. One argument of practitioners is that technical analysis is useful to "disciplinate" the trader and consequently is a method of risk reduction. Short Communication F discusses this argument theoretically and empirically and shows that it is not always right.

In Short Communication G the authors argue the possibility of cumulative depressions by using a monetary optimizing model. For their purpose they develop the money-in-the-utility-function approach. The authors assume the rigidity of the price level in the commodity market, and hence adopt a quantity adjustment mechanism, where the quantity of output moves infinitely fast to clear the commodity market. In addition, the authors presuppose that policy makers follow a constant growth rule for the nominal money supply.

Within the particular model, the authors show that deflationary monetary policy causes a cumulative depression, which appears as a perfect foresight equilibrium path. On this path the consumption level approaches zero eventually. Equally important, they draw attention to the result of inflationary monetary. In this case, policy makers avoid completely the emergence of deep depressions. Namely, inflationary monetary policy is a successful tool for eliminating the cumulative depressions that may arise under deflationary monetary policy.

Finally, the authors discuss the effectiveness of fiscal policy. While an independent use of fiscal policy cannot rule out the cumulative depressions, a combination of fiscal and monetary policies stimulates economic activity. In this sense, fiscal policy is effective in achieving and maintaining the efficiency of the economy.

In: Monetary Growth: Trends, Impacts and Policies
Editors: W.N. Squires et al, pp. 1-34
ISBN: 978-1-60692-305-4

Inflation is always and everywhere a monetary phenomenon (M. Friedman, 1963)

Chapter 1

MONETARY POLICY IN THE US AND THE EUROPEAN UNION: THE ROLE OF MONETARY AGGREGATES

Bernardina Algieri* and Antonio Aquino
Department of Economics and Statistics, University of Calabria, Rende, Italy

Abstract

This chapter examines the monetary policies adopted in the Euro Area, the United States and the UK by their respective Central Banks and tries to depict similarities and differences in their policy actions. In addition, the study investigates the reasons for the different monetary manoeuvres and analyses the links between the growth in monetary aggregates and inflation. The research is motivated by the recent and ongoing debates on the relevance of monetary aggregates in conducting monetary policies. Different from the monetary policy strategies adopted by the U.S. Federal Reserve and several other central banks, which do not give any particular role to monetary aggregates, the European Central Bank has preserved a central role for money in its two-pillar strategy. This chapter therefore contributes to the understanding of the importance of monetary aggregates dynamics for monetary policy choices. Finally, the relationship between inflation, monetary growth and exchange rate dynamics is briefly explored.

1. Introduction

The European Central Bank (ECB), the Bank of England (BoE) and the Federal Reserve (Fed) are pursuing very different policies on inflation fighting and they have a different philosophy concerning the use of monetary aggregates in guiding their policy interventions. Their dissimilar routes mirror both different objectives and dissimilar monetary policy views. The Fed's primary aim is to enhance economic growth, while the ECB and the BoE's targets are price stability by containing inflation at a 2% rate on annual base. The 2007 credit crunch and the fear of recession has led the Federal Reserve to adopt an expansive monetary policy by cutting interest rates by 2% in July 2008, i.e. two points below the inflation rate. This

*E-mail address: b.algieri@unical.it (Corresponding Author)

manoeuvre has not avoided the recession, which magnified in the second half of 2008 and has continued in the first half of 2009 when the FED cut the interest rate to a range of 0 to 0.25%. Conversely, the Bank of England, after a period of declining rates due to the financial turmoil and in order to match the 2% inflation target, kept stable its interest rate at 5% between April and September 2008. Later on, the institution has recognised that the country could have been trapped in a severe recession driven by tight credit and falling house prices and therefore it cut progressively the interest rates to reach a 0.5% in March 2009. The ECB, after almost a year of unchanged rates, opted first for a rise in the interest rate by 0.25 percentage points, bringing the value to 4.25% on July 3rd, 2008 and then it started to reduce the rate bringing it to 1% in May 2009. The first RCB intervention was taken to protect the Euro Area from the fear of overheating, considering that, in the first half of 2008, unemployment rates in Europe were at historically very low levels, while the very strong increase in oil and other primary material prices entailed a rise in the NAIRU (non-accelerating inflation rate of unemployment). The increase in short-term interest rates in the Euro Area was justified by the opportunity to determine an economic slowdown and a reduction in employment in order to reverse inflation expectations. The effectiveness of the ECB decision was amplified by the shrinkage in the long-term interest rates in the Euro Area, due to the positive impact of the significant anti-inflation commitment of the ECB on inflation expectations and hence on long-term interest rates.

Over the years, the former ECB President, Wim Duisenberg, and his successor Jean-Claude Trichet were criticized for putting inflation before growth. Notwithstanding slow growth in much of the Euro Area, the bank frequently declined to give in to European politicians' requests to loosen policy. This happens during a period when the US Federal Reserve, under the leadership of Alan Greenspan first and Ben Bernanke later, was distinguished for its willingness to maintain interest rates low. Two divergent critics have been addressed to the ECB. On the one hand, several US economists put forward that the ECB has an "anti-growth bias"; this would have explained why economic growth in the Euro area averaged only 2.1% per year between 1999 and 2008, against 2.6% in the US (Flanders, 2008). On the other hand, some researchers observed that the ECB monetary policy should have been more restrictive (Zingales, 2008), because at an inflation rate of 4% in 2008, the interest rate was considered to be too low. The Fed Reserve has been also strongly criticised by some observers, for its expansive policy actions. According to Anna Schwartz, this strategy would not only create inflation pressure but could have also been the main cause of the sub-prime crisis. Anna Schwartz argued that the original sin of the Bernanke-Greenspan Fed was to hold rates at 1 percent from 2003 to June 2004, long after the dotcom bubble was over (Telegraph, 2008). In her words "It is clear that monetary policy was too accommodative. Rates of 1 percent were bound to encourage all kinds of risky behaviour".

Against this background, the present chapter aims to discuss and evaluate the different policy actions adopted by the European Central Bank, the Bank of England and the Federal Reserve, to identify the reasons for their different approach in conducting monetary policy and to single out the role of monetary aggregates within their decisions. The plan of the chapter is as follows. Section 2 presents the background of the study and outlines the general principles adopted by the Central banks to conduct their monetary policy actions. Section 3 discusses the role of monetary aggregates and provides some empirical evidence for the Euro Area, the United States and the United Kingdom. Section 4 illustrates the inflation dynamics and the economic growth performances in the three economies. The interest rates, the frequency of policy actions and the links with the exchange rate are explored in section 5. Section 6 provides a brief analysis of the impact of the energy price boom on the economies and describes the possible monetary policy maneuvers to be undertaken. Section 7 offers concluding remarks.

2.1. Monetary Policy, Price Stability and Economic Growth

The primary objective of the ECB's monetary policy, as stated in the Treaty establishing the European Community, is to achieve and maintain price stability in the Euro Area, i.e. to preserve the purchasing power of the euro. In 1998, the Governing Council of the ECB defined price stability as "a year-on-year increase in the Harmonised Index of Consumer Prices* (HICP) for the Euro area of below 2%". In 2003, the Governing Council made clear that, within this definition, the ECB aims at inflation rates of below, but close to 2% over the medium term. This definition clearly highlights that both inflation and deflation are inconsistent with price stability. In the case of deflation, since nominal interest rates cannot fall below zero, a prolonged deflation may render the interest rate policy of Central Banks rather ineffective (Issing, 1999). Further, "...in the actual implementation of monetary policy decisions aimed at maintaining price stability, the Eurosystem+ should also take into account the broader economic goals of the Community. In particular, given that monetary policy can affect real activity in the shorter term, the ECB typically should avoid generating excessive fluctuations in output and employment if this is in line with the pursuit of its primary objective" (Treaty). The pursuit of the primary objective would contribute to a sustainable growth and to increase employment.

The Federal Reserve has a twofold target: stable price and economic growth (including maximum employment), but the top priority is growth.

The objective of the monetary policy adopted by the Bank of England (BoE) is "to deliver price stability—low inflation—and, subject to that, to support the Government's economic objectives including those for growth and employment". Like the ECB, price stability is defined as an inflation target of 2% based on Consumer Price Index (CPI). However, different from the ECB, the inflation target is set by the British government and could be subjected to changes. In any case, inflation below the target of 2% is considered to be just as bad as inflation above the target. The inflation target is therefore symmetrical.

If the target is missed by more than 1 percentage point on either side, that is if the annual rate of CPI inflation is more than 3% or less than 1%, the Governor of the Bank of England has to write an open letter to the Chancellor explaining the reasons why inflation has increased or fallen to such an extent and which are the solutions that the Bank proposes to ensure that inflation comes back to the target.

The BoE seeks to meet the inflation target by setting an interest rate, whose level is decided by the Monetary Policy Committee (MPC), which is made of nine members, five from the Bank of England and four external members appointed by the Chancellor. The MPC is chaired by the Governor of the Bank of England and meets monthly for a two-day meeting, usually on the Wednesday and Thursday after the first Monday of each month. Since 1998,

* The HICP, issued by EUROSTAT, is the fundamental measure for price dynamics among countries. It is based on a representative basket of consumer expenditures in the Euro Area.

+ The 13 National Central Banks in the euro area, together with the ECB, form the Eurosystem.

the BoE is independent to set interest rates, but it is accountable to parliament and the wider public of its *modus operandi* (Bank of England Act). The legislation states that the Government has the power to give instructions to the Bank on interest rates for a limited period, whether in extreme circumstances, the national interest requires it.

2.2. The Transmission Mechanism of Monetary Policy

In general, monetary policy aims to influence the overall level of monetary demand in the economy so that it grows largely in line with the economy's capacity to produce goods and services. This prevents output from rising too quickly or slowly. Interest rates are increased to tone down demand and inflation, while they are reduced to stimulate demand. If rates are set too low, this may bring an inflationary pressure; if they are set too high, demand will be lower than needed to control inflation. Monetary policy operates by influencing the price of money, namely the cost of borrowing and the income from saving. The process through which actions of the Central Bank pass on to the economy and, finally, to prices is called the "transmission mechanism". The transmission mechanism is complex and is based on the fact that monetary growth and inflation are closely related in the medium to long run (ECB, 2004 a). In the short run the central bank can influence real economic developments: a change in the short-term interest rate, in fact, starts a number of mechanisms, mainly because this change produces effects on the consumption, investment and saving decisions of households and firms and ultimately on the real economic variables such as output.

Central Banks set an interest rate at which they lend to financial institutions. This interest rate then shapes the whole range of interest rates determined by other commercial banks and financial institutions for their own savers and borrowers. Interest rates affect both the price of financial assets, such as bonds and shares and the exchange rate, which influences in turn consumer and business demand (Chart 1). In short, when Central Banks modify the official interest rate they affect the whole level of expenditure in the economy.

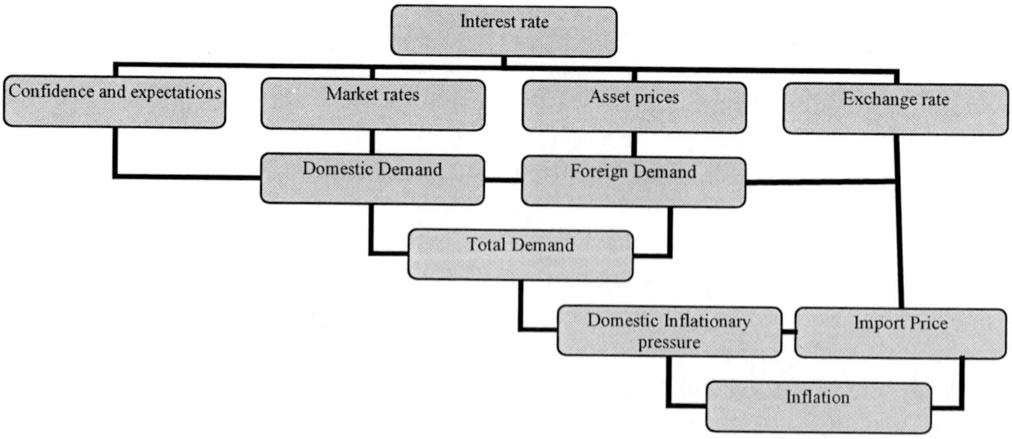

Chart 1. Transmission Mechanism.

For instance, a cut in interest rates renders borrowing more attractive and stimulates spending. Lower interest rates tend to influence households' and firms' cash-flow, i.e. the quantity of cash they have available. Specifically a drop in interest rates lessens the income from savings and the interest payments due on loans. Borrowers tend to spend more of any extra money they have than lenders, so the net result of lower interest rates through this cash-flow channel is to promote higher spending in aggregate. The reverse happens if interest rates boost (Bank of England, 2008).

The price of assets, such as shares and houses, may be influenced by lower interest rates too: increased house prices facilitate the current home owners to broaden their mortgages to finance higher consumption. Higher share prices lift up the wealth of households and this may produce increases in expenditures.

Lower interest rates may have an impact on the exchange rate. An unexpected drop in the rate of interest in the country/area relative to overseas would give investors a smaller return on the country/area assets relative to their foreign-currency equivalents, tending to make assets less attractive. That should decrease the value of the currency in that country/area, i.e. a real depreciation with the consequent increase in competitiveness of that country/ area.

All the changes in financial markets have an effect on consumer and business demand and in turn on output. Besides, adjustments in demand and output bring *in primis* changes in the labour market, affecting employment levels and wage costs, and then changes in the goods and services market through variations in producer and consumer prices.

Since the size of all the effects can vary according to the economic conditions of a given country/area, monetary policy takes quite some time before affecting price dynamics. In general, the overall effect of monetary policy will be more rapid if it is credible. According to some analyses by the Bank of England, the maximum effect on output of a credible monetary policy is estimated to take up to about one year, while the maximum impact of a change in interest rates on consumer price inflation takes up to about two years. Hence, interest rates should be set on the evaluation of future inflation and not on the current level.

In the long run, it is extensively recognized that a variation in the money supply will only be reflected in a change in the general level of prices, but it will not have any impact on real variables such as employment and output. In the ECB words "In the long run a central bank can only contribute to raising the growth potential of the economy by maintaining an environment of stable prices. It cannot enhance economic growth by expanding the money supply or keeping short-term interest rates at a level inconsistent with price stability. It can only influence the general level of prices. Ultimately, inflation is a monetary phenomenon". This general principle is known as "the long run neutrality of money" (Friedman, 1956), in this context, long run variations in real income or employment will be only due to supply-side factors, namely technology changes, population growth and institutional changes.

2.3. General Principles of the ECB Monetary Policy

According to the ECB, a monetary policy to be successful has to satisfy some principles. First, it has to firmly anchor inflation expectations. To this purpose, central banks have clearly specify their objectives, stick to a consistent and symmetric method for determine monetary policy, communicate openly their results and to be transparent. In this way, central banks become credible and credibility is a prerequisite for influencing individual expectations. Second, monetary policy has to be forward-looking, taking into account that the transmission mechanism needs some time to affect price levels, central banks need to establish which policy stance is necessary to maintain price stability in the future. Third, monetary policy has to focus on medium term in order to reduce the fluctuations that occur in the economy. This means that monetary policy cannot aim to adjust price or inflation over the short term because monetary policy affects prices with a time lag. However, in times of wage bargaining to renew labour contracts, lags become shorter, whether actual or expected expansive monetary policy strengthen the inflationist expectations of both workers and firms, and vice versa.

Finally, monetary policy has to be broadly based, in the sense that it has to consider all the relevant information regarding the economic variables and developments and not just a reduced set of indicators or a single model for the economy (Gerdesmeir et al., 2007). The ECB monetary policy strategy is based on two analytical perspectives on the determinants of price developments. These two perspectives are referred as the "two pillars". Pillar one is the economic analysis, which assesses the short to medium term crucial factors of price developments with a focus on real activity (output, demand and labour conditions, fiscal policy, balance of payment, price and cost indicators) and financial conditions (equity and asset prices, financial yields). The attention to asset prices distinguishes the ECB from the U.S. Federal Reserve.

Pillar two is the monetary analysis, which focuses on a longer-term horizon exploiting "the long- run link between money and prices". Put differently, the monetary analysis scrutinises monetary aggregates, their components and counterparts. Pillar two is mainly a mean of cross checking from a short-medium to long term horizon. Hence, monetary and liquidity considerations "allows a central bank to see beyond the traumatic impact of possible shocks". The presence of the economic and monetary analyses, which complement each others, aims at deepening the examination of price dynamics at different horizons in order to guarantee stability by adopting the most appropriate monetary actions. It appears that the ECB's monetary policy strategy is more comprehensive than pure inflation or monetary targeting strategies (Noyer, 2007).

3.1. The Role of Monetary Aggregates

Central banks define and monitor a set of monetary aggregates to a different extent. The ECB assigns a prominent role to money aggregates and money supply. Under pillar two, in fact, the ECB announces a reference value for M3 growth which, if realised on average over the medium term, should in normal circumstances indicate that policy is consistent with the achievement of price stability. Like the ECB, also the Bank of England and other central banks, such as the Bank of Japan, the Canadian, Swedish, Australian and New Zealand Central Banks, pay attention to monetary aggregates. The Bank of England, for instance, in its *Inflation Report* discusses money supply; similarly, the New Zealand, Australia Central Banks deal regularly with money and credit aggregates in their quarterly *Monetary Policy Reports*. Conversely, the Federal Reserve does not give a special status to money and has a different perspective on the usefulness of M3 as indicator of future inflation. On March 23, 2006, the Federal Reserve System ceased publication of its M3 monetary aggregate. The Federal Reserve Statistical Release states, "M3 does not appear to convey any additional information about economic activity that is not already embodied in M2 and has not played a role in the monetary policy process for many years." In any case, M2 is considered by the Fed alike to any other indicator, such as output gap, that conveys information on inflation and future economic conditions, but monetary aggregates have not a key role in defining monetary policy. In this context, Laurence Meyer, a former Fed Governor, explicitly stated that "money plays no role in today's consensus macro-model...and virtually no role in the conduct of monetary policy, at least in the US". We think however that the downgrading of monetary aggregates has gone too far and that the Fed should restore a better status for broad money. The Fed's view is completely different from the ECB, as reported by Issing, a former member of the ECB executive Board and by Trichet, the ECB President "money should never be ignored neither in monetary policy nor in research". As monetary aggregates do not have a major status, the Fed neither define a reference value for M2, like the ECB does for M3, nor conduct an analysis on the impact of money on inflation dynamics and economic activity, such as the Pillar two strategy adopted by the ECB. So while the economic analysis is common to all the Central Banks, the monetary analysis is a special feature of the European Central Bank.

3.2. The ECB Reference Value for Money Growth M3

Since, the long run relation between money and prices has an important role in defining the monetary policy of the ECB, the Governing Council has defined a reference value for the growth of the broad monetary aggregate M3, which is coherent with an inflation target (HICP for the euro area) of 2% on yearly base. The choice of M3 stems from several empirical works that have shown the stability and prediction properties of this monetary aggregate: it appears, in fact, that M3 is the best indicator of future price developments. M3 consists of currency in circulation, overnight deposits, deposits redeemable at a period of notice up to three months, deposits with an agreed maturity up to two years, debt securities with a maturity up to two years, repurchasing agreements and money market fund shares/units. M3 is the closest Euro Area aggregate to M2 in the USA. To understand how the benchmark is set, let consider the velocity money equation expressed in annual percentage variation, formally :

$$\Delta M = \Delta Y - \Delta V + \Delta P \tag{1}$$

According to the ECB forecast (The Monetary policy of ECB, 2004), the real GDP (ΔY) growth rate in the Euro system is of about 2% in the medium-long run. Moreover, the velocity of the aggregate money M3 (ΔV) decreases on average by 0.5% yearly. Formally, this means that $\Delta Y = 2$ and $\Delta V = -0.5$. Substituting these values and the inflation target in equation 1, one gets the benchmark value for M3 growth, i.e. $\Delta M = 4.5\%$. Put differently, given its forecasts on the velocity and GDP growth, the ECB considers that the value of ΔM is the annual monetary growth rate consistent with the target inflation rate. The reference value set in 1998 remains there today. If the information concerning the current and future rates of monetary growth exceeds the benchmark of 4.5%, then there is a signal of incumbent inflation and the Council can decide to adopt a restrictive monetary policy and increase the interest rates. Conversely, if the monetary growth rate is very low and under the 4.5%, then the ECB can decide to implement an expansive monetary policy and decrease interest rates. Indeed, the decisions of ECB will be influenced not only by the indications on the economic growth performances, but also by the news regarding oil prices and requests for wage adjustments and so on. For this reason, even though on some occasions the effective economic growth rate has been above the benchmark value, the ECB has not increased the interest rate. This is because monetary policy does not react mechanically to deviations of M3 growth from the reference value. Having a reference value indicates that ECB strictly monitors the long run relation between growth and inflation.

3.3. Empirical Evidence for the Euro Area

The annual growth rate of M3 remained almost stable between 1999 and 2000; it increased in 2001 and declined between 2003 and 2004. In 2004 the growth in broad money kept on surging and reached the pick of 12.0% in the fourth quarter of 2007. Since the first quarter of 2008, the annual growth rate of M3 has been progressively falling to get to 3.7% in May 2009 (Chart 2), a value far below of the reference value.

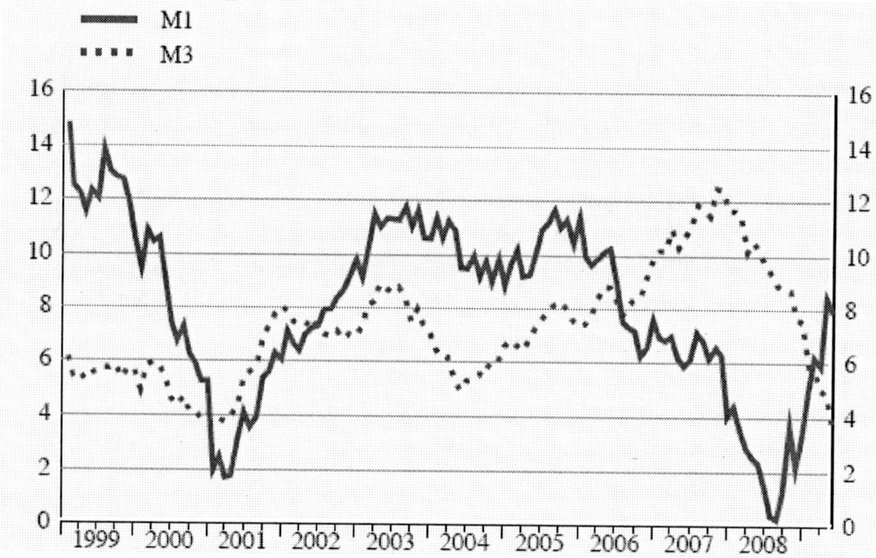

Source: ECB, 2009

Chart 2. Monetary Aggregates, annual growth rate, seasonally adjusted.

It worthwhile noticing that until 2005 the monetary aggregate M1 overstated the pace of M3, except for 2001. From early 2006 until the end of 2008, the Euro area registered a progressive reduction in the annual growth rate of M1, while it experienced a rise in 2009. The downward trend observed in the annual growth rate of M1 demonstrates that the gradual increases in ECB interest rates since late 2005, have had an impact on monetary dynamics. Nevertheless, the persistent growth of loans to the non-financial private sector made strong the underlying monetary dynamics.

Chart 3 sketches the behaviour of the main M3 components, namely M1, "other short term deposits" and "marketable instruments". In the first quarter of 2008 the annual rate of growth of M1 declined at 3.8%, down from 5.9% in the fourth quarter of 2007. The annual growth rate of M1 then weakened further to stand at 2.5% in April and 2.3% in May, levels not seen since early 2001 (ECB, Monthly Economic Bulletin, June-July 2008).

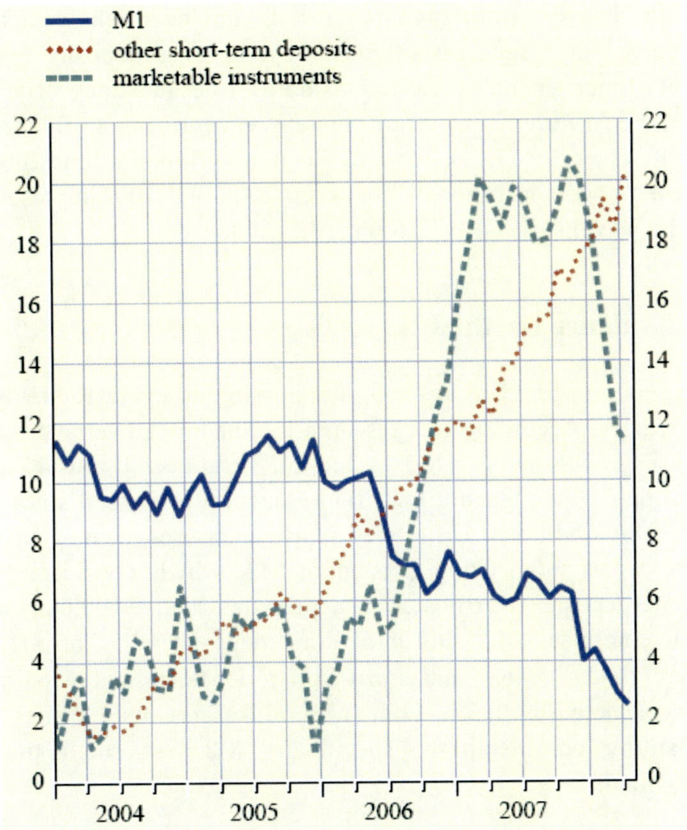

Source: ECB, 2008

Chart 3. Main Components of M3, Annual growth rate, seasonally adjusted.

The descending trend in the growth rate of M1 was mainly ascribed to the rising opportunity cost associated with holding currency and inadequately remunerated overnight deposits in a situation in which short-term interest rates went up. The annual growth rate of overnight deposits declined, de facto, from 5.5% in the last quarter of 2007 to 1.4% in April 2008.

The component "other short-term deposits" accounts for the most relevant contribution to the annual growth in M3. Since 2004, it has been registering significant increases. Its annual growth rate passed from 16.8% in the fourth quarter of 2007 to 18.5% in the first quarter of 2008 reaching 20.2% in April. The impressive growth of other short-term deposits mirrors the dynamics of short-term time deposits (specifically, deposits with an agreed maturity of up to two years), the annual growth rate of which stood at 41.7% in the first quarter of 2008, the highest quarterly growth rate since the start of Stage Three of Economic and Monetary Union (ECB, Monthly Economic Bulletin, June 2008). Short-term savings deposits (i.e. deposits redeemable at notice of up to three months) continued to decline, but did so at a reduced rate, thereby also contributing to the strengthening of growth in other short-term deposits.

The particularly strong dynamics of short-term time deposits stem from the current term structure of interest rates: their remuneration, in fact, follows closely the increases in the money market rates. Given that the increases in the interest rates on overnight and savings deposits have been considerably more moderate, the spread between the remuneration of short-term time deposits and that of other deposit categories is amplified. This leads to shifts into short-term time deposits from savings deposits and overnight deposits. Furthermore, since the yield curve stays relatively flat, short-term time deposits become also more attractive than other longer-maturity assets outside M3, because they offer greater liquidity and less risk at little cost in terms of return, thereby encouraging shifts into this instrument from longer-maturity assets too (ECB, Monthly Economic Bulletin, June 2008).

The component "market instruments" between 2006 and 2007 represented the bulk of M3 growth rate, and its value reached 11.6% in May 2008.

3.4. Empirical Evidence for the US

Albeit the Fed ceased reporting M3 in 2006, it is possible to evaluate the dynamics of some US monetary aggregates. According to a research by Shadow Government Statistics (2009), the estimated annual growth level of M3 in mid-2008 has been a plus 15% to fall to about 12% in the second half 2008 . Such a high figure has not been seen since August 1971. In Charts 4 is reported the traditional US money supply measures, namely M1, which includes cash and demand deposits (checking accounts); M2, which considers M1 plus savings accounts, small time deposits (certificates of deposit less than $100,000) and retail money funds; M3, which comprises M2 plus large time deposits (CDs of $100,000 or more), institutional money funds, repos* and Euro-Dollar deposits; and Money Zero Maturity (MZM), which is calculated by the St. Louis Federal Reserve and consists of cash accounts that have no maturity considerations, specifically M2 less small time deposits plus institutional money funds.

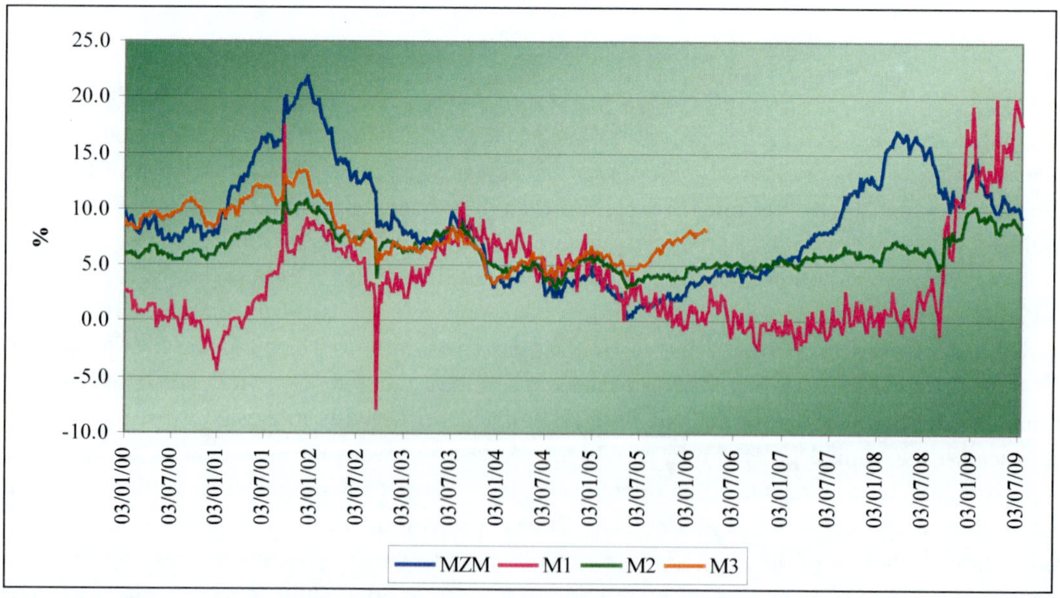

Source: Elaborations on Louis Federal Reserve

Chart 4. M1, M2, M3 and MZM. % change from year ago.

* A repo is a repurchase agreement through which the seller of securities, such as Treasury Bills, agrees to buy them back at a specified time and price.

According to some observers (Williams, 2008) the Fed stopped publishing M3 figures to avoid that upsurges in broad money growth would have add to the already rising inflation concerns and alarms. The fact that large time deposits and institutional money funds are not included in M2, renders M2 growth artificially low.

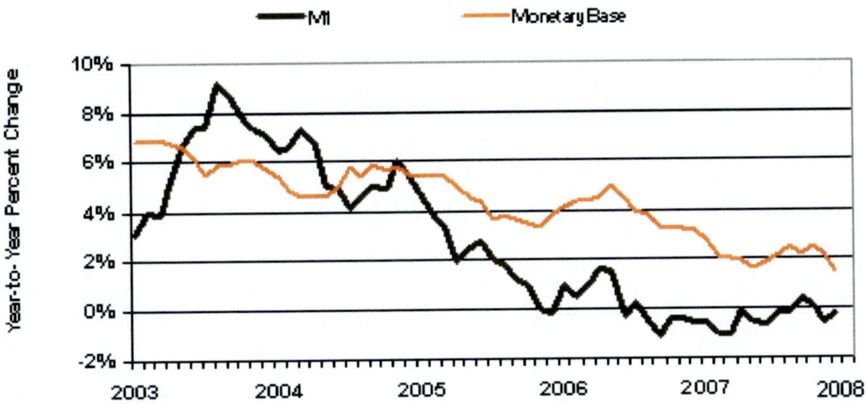

Source: Louis Federal Reserve

Chart 5. Money Supply Growth –M1 vs. Monetary Base. Monthly average year to year % change.

It is interesting noticing that while annual M3 growth stood at 15.2% in 2008, the monetary base, i.e. bank reserves plus currency, shows an annual growth of just 1.5% during the same period. There are a number of reasons explaining this. Firstly, the correlation between monthly or annual growth of the monetary base and M3 has been always very low (-14% for 1970 to 2007). A relatively high M3 growth versus low-growth monetary base, however, has been frequent to most recessions since 1970 with the exception of 1990-1991. Conversely, the monetary base has a rather strong correlation with M1 (68% for 1970 to 2007), whose values have decreased over time. Secondly, the sustained growth in M3 has been fuelled by growing foreign investments in US Treasury securities.

3.5. Empirical Evidence for the UK

The Bank of England uses two money aggregates to measure money supply: the base money (M0) and the broad money (M4), whose behaviour is reported in Chart 6. Base money includes the currency held by the public and the reserves retained by the commercial banks. M4 comprises M3 plus pension funds, treasury bills and negotiable bonds. This aggregate is called "very broad money" and it is used as a measure for fairly liquid assets. The BoE considers also another monetary aggregate, M3H, to harmonize it with the Euro Area's M3 figures. The purpose of the monetary aggregate M3H is in fact, to coordinate the meaning of broad money within the union, as BoE is part of the European System of Central Banks (Hylton, 2006).

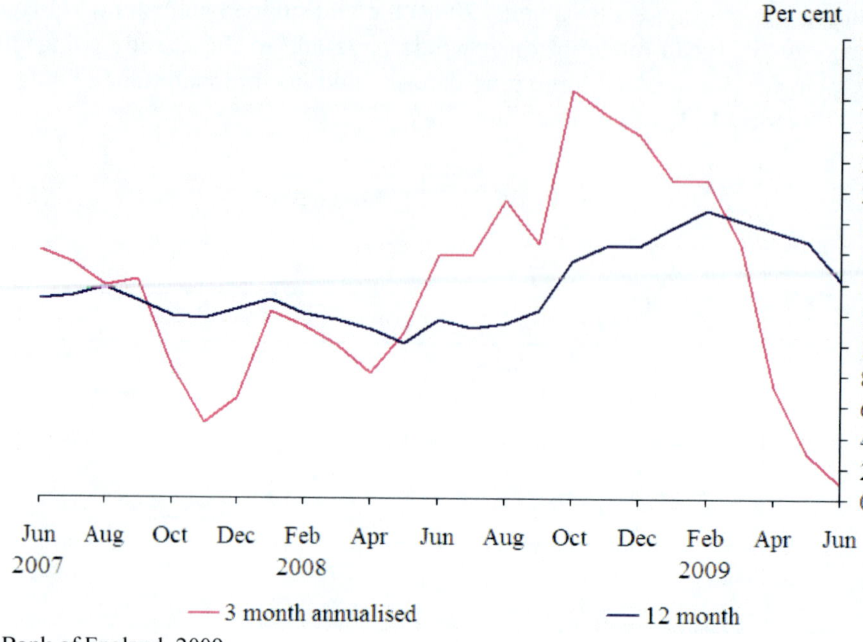

Source: Bank of England, 2009

Chart 4. Growth rate of M4. % Values.

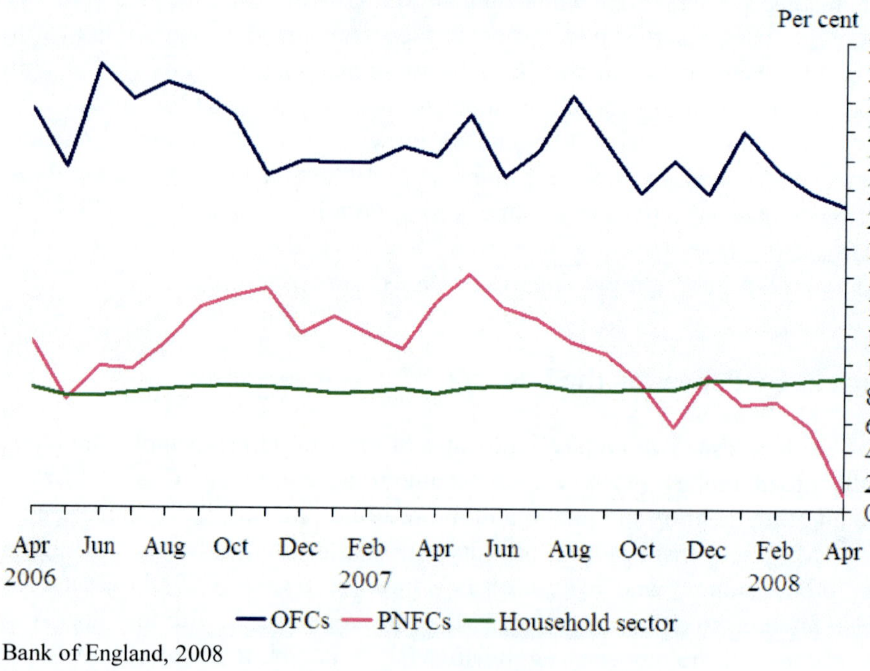

Source: Bank of England, 2008

Chart 7. Growth rate of sectoral M4. % Values.

Chart 7 sketches the dynamics of the main M4 components, namely the household sector's holdings, the Private non-financial corporations' (PNFCs) and other financial corporations' (OFCs) holdings. The annual growth rate of the household sector's holdings of

M4 has been almost stable during April 2006 and April 2008 with a value in a range of 8.0 to 9.0%. Private non-financial corporations' (PNFCs) holdings recorded their lowest values in April 2008; their annual growth rate passed from plus 15% in May 2007 to 1.0% in April 2008. Holdings of M4 by other financial corporations (OFCs) represent the major component within M4 and have been subjected to various fluctuations over time.

Chart 8 depicts the evolution of M4 and M4 less intermediate OFC deposits between 1999 and 2009. Since 2001, the two variables have been growing significantly, reaching a pick at the beginning of 2006. Their values start falling in 2008, albeit M4 growth accelerated at the end of the same year and their divide widened.

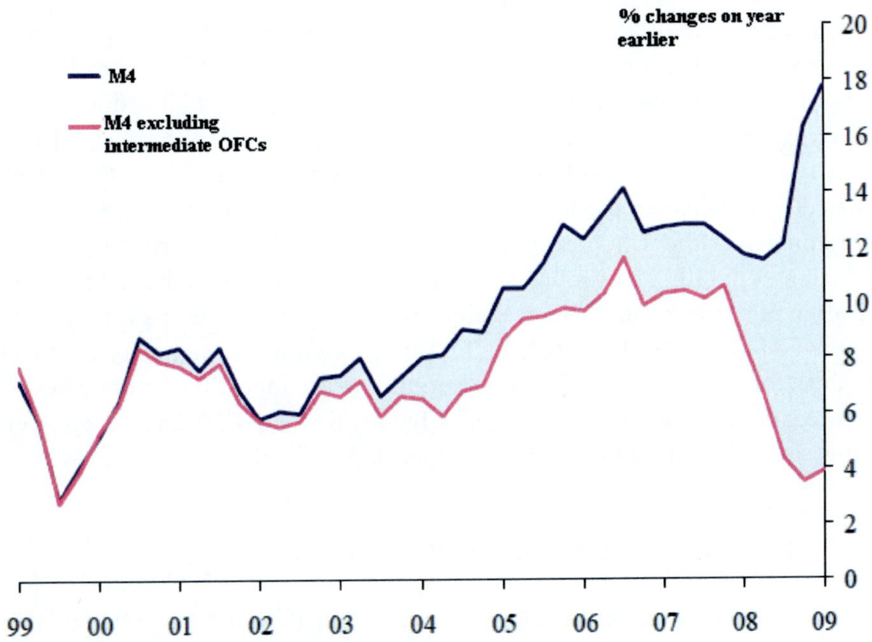

Source: Bank of England, 2009

Chart 8. Evolution of M4 between 1999 and 2009.

3.6. The Different Role of Monetary Aggregates

The different role given by the ECB and the Fed to monetary aggregates, and their different approach in conducting monetary policy can be ascribed to their divergent institutional histories and their dissimilar economic contexts and philosophies (Kahn and Benolkin, 2007). The Fed is an old institution created in 1913 which matured a line of actions according to its gained experience throughout the years. From its foundation until the 30s, money supply statistics did not exist. Between 30s and 60s, the interest in measuring money supply grew up and the Fed staff started compiling data on monetary aggregates. In the 70s and early 80s, the central bank paid a particular attention to money growth as a consequence of high inflation registered in those years. In particular, money supply had its "moment of glory" in Fed policy in 1979, when the Chairman Paul Volcker used it as mean of curbing an upsurging inflation. Mr. Volcker moved to hike dramatically interest rates in order to eradicate rampant inflation but this contributed to the recession of the early 1980s. However, the result of the Fed's tight-money policy was a far faster reduction in inflation than most economists thought feasible. From 12.5 percent in 1980, it fell to 8.9 percent in 1981, and 3.8 percent in 1982. Afterwards, money aggregates lost their status and the Fed downgraded the importance of money measures, considering them as others economic indicators. As stated by Ben Bernanke "heavy reliance on monetary aggregates as a guide to policy would seem to be unwise in the US context…the empirical relationship between money growth and variables such as inflation and nominal output growth has continued to be unstable" (Herald Tribune, 2006). Certainly, the Fed staff keeps on researching and collecting data on money supply, but these data do not represent a point of concern among policy makers. As regards the economic context, from the empirical analysis it turns out that money is a leading indicator for the prediction of future inflation in the Eurozone, while it is not so relevant for the understanding of the future price dynamics in the States. There are several studies looking at how well monetary indicators predict inflation*. The correlation between money and inflation, is indeed higher for the Euro Area than the US and also the relation between money growth and other economic variables is more stable for the Eurozone than the US. Differently from the US, money growth helps to easily forecast inflation in the EU in a simple econometric model, whilst forecast errors for money growth are often relevant for the United States. This brings the ECB to give a central role to money and the Fed to limit it. In effect, the ECB put forward that monetary aggregates are a necessary guide for everyday policy if two conditions are met. First, money supply has to be able to forecast future movements in price levels. Second, the relation between money supply, output and prices has to be stable, or at least, predicable (OECD, 2007).

4.1. Inflation Dynamics and Economic Performances

In the first half of 2008, inflation was elevated internationally. Taken as a whole, the average world inflation rate rose to 5.5% in May 2008, its maximum percentage since 1999 (The Economist, 24, May, 2008). In the Euro Area inflation rate stood at 4% in July 2008, this was the highest value since the establishment of the ECB, a similar value was experienced in 1993 (Chart 9). The strong contribution of the energy sector, mainly oil-related products (for transport and heating), was the driving factor of the rise in the Euro Area annual HICP inflation. The other main forces pushing inflation up were food prices and spiking broad money growth, as analysed in the previous paragraphs. In particular, concerning food prices, fruit, vegetable and meat prices have followed a continuous upward trend between mid-2007 and mid-2008. In the second half of 2008, the prices of most commodities fell dramatically on expectations of diminished demand in a world recession. Many economies therefore experienced deflation. The main components of HICP for the Euro Area are reported in Chart 10 and a more detailed disaggregation is presented in Table 9.

* See Masuch et al. for a review.

Table 9. Inflation Statistics for the Euro Area

	HICP - Overall index	HICP - Processed food incl. alcohol and tobacco	HICP - Goods	HICP - Industrial goods	HICP - Energy	HICP - Services	HICP - All-items excluding energy and unprocessed food
1999:1	0,8	1.2	0.3	-0.2	-4.4	1.7	1.3
1999:2	0,8	1.3	0.3	-0.3	-4.3	1.6	1.2
1999:3	1,0	1.1	0.5	0.1	-2.8	1.7	1.2
1999:4	1,1	1.1	0.8	0.6	0.3	1.6	1.2
1999:5	1,0	0.8	0.6	0.6	0.5	1.5	1
1999:6	0,9	0.7	0.6	0.8	1.5	1.5	1
1999:7	1,1	0.7	0.7	1.2	3.2	1.6	1.1
1999:8	1,2	0.7	0.9	1.5	5	1.4	1
1999:9	1,2	0.7	1.1	1.7	6.4	1.4	0.9
1999:10	1,4	0.9	1.3	1.8	6.5	1.3	0.9
1999:11	1,5	0.9	1.5	2	7.2	1.4	1
1999:12	1,7	1	1.8	2.6	10.1	1.5	1.1
2000:1	1,9	1.1	2	2.9	12.1	1.6	1.1
2000:2	1,9	1.1	2.2	3	13.5	1.4	0.9
2000:3	1,9	1	2.4	3.4	15.2	1.3	0.9
2000:4	1,7	0.9	1.8	2.4	10.1	1.6	1
2000:5	1,7	1	2.1	2.7	11.9	1.3	0.9
2000:6	2,1	1.1	2.6	3.3	14.4	1.4	0.9
2000:7	2,0	1.1	2.4	2.8	13.2	1.4	0.9
2000:8	2,0	1.2	2.4	2.7	11.6	1.4	1
2000:9	2,5	1.3	3.1	3.5	15.1	1.4	1
2000:10	2,4	1.3	2.9	3.4	14.1	1.5	1.1
2000:11	2,5	1.4	3.1	3.5	14.7	1.3	1.1
2000:12	2,5	1.5	2.7	2.8	10.7	2.2	1.5
2001:1	2,0	1.6	2	1.7	7.2	1.9	1.2
2001:2	1,9	2	1.9	1.4	7.5	2.1	1.2
2001:3	2,2	2.2	2.3	1.5	4.9	2.1	1.5
2001:4	2,7	2.5	3	2.4	7.2	2.3	1.9
2001:5	3,1	2.7	3.5	2.7	7.9	2.5	2
2001:6	2,8	3	3.1	2	4.9	2.5	2.1
2001:7	2,6	3.2	2.5	1.2	2.4	2.5	2
2001:8	2,3	3.4	2.1	0.8	1.5	2.6	1.9
2001:9	2,2	3.4	1.9	0.4	-1.7	2.7	2.1
2001:10	2,2	3.5	1.9	0.4	-3	2.8	2.4
2001:11	2,0	3.4	1.4	0	-5.3	2.9	2.4
2001:12	2,0	3.4	1.6	0.1	-4.7	2.8	2.4
2002:1	2,6	3.8	2.4	0.8	-1.9	2.9	2.6
2002:2	2,5	3.4	2.1	0.7	-2.9	3	2.6
2002:3	2,5	3.3	2	1	-1.5	3.2	2.7
2002:4	2,3	3.3	2	1.2	-0.5	2.9	2.5
2002:5	2,0	3.2	1.3	0.6	-2.8	3.3	2.6
2002:6	1,9	3.1	1	0.4	-3.6	3.2	2.6
2002:7	2,0	3	1.2	0.7	-1.6	3.2	2.5
2002:8	2,1	3	1.4	0.9	-0.3	3.3	2.5
2002:9	2,1	2.8	1.4	0.9	-0.2	3.2	2.4
2002:10	2,3	2.6	1.7	1.5	2.6	3.1	2.3

Table 9. Continued

	HICP - Overall index	HICP - Processed food incl. alcohol and tobacco	HICP - Goods	HICP - Industrial goods	HICP - Energy	HICP - Services	HICP - All-items excluding energy and unprocessed food
2002:11	2,3	2.6	1.8	1.5	2.4	3.1	2.3
2002:12	2,3	2.7	1.9	1.7	3.8	3	2.3
2003:1	2,1	2.8	1.6	1.7	6	2.8	2
2003:2	2,4	3.2	2.1	2.2	7.7	2.7	2
2003:3	2,5	3.3	2.2	2.2	7.5	2.6	2
2003:4	2,1	3.3	1.5	1.1	2.2	2.9	2.1
2003:5	1,8	3.3	1.4	0.9	0.6	2.5	2
2003:6	1,9	3.2	1.6	1	1.6	2.5	2
2003:7	1,9	3.1	1.6	1	2	2.3	1.8
2003:8	2,1	3.1	1.7	1	2.7	2.5	1.9
2003:9	2,2	3.1	1.8	1	1.6	2.5	2
2003:10	2,0	3.5	1.7	0.8	0.7	2.5	2
2003:11	2,2	4	2	1.1	2.2	2.4	2
2003:12	2,0	3.8	1.8	0.9	1.8	2.3	1.9
2004:1	1,9	3.3	1.3	0.4	-0.4	2.5	1.9
2004:2	1,6	3.2	1	0.2	-2.2	2.6	2
2004:3	1,7	4.1	1.1	0.1	-2	2.5	2.1
2004:4	2,0	3.9	1.8	1.2	2	2.5	2.1
2004:5	2,5	3.9	2.4	2.1	6.7	2.6	2.1
2004:6	2,4	3.8	2.2	2	5.9	2.6	2.2
2004:7	2,3	3.8	2.1	1.8	6	2.7	2.1
2004:8	2,3	3.6	2.1	2.1	6.5	2.7	2.2
2004:9	2,1	3.3	1.8	2	6.4	2.6	2
2004:10	2,4	2.8	2.2	2.7	9.8	2.6	2
2004:11	2,2	2.3	2	2.5	8.7	2.7	1.9
2004:12	2,4	3.2	2	2	6.9	2.7	2.1
2005:1	1,9	2.8	1.6	1.7	6.2	2.4	1.8
2005:2	2,1	2.7	1.8	1.8	7.7	2.4	1.6
2005:3	2,1	1.6	1.9	2.1	8.8	2.5	1.6
2005:4	2,1	1.7	2	2.4	10.1	2.2	1.4
2005:5	2,0	1.5	1.6	1.7	6.8	2.5	1.6
2005:6	2,1	1.5	1.8	2.2	9.4	2.2	1.4
2005:7	2,2	1.6	2.1	2.6	11.7	2.3	1.3
2005:8	2,2	1.7	2.2	2.5	11.5	2.2	1.3
2005:9	2,6	2.3	2.9	3.4	15	2.2	1.4
2005:10	2,5	2.4	2.6	2.9	12.1	2.2	1.5
2005:11	2,3	2.6	2.4	2.5	10	2.1	1.5
2005:12	2,2	1.8	2.4	2.7	11.2	2.1	1.4
2006:1	2,4	1.9	2.7	3.1	13.6	2	1.3
2006:2	2,3	1.9	2.6	3	12.5	2	1.3
2006:3	2,2	2.3	2.4	2.8	10.5	1.9	1.4
2006:4	2,5	2.2	2.6	3	11	2.2	1.6
2006:5	2,5	2.2	2.9	3.4	12.9	1.8	1.5
2006:6	2,5	2.2	2.8	3.1	11	2	1.6
2006:7	2,4	2.3	2.7	2.7	9.5	2.1	1.6
2006:8	2,3	2.2	2.5	2.4	8.1	1.9	1.5

Table 9. Continued

	HICP - Overall index	HICP - Processed food incl. alcohol and tobacco	HICP - Goods	HICP - Industrial goods	HICP - Energy	HICP - Services	HICP - All-items excluding energy and unprocessed food
2006:9	1,7	1.8	1.6	1	1.5	2	1.5
2006:10	1,6	2.3	1.3	0.5	-0.5	2.1	1.6
2006:11	1,9	2.2	1.7	1.1	2.1	2.1	1.6
2006:12	1,9	2.1	1.8	1.4	2.9	2	1.6
2007:1	1,8	2.2	1.5	0.9	0.9	2.3	1.8
2007:2	1,8	2.1	1.5	1.1	0.8	2.4	1.9
2007:3	1,9	1.9	1.7	1.4	1.8	2.4	1.9
2007:4	1,9	1.9	1.5	1	0.4	2.5	1.9
2007:5	1,9	1.9	1.4	0.9	0.3	2.6	1.9
2007:6	1,9	2	1.5	1	0.9	2.6	1.9
2007:7	1,8	1.9	1.2	0.7	0	2.6	1.9
2007:8	1,7	2.5	1.2	0.6	-0.9	2.6	2
2007:9	2,1	3.1	1.9	1.5	3	2.5	2
2007:10	2,6	3.8	2.6	2.1	5.5	2.5	2.1
2007:11	3,1	4.6	3.4	3.2	9.7	2.5	2.3
2007:12	3,1	5.1	3.4	3	9.2	2.5	2.3
2008:1	3,2	5.9	3.7	3.1	10.6	2.5	2.3
2008:2	3,3	6.5	3.8	3.1	10.4	2.4	2.4
2008:3	3,6	6.8	4.1	3.4	11.2	2.8	2.7
2008:4	3,3	7	4	3.2	10.8	2.3	2.4
2008:5	3,7	6.9	4.5	3.9	13.7	2.5	2.5
2008:6	4,0	7.0	5.0	4.5	16.1	2.6	2.5
2008:7	4,0	7,2	5,1	4,6	17,1	2,7	2,6
2008:8	3,8	6,8	4,6	4,2	14,6	2,6	2,5
2008:9	3,6	6,2	4,4	4,0	13,5	2,6	2,4
2008:10	3,2	5,1	3,5	3,1	9,6	2,6	2,2
2008:11	2,1	4,2	1,8	0,8	0,7	2,6	2,1
2008:12	1,6	3,5	0,9	-0,3	-3,7	2,4	1,8
2009:1	1,1	2,7	0,2	-1,0	-5,3	2,4	1,7
2009:2	1,2	2,0	0,3	-0,7	-4,9	1,9	1,5
2009:3	0,6	1,6	-0,4	-1,5	-8,1	2,5	1,7
2009:4	0,6	1,2	-0,7	-1,7	-8,8	2,1	1,5
2009:5	0,0	1,0	-1,4	-2,5	-11,6	1,9	1.3
2009:6	-0,1	1,1	-1,5	-2.7	-11,8	2,7	2,6

Source: ECB data Statistics, 2009

In the United Kingdom annual Consumer Prices Index inflation—the Government's target measure of inflation—rose considerably from 3% in April to 5.2% in September 2008, owing largely to food and energy prices. Afterwards, the inflation rate fell progressively to reach 1.8% in June 2009. The overall dynamics from 1996 to 2009 are reported in Chart 11. While until 2006 the BoE fulfilled its inflation target, later it faced the same problems of many other worldwide economies. In 2007, upward pressures came from housing and household services due to the increase in gas, electricity bills and heating oil prices. Further increases were registered in the recreation and culture sector. The main rising pressures hailed

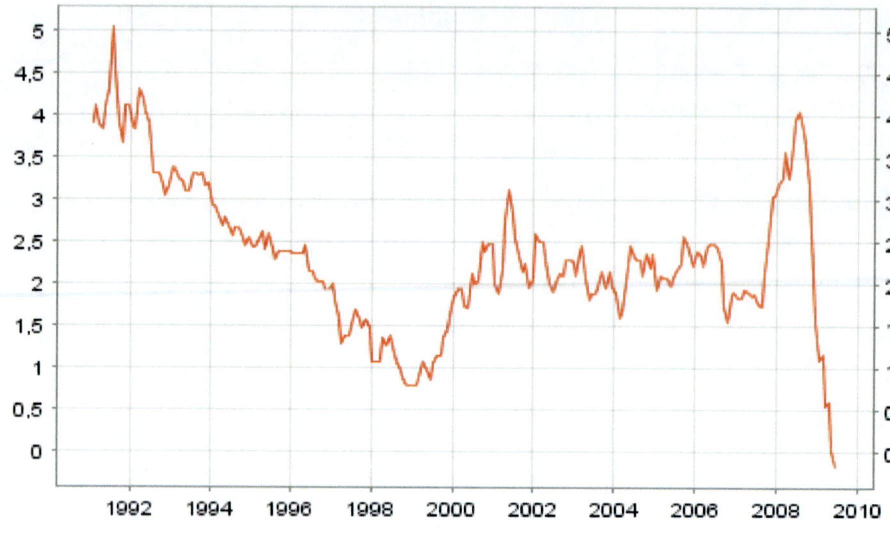

Source: ECB data Statistics, 2009

Chart 9. Evolution of HICP in the Euro Area, % change.

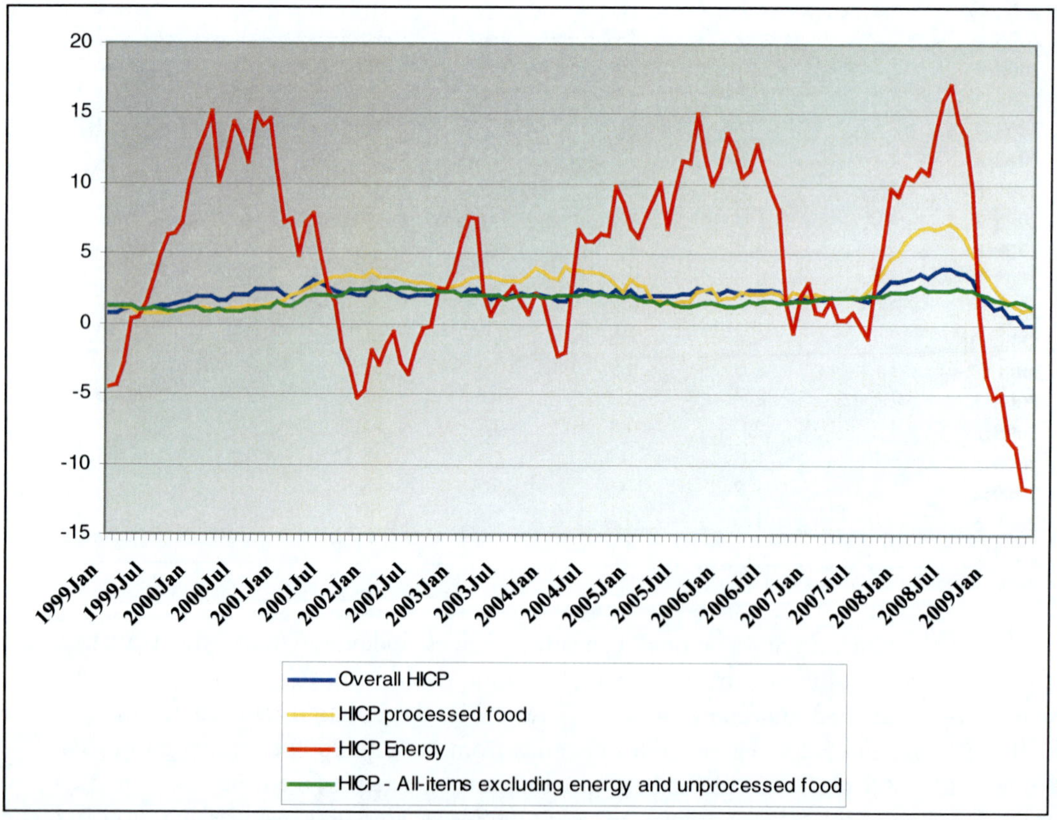

Source: Own Elaboration on ECB data Statistics, 2009

Chart 10. Euro Area Inflation rate and its main component, Annual rate of change.

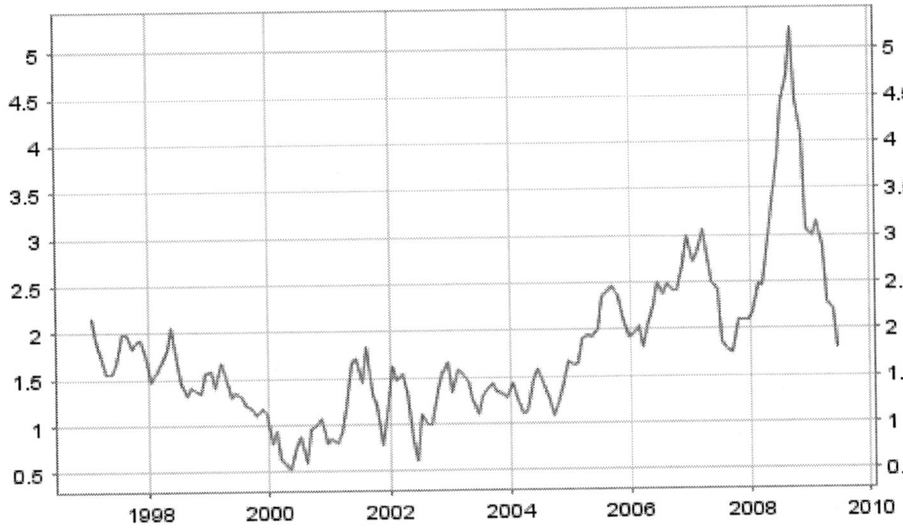

Source: ECB data Statistics, 2009

Chart 11. Evolution of consumer price index inflation in the UK (% change).

from books, newspapers and foreign holidays. In May 2008 producer prices also reached new highs, driven to a large extent by higher petroleum product and food prices. Subsequently, HICP inflation declined significantly. This was mainly the result of shrinking house prices which have been falling since the start of the financial crisis in mid-2007. Looking ahead, inflation is expected to decline further and to fall below the Bank of England's target of 2% (ECB, Economic Bulletin July 2009).

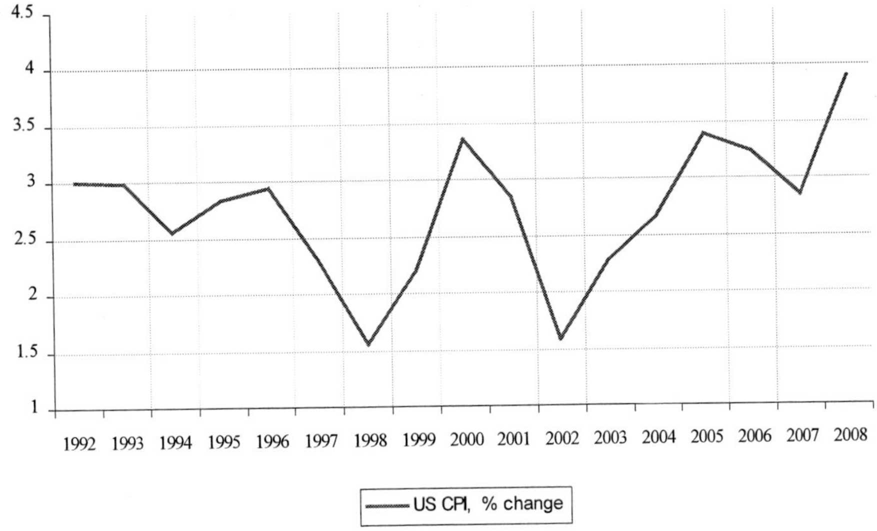

Source: Own Elaboration on OECD Statistics, 2009

Chart 12. Evolution of consumer price index inflation in the US.

In the United States, headline CPI inflation was on average 4.2% in the first half of 2008 while the inflation rate of the personal consumption expenditures (PCE) index was 3.2% during the same period. In the second half of that year, annual CPI inflation decreased substantially, falling to -0.7% in April, -1.3% in May and to -1.4 in July 2009. The decline was driven by base effects linked to energy prices and to the downturn in global economic activity.

As regards economic growth, global economic activity has been first hampered by the economic weakness in the United States, and then by the consequences of the financial crisis and its worldwide domino effects. The slowdown in economic growth has also impacted on emerging markets.

In the US, economic growth has been registering a declining trend since 2004 (Chart 13). According to Bureau of Economic Analysis (BEA), in the first quarter 2008 real GDP increased at a annualised rate of 0.9%, compared with -0.2% in the final quarter of 2007 (Table 1). Final domestic demand slowed, reflecting both a weakening in the growth rate of personal consumption expenditure and a significant decline by 24.6% in residential investment. The largest contribution to GDP growth came from net exports, which added 0.8 percentage point. In 2009, economic activity remained subdued. Specifically, real GDP contracted by 5.5% in annualised terms in the first quarter of 2009, after 6.3% in the preceding quarter. Exports, inventories and private fixed investment continued to be a haul on the economy, which was only moderately counterbalanced by lower imports and relatively vigorous consumer spending.

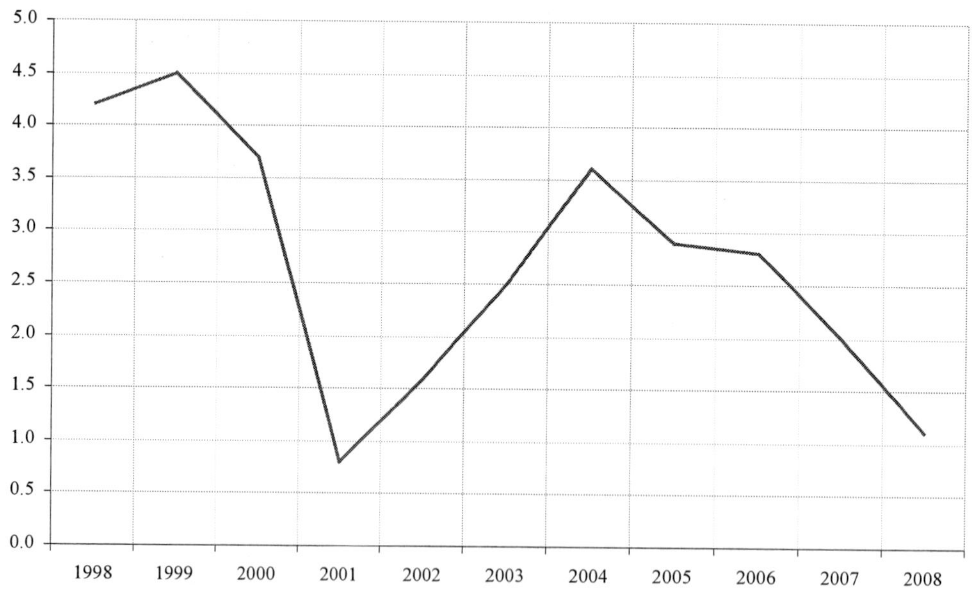

Source: Own Elaboration on BEA Statistics, 2009

Chart 13. Evolution of GDP growth in the US, % change from preceding period based on chained 2000 dollars.

Table 1. Real GDP variations in the US. Percentage values

1999q1	1999q2	1999q3	1999q4	2000q1	2000q2	2000q3	2000q4	2001q1	2001q2	2001q3	2001q4	2002q1
3.4	3.4	4.8	7.3	1.0	6.4	-0.5	2.1	-0.5	1.2	-1.4	1.6	2.7
2002q2	**2002q3**	**2002q4**	**2003q1**	**2003q2**	**2003q3**	**2003q4**	**2004q1**	**2004q2**	**2004q3**	**2004q4**	**2005q1**	**2005q2**
2.2	2.4	0.2	1.2	3.5	7.5	2.7	3.0	3.5	3.6	2.5	3.0	2.6
2005q3	**2005q4**	**2006q1**	**2006q2**	**2006q3**	**2006q4**	**2007q1**	**2007q2**	**2007q3**	**2007q4**	**2008q1**	**2008q2**	**2008q3**
3.8	1.3	4.8	2.7	0.8	1.5	0.1	4.8	4.8	-0.2	0.9	2.8	-0.5
2008q4	**2009q1**											
-6.3	-5.5											

Source: BEA Statistics, 2009

The outlook for the Euro Area economy is presented in Table 2 and Chart 14. GDP growth rate averaged 3.7% between 1998 and 2000. From a pick of plus 4.61% in 2000, GDP growth decelerated to 0.48% in the second quarter of 2003 to improve again in 2006, when it expanded by 3.26% in the second quarter 2006, and to loose pace at the end of 2007 and throughout 2008. In the last quarter of 2008 and in 2009 the Euro Area entered into recession.

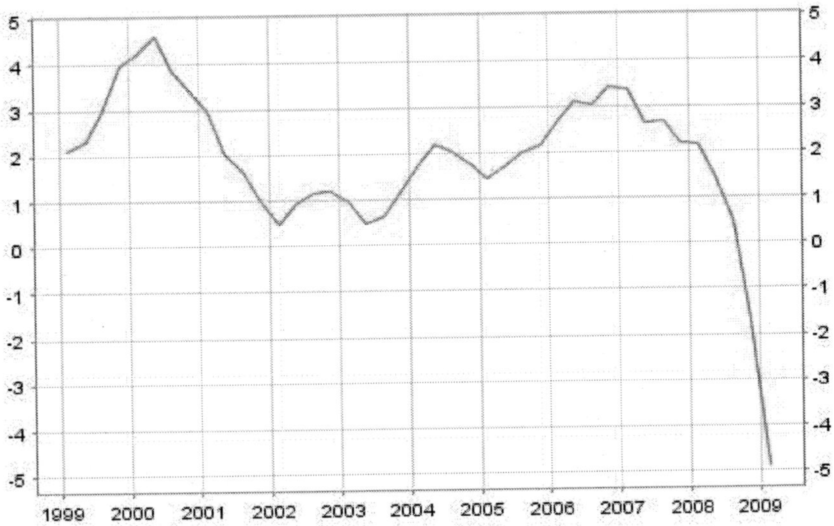

Source: Own Elaboration on ECB Statistics, 2009

Chart 14. Evolution of GDP growth in the Euro Area. GDP in previous year's prices (% change).

Table 2. Real GDP variations in the Euro Area. Percentage values

1998q4	1999q1	1999q2	1999q3	1999q4	2000q1	2000q2	2000q3	2000q4	2001q1	2001q2
1.84	2.09	2.27	2.97	4.02	4.24	4.61	3.85	3.38	2.98	2.06
2001q3	**2001q4**	**2002q1**	**2002q2**	**2002q3**	**2002q4**	**2003q1**	**2003q2**	**2003q3**	**2003q4**	**2004q1**
1.64	1.00	0.51	0.,88	1.17	1.12	0.93	0.48	0.65	1.17	1.66
2004q2	**2004q3**	**2004q4**	**2005q1**	**2005q2**	**2005q3**	**2005q4**	**2006q1**	**2006q2**	**2006q3**	**2006q4**
2.10	1.94	1.69	1.45	1.63	1.93	2.08	2.60	2.99	2.90	3.26
2007q1	**2007q2**	**2007q3**	**2007q4**	**2008q1**	**2008q2**	**2008q3**	**2008q4**	**2009q1**		
3.25	2.58	2.67	2.18	2.16	1.47	0.49	-1.68	-4.85		

Source: ECB Statistical Data Warehouse, 2009

In the United Kingdom after 16 years of increasing GDP growth, the economy registered a halt. Business and economic surveys (The Economist, July 5th 2008) have signalled bad news: there is a sinking economy characterised by low consumer confidence and stagnating living standards. Furthermore, an economy that relies heavily—as the UK's did—on finance has been manifestly exposed to an extended banking crisis. The time in which GDP growth was triggered by a strong financial sector is over. Quarterly real GDP growth contracted by 2.4% in the first quarter 2009.

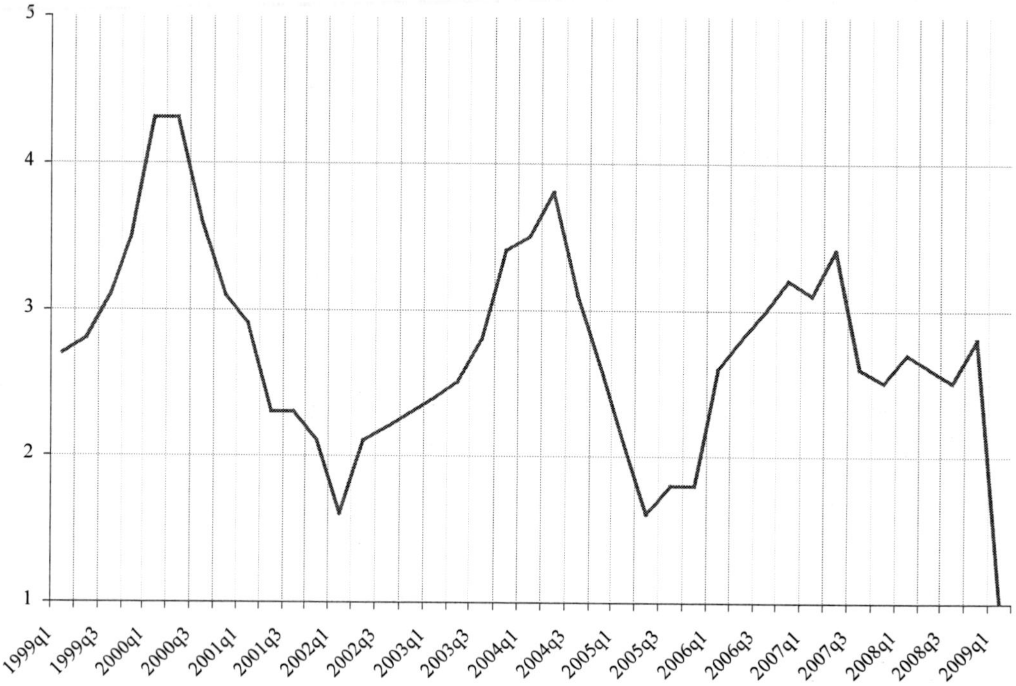

Source: Own Elaboration on Office for National Statistics, UK, 2009

Chart 15. Real GDP in UK, quarter on same quarter of previous year.

Table 3. Real GDP variation in UK. Percentage values

1999q1	1999q2	1999q3	1999q4	2000q1	2000q2	2000q3	2000q4	2001q1	2001q2	2001q3	2001q4	2002q1	2002q2
2.7	2.8	3.1	3.5	4.3	4.3	3.6	3.1	2.9	2.3	2.3	2.1	1.6	2.1
2002q3	**2002q4**	**2003q1**	**2003q2**	**2003q3**	**2003q4**	**2004q1**	**2004q2**	**2004q3**	**2004q4**	**2005q1**	**2005q2**	**2005q3**	**2005q4**
2.2	2.3	2.4	2.5	2.8	3.4	3.5	3.8	3.1	2.6	2.1	1.6	1.8	1.8
2006q1	**2006q2**	**2006q3**	**2006q4**	**2007q1**	**2007q2**	**2007q3**	**2007q4**	**2008q1**	**2008q2**	**2008q3**	**2008q4**	**2009q1**	
0.9	0.7	0.7	0.9	0.7	0.6	0.5	0.5	0.8	-0.1	-0.7	-1.8	-2.4	

As regards unemployment rates, the Euro area started with an average rate of above 10% in 1998 to finish with a value of about 7% in 2008 and of 9.5% in May 2009. For the United States, the unemployment rate for June 2009 was 9.5%, 0.1 percentage point higher than the previous month and 3.9 percentage points higher than a year earlier. The UK, after keeping an almost stable unemployment rate of about 5% over time, registered a rate of 7.2% in March 2009, 0.1 percentage point higher than the previous month and 2.0 percentage points higher than in March 2008. The deep financial crisis is having thus a negative effect on the labour market on global basis. Chart 16 shows the dynamics of the unemployment rate for the three economies.

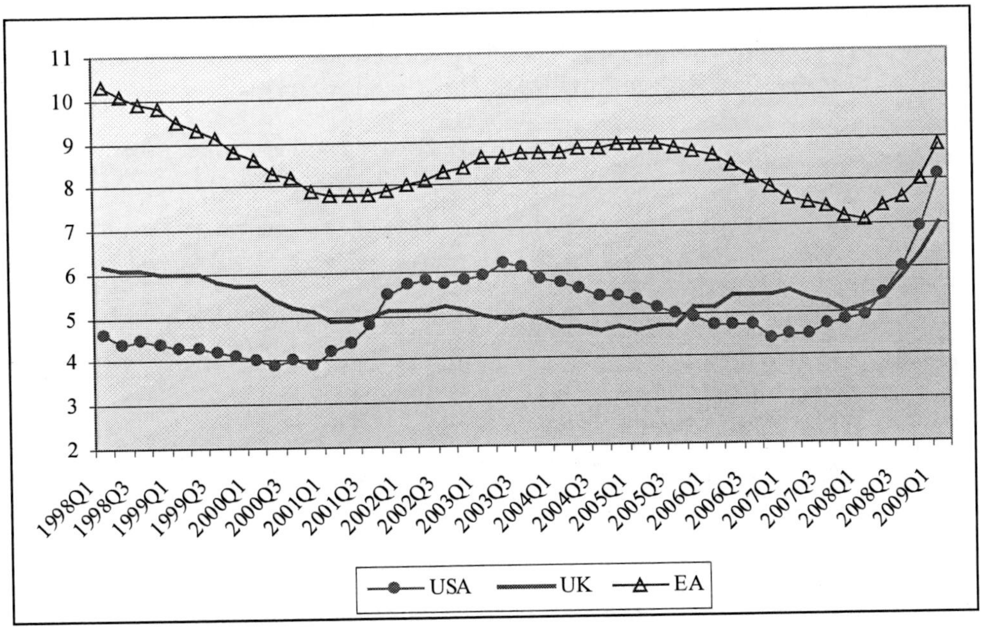

Source: Own Elaboration on OECD, Main Economic Indicators, 2009

Chart 16. Standardised unemployment rate, % Values.

5.1. Interest Rate and the Frequency of Policy Action

Chart 17 shows the nominal interest rate dynamics (all short-term funding rates) as managed by the ECB (Main Refinancing Operations), the Fed (Federal Fund rate) and BoE (Official Bank Rate). In table 10 are reported the interest rates for long-term government bonds denominated in national currencies for the EU Member States.

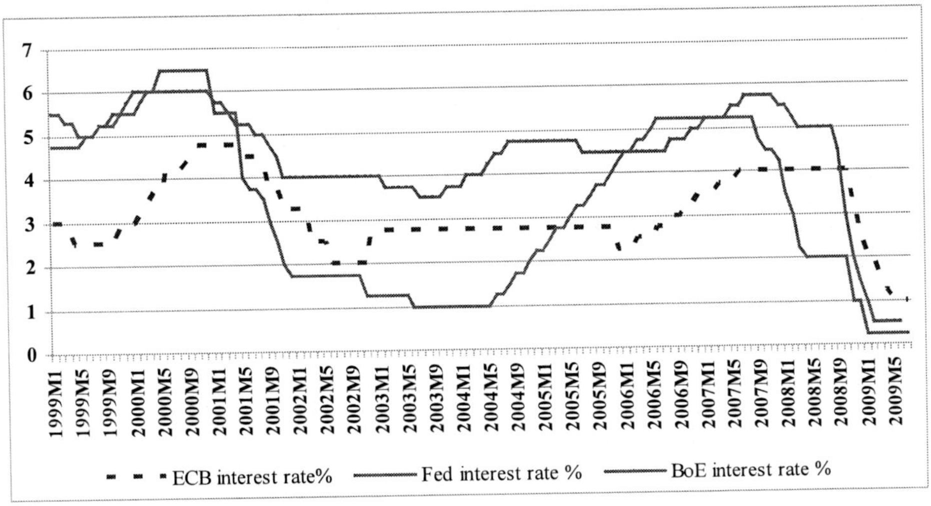

Source: Own Elaboration on ECB, Fed and BoE data.

Chart 17. ECB, Fed and BoE Interest rates % value.

Table 10. Harmonised long-term interest rates (percentages per annum; period averages; secondary market yields of government bonds with maturities of close to ten years)

Countries	June 07	July 07	Aug. 07	Sep. 07	Oct. 07	Nov. 07	Dec. 07	Jan. 08	Feb. 08	Mar. 08	Apr. 08	May 08	June 08
						Euro area							
Belgium	4.64	4.62	4.44	4.39	4.42	4.28	4.41	4.25	4.23	4.23	4.37	4.51	4.84
Germany	4.56	4.5	4.3	4.22	4.28	4.09	4.21	4.03	3.95	3.8	4.04	4.2	4.52
Ireland	4.62	4.59	4.4	4.32	4.39	4.31	4.45	4.25	4.21	4.17	4.44	4.58	4.91
Greece	4.8	4.79	4.62	4.56	4.58	4.43	4.53	4.4	4.36	4.42	4.54	4.74	5.17
Spain	4.62	4.6	4.4	4.36	4.38	4.25	4.35	4.18	4.15	4.12	4.32	4.43	4.79
France	4.62	4.58	4.39	4.36	4.4	4.23	4.35	4.15	4.08	4.02	4.27	4.41	4.73
Italy	4.77	4.76	4.58	4.57	4.59	4.45	4.54	4.4	4.35	4.38	4.53	4.7	5.11
Cyprus (1)	4.44	4.44	4.44	4.45	4.6	4.6	4.6	4.6	4.6	4.6	4.6	4.6	4.6
Luxembourg (2)	4.85	4.84	4.68	4.64	4.63	4.56	4.68	4.47	4.42	4.37	4.55	4.67	4.98
Malta	5.12	5.18	4.94	4.85	4.92	4.72	4.81	4.63	4.6	4.49	4.77	4.91	5.26
Netherlands	4.61	4.57	4.38	4.34	4.38	4.21	4.34	4.13	4.05	3.97	4.21	4.35	4.73
Austria	4.62	4.58	4.39	4.33	4.43	4.21	4.34	4.16	4.08	3.99	4.22	4.38	4.74
Portugal	4.75	4.73	4.56	4.5	4.52	4.36	4.47	4.31	4.27	4.36	4.52	4.63	4.96
Slovenia	4.79	4.72	4.82	4.69	4.59	4.4	4.55	4.39	4.32	4.33	4.47	4.61	4.95
Finland	4.62	4.59	4.39	4.34	4.38	4.22	4.34	4.14	4.06	4	4.22	4.47	4.78

Sources: ECB and European Commission.

(1) For Cyprus, primary market yields are reported. The same applies to Slovenia up to October 2003.

(3) Due to the fact that the Luxembourg Government does not have outstanding long-term debt securities with a residual maturity of close to ten years, the indicator is based on a basket of long-term bonds. This basket has an average residual maturity of close to ten years. The bonds are issued by a private credit institution and the indicator is thus not fully harmonised.

As regards the frequency of the policy actions, the Eurosystem has changed its policy rate (the interest rate on the main refinancing operations, MRO) 32 times since the adoption of the Euro in 1999 (MRO is at 1% in July 2009). Explicitly, there were 15 cuts and 17 spikes. This means that on average the ECB changes interest rate every 4 months, and this value is near to the average frequency of interest rate changes recorded by the other central banks of industrialized countries (i.e. 5 months, value highlighted by Clerc and Yeats, 1999 and Noyer, 2007).

Conversely, the BoE and the Fed during the same period show a higher frequency of policy actions, the interest rate was changed 36 and 45 times respectively, meaning an average change each 3.6 months for the BoE and 2.9 months for the Fed. Within the 36 time changes by BoE, there were 15 hikes and 21 drops, within the 45 time changes by the Fed, there were 23 increases and 22 drops of the interest rate (Fed, 21 July, 2009). Particularly, the Fed targets the level for the federal funds rate, i.e. the interest rate at which depository institutions lend balances at the Federal Reserve to other depository institutions overnight. The federal funds rate, in turn, affects monetary and financial conditions, which ultimately influence employment, output, and the overall level of prices (Fed, 2008).

To have a more comprehensive picture on the type of policy maneuvers, we have calculated the standard deviation of interest rate throughout the same time horizon. From table 5, it can be noticed that the US policy actions have been more active (s.d. 1.93) than those adopted by the Euro Area (s.d. 0.85) and UK (s.d. 1.21).

Table 4. ECB Interest rate on the main refinancing operations. % Values

04/01/1999	22/01/1999	09/04/1999	05/11/1999	04/02/2000	17/03/2000	28/04/2000	09/06/2000	01/09/2000
3	3	2.5	3	3.25	3.5	3.75	4.25	4.5
06/10/2000	**11/05/2001**	**31/08/2001**	**18/09/2001**	**09/11/2001**	**07/03/2002**	**06/06/2002**	**06/12/2002**	**06/12/2005**
4.75	4.5	4.25	3.75	3.25	2.5	2	2.75	2.25
08/03/2006	**15/06/2006**	**09/08/2006**	**11/10/2006**	**13/12/2006**	**14/03/2007**	**13/06/2007**	**09/07/2008**	**15/10/2008**
2.5	2.75	3	3.25	3.5	3.75	4	4.25	3.75
12/11/2008	**10/12/2008**	**21/01/2009**	**11/03/2009**	**08/04/2009**	**11/05/2009**			
3.25	2.5	2	1.5	1.25	1			

***Note**: On 8 June 2000 the ECB announced that, starting from the operation to be settled on 28 June 2000, the main refinancing operations of the Eurosystem would be conducted as variable rate tenders. The minimum bid rate refers to the minimum interest rate at which counterparties may place their bids. Before June 28, 2000 the main refinancing operations of the Eurosystem was conducted as fixed rate tenders. On October, 9th 2008 the ECB announced that the main refinancing operations of the Eurosystem is again conducted as fixed rate tenders.

Source: ECB, 2009

Table 5. Standard Deviation (s.d.) of interest rate

EA	US	UK
0.847	1.935	1.209

Source: Own Elaboration on ECB, Fed and BoE data.

Table 6. Fed Interest rate, Federal Fund rates. % Values

30/06/1999	24/08/1999	16/11/1999	01/02/2000	21/03/2000	16/05/2000	03/01/2001	31/01/2001	20/03/2001
5	5.25	5.5	5.75	6	6.5	6	5.5	5
18/04/2001	**15/05/2001**	**27/06/2001**	**21/08/2001**	**17/09/2001**	**02/10/2001**	**06/11/2001**	**11/12/2001**	**06/11/2002**
4.5	4	3.75	3.5	3	2.5	2	1.75	1.25
25/06/2003	**30/06/2004**	**10/08/2004**	**21/09/2004**	**10/11/2004**	**14/12/2004**	**02/02/2005**	**22/03/2005**	**03/05/2005**
1	1.25	1.5	1.75	2	2.25	2.5	2.75	3
30/06/2005	**09/08/2005**	**20/09/2005**	**01/11/2005**	**13/12/2005**	**31/01/2006**	**28/03/2006**	**10/05/2006**	**29/06/2006**
3.25	3.5	3.75	4	4.25	4.5	4.75	5	5.25
18/09/2007	**31/10/2007**	**11/12/2007**	**22/01/2008**	**30/01/2008**	**18/03/2008**	**30/04/2008**	**30/10/2008**	**01/01/2009**
4.75	4.5	4.25	3.5	3	2.25	2	1.00	0.25

Source: FED, 2009

Normally, the amplitude of policy changes depends on the state of the economy, and the monetarist or Keynesian approach adopted by the banks. This means that according to a Keynesian view, monetary policies have to be very dynamic and require quickly and frequently changes in interest rates and money growth in order to mitigate the cycle fluctuations of the real economy. In a monetarist perspective instead, monetary policies should be more silent, because when they are too much active they can be the cause of fluctuations in the economies. The ECB shares more a monetarist view, while the Fed is more Keynesian driven. In any case, some economists argue that the more gradual policy adopted by the ECB could be due to the less pronounced cycle's fluctuations compared to the United States. In this perspective, since the Euro Area shows an higher degree of price stickiness in labour markets, a more gradual monetary approach would be recommended instead of a "cold turkey" policy.

The highest interest rate in the US was recorded in May 2000 (6.5%), the lowest values were registered first in June 2003 (1%) when, after the 2001 recession, Greenspan kept cutting interest rates for more than two years to avoid deflation, and later on in January 2009 (0.25%) with the financial crash and the recession. The maximum interest rate value in the Euro Area was set in October 2000 (4.75%) the minimum in May 2009 (1%), while the top interest rate in the UK was fixed in February 1999 and February 2000 (6%), the lowest in March 2009 (0.50%).

Table 7. BoE Interest rate. % Values.

07/01/1999	04/02/1999	08/04/1999	10/06/1999	08/09/1999	04/11/1999	13/01/2000	10/02/2000	08/02/2001
6.00	5.50	5.30	5.00	5.25	5.50	5.75	6.00	5.75
05/04/2001	**02/08/2001**	**18/09/2001**	**04/10/2001**	**07/11/2001**	**06/02/2003**	**10/07/2003**	**06/11/2003**	**05/02/2004**
5.50	5.00	4.75	4.50	4.00	3.75	3.50	3.75	4.00
06/05/2004	**10/06/2004**	**05/08/2004**	**07/07/2005**	**03/08/2006**	**09/11/2006**	**11/01/2007**	**10/05/2007**	**05/07/2007**
4.25	4.50	4.75	4.50	4.75	5.00	5.25	5.50	5.75
06/12/2007	**07/02/2008**	**10/04/2008**	**08/10/2008**	**06/11/2008**	**04/12/2008**	**08/01/2009**	**05/02/2009**	**05/03/2009**
5.50	5.25	5.00	4.50	3.00	2.00	1.50	1.00	0.50

Source: BoE, 2009

5.2. The Financial Crisis and Monetary Policies

The financial crisis which started in 2007 and blew up in September 2008 has entailed some dramatic changes in the conduit of central banks' monetary policies. Traditionally central banks concentrated on controlling mainly a single tool, interest rates, in order to pursue a single goal, price stability. The financial crisis has caused so a strong decrease in aggregate demand of good and services, and a world deflationary bias, which, according to some estimates, on the basis of the Taylor rule official interest rates, should have been in the first half of 2009 about -6%. In order to counteract such a deflationary bias the US Federal Reserve, the European Central Bank and the Bank of England, after having diminished official interest rates in the range from zero to 1 per cent, have adopted various forms of unorthodox monetary policies, mainly in the form of "quantitative easing". While usually Central Banks give credits only to banks at very near terms (about one or two weeks), in 2009 they have extended credits to banks for as long as one year. They have also sometimes given credit to operators other than banks, buying some types of assets directly in financial markets. The Fed has even bought up government bonds with newly printed money.

In March 2009 the Fed decided to buy $ 300 billion in Treasury bill, 200 $ billion in bond issued by Fannie Mae and Freddie Mac, the America's two housing-finance giants, and $ 1,25 trillion of their mortgage based securities. The purchases were meant to drive down long-term interest rates, and at first they did. Ten-year Treasury yields fell from 3% to 2.5%; they however increased to 3.5% in June 2008, perhaps because of higher inflation expectations. Inflation-protected bonds implied in June 2009 inflation expectations of 2%, up from close to zero in June 2008. The Fed has financed its assets purchases by creating new reserves for the banking system, which is like printing money. Reserves rocketed to almost $900 billion in

June 2009, up from an average of $ 11 billion in the year to September 2008[1]. Many analysts see these excess reserves as a pool of inflationary fuel. The Fed, however, is convinced that it will be able to absorb excess reserves as soon as the inflation risk materializes; even more so, since it has received authority to pay interest on reserves as other central banks have long been able to do.

In March 2009 the Bank of England lowered the base rate to 0.5%, reaching what is supposed to be the limit of the usual way of stimulating aggregate demand by monetary policy. Since this was not sufficient, the Bank decided an injection of newly created money into the economy by buying assets. Similar unorthodox monetary policies were decided by the US Federal Reserve and the European Central Bank. These kinds of monetary policies are controversial, since they recollect the sort of policies typical of inflation-ridden states, as Argentina frequently was during the 20th century. In this crisis, however, these policies seem to be justified by the fact that, owing perhaps to a malfunctioning credit system, even very low official rates are not sufficient to revive aggregate demand, and, at least for the moment, the main worry is deflation rather than inflation[2]. In particular, the Bank of England decided to buy £ 125 billion of assets, mainly gilt-edged government bonds, paid by central bank money.

Even at the height of the financial crisis the European Central Bank has maintained its refinancing rate at a minimum level of 1 per cent, somewhat higher than the other most important central banks, some of which reduced official rates close to zero. However, the level of market rates seems to suggest that overall monetary-policy stance in the euro area is as loose as anywhere else. In October 2008 the ECB decided that it would offer banks as much cash as they wanted, at the refinancing rate, against a wider range of securities than usual, for up to six months. In May 2009 the ECB decided to extend the offer of fixed-rate cash to one year; at the first 12-month refinancing operation in June 2009 the euro-zone banks borrowed euro 442 billion. With so much cash splashing around, overnight interest rates in the euro zone (EONIA) have fallen to 0,3 per cent on an annual basis, about the same as in the USA. Before the crisis the ECB aimed to keep overnight interest rates close to the refinancing rate; since it moved to unlimited fixed-rate funding, the ECB has allowed the overnight rate to drift much lower than the policy rate, in an interval between the refinancing rate and the rate the ECB pays on banks' deposits with it (0.25% in July 2009). The ECB has not done more to ease credit conditions by buying government and corporate bonds, as the bank of England and the Fed have done. The decision of July 2009 to purchase euro 60 billion of the safest bank bonds is quite modest in comparison with analogous decisions by the Fed and the Bank of England. The ECB focus on banks depends on the fact that in the euro-zone business and homebuyers rely more on banks than capital markets for credit. In a sense, the measure of "quantitative easing" implemented by the ECB can be also seen as a monetisation of public debt at a remove, since banks, flush with central-bank money, are keen buyers of public debt.

---

[1] At the end of July 2009 reserves stood at $780 billion, compared with a typical level of around $ 10 billion before the crisis.

[2] One the first experiments of such a sort of "quantitative easing" was made in Japan in the first years of this century. The Bank of Japan bought with central bank money assets for a value corresponding to 7% of GDP over a three years period, while the Bank of England intervention was about 9 per cent of GDP in less than 6 months.

5.3. Interest Rate and Exchange Rate

Capital Economics' Jessop has noted that two of the strongest currencies are in countries whose central banks have kept rates low: Japan and Switzerland. Conversely, *The Economist* showed (Chart 18) that, "countries whose currencies have gained most [against the dollar] are high interest-rate economies, such as Turkey, Brazil and New Zealand, commodity producers, such as Canada, or a mixture of both, such as Australia" (The Economist August, 9th 2007). Central-bank interest rates are 16.75% in Turkey, 11.25% in Brazil, 8.25% in New Zealand, 6.75% in Australia and 5.00% in the U.K.

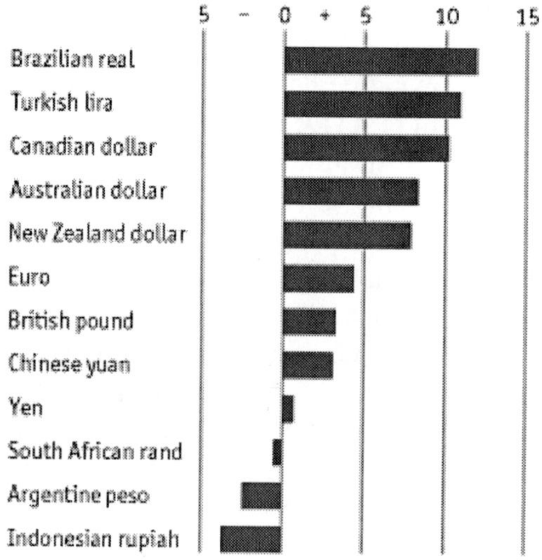

Source: The Economist, 2007

Chart 18. Exchange rate against the dollar. % Change December 29th, 2006- August 7th, 2007.

High interest rates may contribute to the appreciation of a given currency for a while by attracting money from abroad. But extraordinary interest rates, such those in Turkey and Brazil, are usually a symptom of inflation-prone monetary policies.

Currencies of commodity exporters likewise fall or rise when commodity prices plunge or boost independently from the interest rate dynamics. For instance, when the price of oil chopped down in early 1986, late 1998 and 2001, the Canadian dollar recorded a significant depreciation, even though central-bank interest rates were higher in Canada than in the U.S.

That gap between U.S. and Euro interest rates widened in 2005 and early 2006 (tables 4 and 6). Predictably, the Euro declined to 1.195 per dollar from November 2005 to March 2006, i.e. the depreciation was of about 16% from the end of 2004 (Reynolds 2007). The Fed brought to a halt raising interest rates after June 2006, while the ECB carried on a tighter monetary policy. As a result, the gap between U.S. and Euro interest rates first lessened and then disappeared as the Fed eased. Therefore, the Euro appreciated. The Euro's strength involved betting on the expectations, that later came true, that the Fed would have cut interest rates, but also that the ECB would have not followed the Fed's manoeuvre. In general, the ECB went often along with the Fed's interest-rate moves, though with some lags. The ECB started decreasing interest rates after May 2001, about five months later than the Fed. At the same time, the ECB did not increase interest rates above 2% until December 2005, meaning a year later than the Fed.

During the periods of oil shocks, in 1974, 1980 and 2000, all major central banks moved up interest rates jointly together. This always led to a world recession, which was gradually followed by profound cuts in central bank interest rates (Reynolds 2007).

"Those calling for higher central-bank interest rates when oil prices rise should realize that such policies have, in the past, resulted in interest rates of 1%-2% two or three years later (arguably too low and too late), after global industrial slumps slashed the price of oil" (Reynolds 2007).

In this scenario, the Fed was the first to cut interest rates, unilaterally. That obviously affected exchange rates and had an impact on other emerging countries. Since the Fed diminished its interest rates, indeed several Asian emerging countries that have closely aligned their currency to the US dollar, were obliged to adopt an expansive monetary policy. This fuelled major price rises in their economies. Prices rocketed at 8.5% in China, 11.4% in India, 10.4% in Indonesia, 9.6% in the Philippines and 7.6% in Thailand in mid 2008 (The Economist, 24 May 2008; Sole24Ore 6 July 2008). This alignment of Asian currencies to the US dollar has created a sort of monetary Union for the "Dollarlandia", therefore the monetary policy actions taken at the Fed had a repercussion on these countries, pushing inflation up.

Table 8. Inflation rate and interest rate in emerging Asian countries, mid- 2008

	inflation rate %	**interest rate %**
China	8.5	7.47
Hong Kong	5.7	2.35
South Korea	4.9	5
India	11.4	8.5
Thailand	7.6	3.25
Taiwan	3.7	3.63
Philippines	9.6	5.25
Malaysia	3.8	3.5
Singapore	7.5	1.25

Source: CEIC

In 2007 and in the first half of 2008, many analysts observed that loose money in USA and rigid exchange rate could have been a dangerous combination. The longer emerging economies would have held down their exchange rate, the greater the risk of soaring global inflation. At the same time appreciation would be not a simple remedy because an increase in interest rate and the expectation of further appreciation in exchange rate could have, in turn, produced more inflation by attracting more capital from abroad.

Afterwards, the financial and economic crisis changed the economic scenario. The crisis hit emerging market economies (EMEs) with full force in the final quarter of 2008. Exchange rates in many countries depreciated, equity prices declined and the cost of external financing rose sharply. The plunge in commodity prices and the increased economic slack resulting from the sharp slowdown in growth have reduced the high rate of EME inflation, which is forecast to decline from 6.0% in 2008 to less than 5% in 2009. Headline and core inflation have fallen abruptly in Asia, and underlying inflation in China and Thailand has exhibited deflationary tendencies in recent months (BIS, 2009).

6. The Impact of Oil Price Spikes on the Economy

The steep increases in oil and energy prices over the period 2000 mid-2008 had a significant impact on consumers, producers and policy choices. In premise, since oil and natural gas are crucial inputs to a great variety of production processes, transportation and heating systems, higher energy prices will translate into higher costs because it is difficult to adjust the amount of energy that people use at least in the short run. In the long run, if energy consumption is altered by, for instance, adjusting the production or transportation techniques, then the effects of a supply shock could be mitigated. In general, higher relative price of oil and energy produces many economic consequences.

Higher oil price tends to lessen the productive capacity of a country or area, because high energy costs discourage investments or cause some existing capital to become economically obsolete. These effects tend to hold back the growth in labor productivity, which leads to lower real wages and profits. In addition, higher cost of imported oil is likely to deteriorate the terms of trade of a given country, that is, a country will have to sell more goods and services abroad to pay for a given quantity of oil and other imports (Bernanke, 2006). Put differently, an oil price increase shifts the terms of trade between net-importing and net-exporting economies in favor of the latter. Fundamentally, this entails a real income transfer from consuming to producing countries. Dwindling real incomes in countries tackling larger oil and energy costs, in turn, indicate less income to spend on other commodities, which translates into poorer domestic demand unless toned with reduced domestic savings and/or higher export demand (United Nation, 2005). In other terms, an upsurge in oil prices squeezes economic growth primarily through its effects on consumer spending, because an increase in oil prices is broadly equivalent to the imposition of a tax on residents, with the revenue from the tax going to oil producers abroad. Some empirical evidences show that the tendency of oil-producing countries to consume from current income is low relative to consuming economies. Oil price booms have historically been accompanied by widening current-account surpluses in oil-exporting countries, meaning that the extra revenues going to producers is not immediately and completely spent.

In addition, higher oil prices raise inflation in the short run, because of the pass through on refined products such as gasoline, heating oil and diesel with a consequent increase in cost of livings. This direct effect of higher oil prices on the cost of living is called the *first-round effect* on inflation. Moreover, higher oil prices could produce a *second-round effect* on inflation if workers and unions respond to the increase in the cost of living by demanding higher nominal wages or if firms rise consumer prices for non-energy goods or services as result of increased production costs. To be more explicit, a higher rate of inflation generates a loss of real income unless nominal wages increase alongside consumer prices. If worker unions successfully bargain for higher wages in order to offset the real income losses, the result is an additional upward pressure on the price level since firms will try to transfer rising labor costs on consumer prices. If workers judge that their recently negotiated wages do not proper reflect the rising price level, then they enter the next round of wage bargaining with further aspirations. Such a situation could bring either to a wage-price spiral resulting in accelerating inflation, or to embed higher inflationary expectations in the economy's wage bargaining processes, involving a permanently higher inflation rate compared to the initial situation. Simply, an oil price hike pushes people's expectations on inflation up, contributing to additional upward pressure on inflation.

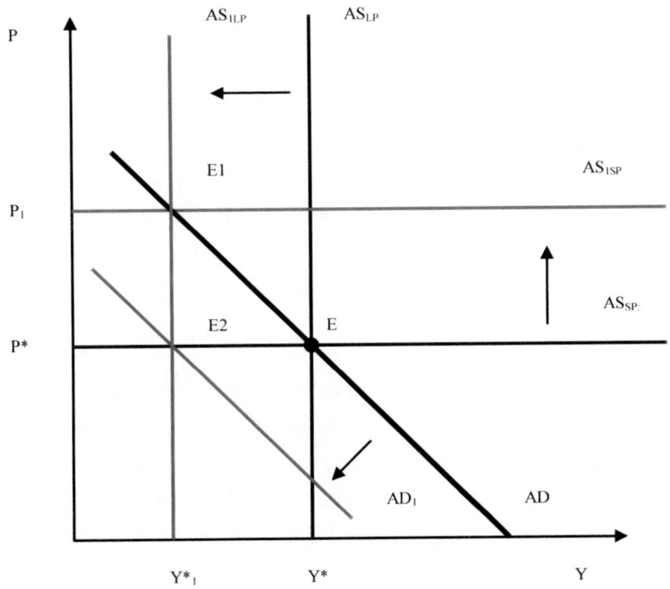

Note: The vertical axis reports the aggregate price level (P). The horizontal axis reports the total output in the economy (Y).
Source: Own Elaborations

Chart 19. Supply shock within AD-AS model.

A monetary policy intervention that aims at halting the effects of an energy price shock is called stabilization policy. To understand how a stabilization measure works, one can use the macroeconomic tools of aggregate demand (AD) and supply (AS) in the short (SR) and long run (LR). Starting from the long run equilibrium in point E (Chart 19) where there is the potential output (Y*) and the optimal price level (P*), an oil shock like the current one, will produce a shift of AS_{SR} curve in AS_{SR1}, in this new situation the equilibrium will move from E to E1 where prices (P) increase and the effective production (Y) drops under the potential ones, with a consequent negative output gap. Soon after, the AS in the long run moves inward in AS1, meaning that the new potential output will decrease as a consequence of decreasing productivity due to the oil shock. At that point also the production will shift from Y* to Y^*_1, while NAIRU (non accelerating inflation rate of unemployment) will increase. Without any policy interventions, the economy will come back to its initial equilibrium E after the oil shock will be completely absorbed and only after a period of stagflation that could be particularly dangerous for the households and firms, because it implies a long period of sacrifice in terms of high inflation, unemployment and GDP deceleration. In this situation, a virtuous monetary policy would produce a shift of AD in AD1 as soon the shock materializes. The reduction of AD can be caused only by a restrictive monetary action. This tighten monetary intervention would offset the negative impact of an oil price escalation and would establish a new equilibrium in point E_2. Explicitly, considering the velocity money equation, an increase in price due to an oil shock, for a given potential output and constant velocity of money, can be counterbalanced only by a fall in the money supply. This theoretical framework could be applied to the Euro Area. Therefore, it would be convenient for the ECB to take a more restrictive policy in order to reach point E2. For the Fed and the Bank of England the same reasoning cannot be applied as a whole, because the oil shock has been accompanied by the financial turmoil.

7. Conclusions

The present chapter has analysed the different monetary policy measures adopted by the ECB, Fed and BoE from 1999 onwards. Each Central Bank sets its own official interest rate in order to influence the overall level of expenditure in the economy. When the amount of money growth increases more rapidly than the volume of domestic production, inflation is the result. At the same time, oil and energy price upsurges, such as those recorded between 2000 and 2008, put further pressure on price level and inflation expectations through the so-called first and second round effect. Changes in interest rates are therefore necessary to control inflation. The three considered Central Banks have adopted different interest rate strategies to cope with the new economic scenario, explicitly the Fed decreased the interest rate, the ECB increased it and the BoE kept it constant between 2007 and the first half of 2008. Their different behaviours mirrored both their dissimilar philosophies and their divergent economic context. For instance, the Fed is more Keynesian oriented, the ECB is more monetarist driven and the BoE is a mix of both. For this reason, while the ECB monitors accurately the evolution of M3 and gives a special role to money, the Fed does not reserve any particular status to the monetary aggregates. The BoE keeps an eye on money supply more firmly than the Fed, but less strictly than ECB. Moreover, since the economic and financial situation differs in the three areas, their monetary approach also tends to not converge. While in the US the financial turmoil has been accompanied by an increase in the unemployment rate, falling asset prices and weak dollar, the expansive Fed manoeuvre seems more appropriate to avoid an exacerbation of the economic slowdown. This of course produces more inflation, but it could avoid a strong recession. As for the Euro Area, since the economy experiences no financial crisis, enjoys an unemployment rate at its minimum historical level and a strong currency, a more restrictive policy should be suitable to curb inflation. For the UK, it would be reasonable to leave things unchanged, as the economic scenario does not appear very healthy due to the risk of financial contagion. Diverging monetary policy actions seems reasonable because it has been empirically verified that during the periods of oil shocks, in 1974, 1980 and 2000, all main central banks that moved up interest rates jointly together produced a world recession, which was gradually followed by deep cuts in their interest rates.

References

[1] Bank of England (2008), *How do interest rates affect inflation?*, extracted from http://www.bankofengland.co.uk/education/targettwopointzero/inflation/ratesAffectInflation.htm

[2] Bank for International Settlements, BIS, (2009), BIS Annual Report 2009, http://www.bis.org/publ/arpdf/ar2009e5.pdf

[3] Bernanke B. (2006-2009) Various Speeches.

[4] Bureau of Economic Analysis (2009), http://www.bea.gov/national/index.htm#gdp

[5] *Business Week* (2008), Special Report The Financial Crisis, Mc Graw-Hill Company, March 31st.

[6] Clerc, L. and Yates T. (1999), "Interest Rate Stepping: Some Puzzles and Facts," mimeo, Bank of England.

[7] Davey, N, 2005, 'A work programme in financial statistics – April 2005', *Monetary & Financial Statistics*, April, pp. 4-8.

[8] ECB (2003), "The ECB's Monetary Policy Strategy", Press Release, 8 May 2003.

[9] ECB (2004, a), "The Monetary Policy of ECB", ECB Frankfurt am Main, Germany.

[10] ECB (2004, b), "Monetary Analysis in Real Time", *Monthly Bulletin* October, pp. 43-63.

[11] ECB (2005), "Money Demand and Uncertainty", *Monthly Bulletin* October, pp. 57-74.

[12] ECB (2008-2009), "Monthly Economic Bulletin", several issues.

[13] Federal Reserve (2008-2009), http://www.federalreserve.gov/

[14] Fischer, B.; Lenza, M.; Pill; H. and Reichlin, L. (2006), Money and monetary policy: The ECB experience 1999-2006, paper presented at the *4th ECB Central Banking Conference*, 9&10 November 2006 in Frankfurt.

[15] Flander S. (2008), The ECB's progress 10 years on, BBC news, 1 June, http://news.bbc.co.uk/2/hi/business/7430240.stm

[16] Friedman, M. (1956) "The quantity theory of money: a restatement," in *Studies in the Quantity Theory of Money,* ed. M. Friedman. Chicago: University of Chicago Press.

[17] Gerdesmeier D., Mongelli F.P. and Roffia B. (2007), "The Eurosystem, the US Federal Reserve and the Bank of Japan: similarities and differences", in *Journal of Money, Credit, and Banking*. October; 39(7): 1785-1819.

[18] *Herald Tribune* (2006-2009), several issues.

[19] Hofmann, B. (2006), "Do monetary indicators (still) predict euro area inflation?" *Bundesbank Discussion paper* No. 18/2006.

[20] Hylton, M, nd, 'Measurement of Money Supply', viewed 2 May 2006

[21] http://www.boj.org.jm/uploads/pdf/papers_pamphlets/papers_pamphlets_The_Measurement_of_Money_Supply_.pdf

[22] Issing, O. (1999), The monetary policy of the ECB in a world of uncertainty, Contribution to the policy panel at the conference on *"Monetary policy-making under uncertainty"* organised by the European Central Bank and the Center for Financial Studies, 3-4 December, Frankfurt am Main.

[23] Issing, O. (2005), "The role of money in the monetary policy strategy of the ECB", speech delivered at the workshop entitled "What central banks can learn from money and credit aggregates", Eltville, 28 October 2005.

[24] Issing, O. (2006), "The ECB's monetary policy strategy: why did we choose a two-pillar approach?", address given at the *4th ECB Central Banking Conference*, 9&10 November 2006 in Frankfurt.

[25] Kahn, A. and Benolkin, S. (2007), "The Role of Money in Monetary Policies: Why the Fed and ECB see it so Differently", Federal Reserve Bank of Kansas City.

[26] King, M. (2002), "No money, no inflation – the role of money in the economy", Bank of England, *Quarterly Bulletin*, Summer, pp. 162-177.

[27] Lenza, M. (2006), "Does money help forecasting inflation in the euro area?" DG-Research, mimeo.

[28] McCandless, G.T. and Weber, W.E. (1995), "Some Monetary Facts", *Federal Reserve of Minneapolis Review*, Vol. 19, No. 3, pp. 2-11.

[29] Nicoletti Altimari, S. (2001), "Does money lead inflation in the euro area?" *ECB Working Paper* Nr. 63.

[30] Noyer C. (2007), "The Eurosystem's Monetary policy: a View from the Inside", Speech at the *Swedbank's Annual Global Business Outlook Conference*, Stockholm, October 8.

[31] OECD (2007), economic survey of the euro area 2007: the role of Monetary Aggregates in Monetary Policy, OECD Paris.

[32] Pill, H. und Rautanen, T. (2006), "Monetary Analysis: The ECB Experience", *Paper presented at the Conference: the ECB and its Watchers,* held on 5 May 2005 in Frankfurt, mimeo.

[33] Reynolds A. (2007), Interest Rates and Dollar Fundamental,s in *The Wall Street Journal*, November 15.

[34] Shadow Government Statistics (2008) New record money Growth thretens monetary inflation, January http://www.shadowstats.com/

[35] Tabellini G. (2008), Either The ECB or The Fed Is Making a Mistake, in Real Clear Markets, 23 June.

[36] Telegraph (2008), Anna Schwartz blames Fed for sub-prime crisis, 9 July.

[37] *The Economist* (2006-2009), several issues.

[38] Tootell, G, 2002, 'The Bank of England's Monetary Policy', *New England Economic Review*, issue Q 2, pp. 61-64.

[39] United Nations (2005), *Trade and Development Report*, UNCTA September 7th.

[40] Williams J. (2008), New record money Growth thretens monetary inflation, in Financial Sense Editorials, http://www.financialsense.com/editorials/williams_j/2008/0114.html

In: Monetary Growth: Trends, Impacts and Policies
Editors: W.N. Squires et al, pp. 35-49
ISBN: 978-1-60692-305-4

Chapter 2

INTERACTIONS BETWEEN MONETARY AND FISCAL POLICIES: THE CASE OF THE EUROPEAN MONETARY UNION

Maria-Soledad Castaño Martínez*
Inmaculada Carrasco Monteagudo, University of Castilla-La Mancha,
Plaza de la Universidad, Albacete (Spain)

Abstract

The European Monetary Union (EMU) creation has opened a new source of studies about interactions between monetary and fiscal policies. It has been especially interesting the study of fiscal policy influences in the credibility of European monetary policy because budget deficits could affect the achievement of the main monetary policy goal: price stability. It has also been attention-grabbing the study of fiscal policy as stabilisation means when country-specific shocks occur in this new political framework.

Central bankers consider fiscal discipline and coordination as a prerequisite for a successful monetary union. Fiscal discipline idea was included in the Delors Report (1989), the Treaty on European Union (1992) and the Stability and Growth Pact (SGP) (1997). Some fiscal limits have been imposed and, since December (1999) Helsinki Council, the Euro-area fiscal policies coordination has been increased. A part of the literature has criticized those constrains and doubt about the efficacy of fiscal policy when individual shocks could occur.

This paper presents a brief summary of monetary and fiscal policies implementation in the EMU. It also collects a survey of the literature about interactions between monetary and fiscal policies in the context of EMU. Finally, some empirical evidence of these interactions is analysed. This evidence supports the idea that European policy mix has been well performed, but some doubts have appeared in the new crisis panorama, especially on public finances sustainability.

1. Introduction

After the creation of European Monetary Union, literature has been worried about interactions between monetary and fiscal policies in the European framework. It has especially been interesting

[1] E mail address: MariaSoledad.Castano@uclm.es

the study of how fiscal policy can influence the single monetary policy credibility, because budget deficits can hinder the achieving of the main monetary policy goal: the price stability. They also have been worried about how fiscal policy can or should stabilise country-specific shocks.

Central bankers use to consider fiscal discipline as a prerequisite for the success of a monetary union. This idea was included in the Delors Report (1989), the Treaty on European Union (1992) and the Stability and Growth Pact (SGP) (1997). Coordination of fiscal policies has been also considered as necessary for a monetary union success. Since December (1999) Helsinki Council, the coordination of fiscal policies in Euro area was increased. But the fiscal criteria establised to achieve the third stage of EMU have been frequently criticized by the economists.

In this paper, it will be presented a summary of the single monetary policy strategy and implementation. It will also be presented a summary of the fiscal limits imposed to EMU countries. In addition, a survey of the literature studying the interactions between monetary and fiscal policies will be presented. Special attention to EMU study cases will be made. After that, an analysis of EMU empirical data will be made. Finally, some reflections about public finances sustainability and its influences on single monetary policy will be made. A section collecting the main conclusions will close the chapter.

2. Strategy and Implementation of the Single European Monetary Policy

Eurosystem monetary policy's strategy has been organised over three basic elements: a main goal (price stability) and two basic pillars (the analysis of economic dynamics and shocks and the analysis of monetary trends).

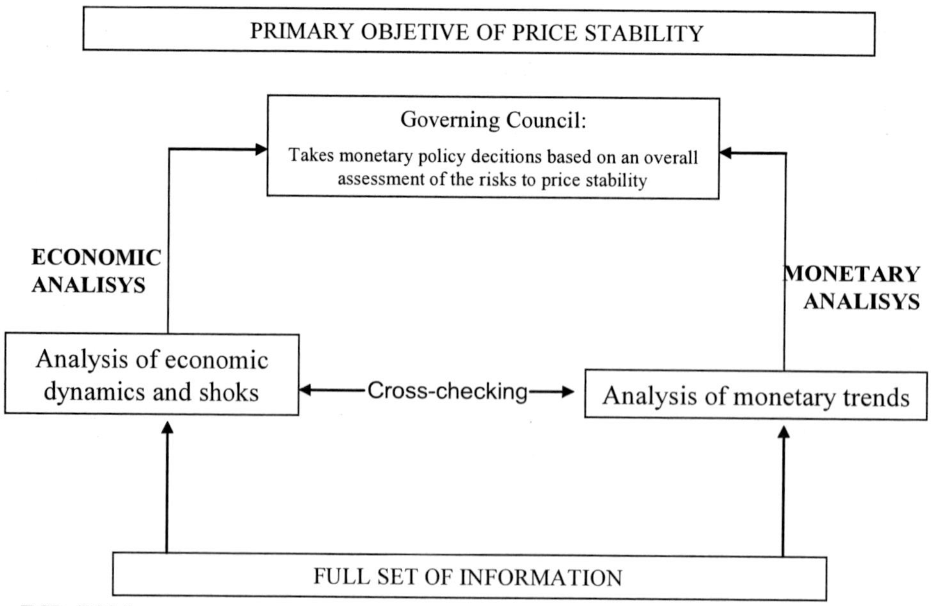

Source: ECB (2004)

Chart 1. The stability-oriented monetary policy strategy of the ECB.

2.1. The Primary Objective

In order to give an anchor to inflation expectations, the task entrusted by the Maastricht Treaty to the Euro-system is to maintain the price stability. The ECB's Governing Council defined "price stability" in quantitative terms as a year-on-year increase in the Harmonised Index of Consumer Prices (HICP) for the euro area of below 2 %. This price stability goal has to be maintained over the medium term (ECB, 1999-a: 53).

The HICP was primarily created as a tool for the study of the prices' convergence among countries in the European monetary integration process. They decided to use it for the European monetary policy implementation because people use to measure the growth of prices by consumer prices indexes. The employment of HICP shows clearly the European Central Bank (ECB) intentionality: European monetary policy responds to prevailing conditions in the Euro-area as a whole, nor in concrete regions or countries.

On the other hand, when they affirm that price stability is to be maintained over the medium term, they implicitly recognise that prices are volatiles on the short term, due to some non-monetary perturbations hardly controllable by the monetary policy, such us changes in indirect taxes or changes in the rough material prices. The medium-term orientation facilitates (i) the achievement of the goal and so that the Euro-system's requisite of balance, and (ii) a gradual response of monetary policy, that's to say, a major flexibility to respond in a more appropriate manner to the different economic shocks.

In order to achieve its goal, the ECB organises, evaluates and cross-checks the more relevant information about risks to prices stability in an eclectic framework based on two analytical perspectives, the two pillars.

2.2. The First Pillar

The first pillar analyses the short and medium-term risks to price stability on real economy. This analysis is centred in economic and financial variables that have the character of advanced indicator, such as the developments in overall output, the aggregate demand and its components, the fiscal policy, the conditions of capital and labour markets, cost and prices indicators, exchange rates, the developments of the balances of payments, the developments of financial markets, etc. It tries to identify the nature of shocks that hit the economy and their possible effects.

Therefore, high quality statistics relating economic and financial developments are very important for EMU implementation, because it needs a reliable picture of the economy. It is vital to identify correctly the strengths that should lead the prices evolution, and to distinguish between the temporary and the underlying strengths.

2.3. The Second Pillar

Money has been singled out from the sample of the above mentioned indicators, because it is recognised that money and prices are strongly related in the long term. Money is, then, a natural, stable and reliable nominal anchor for inflation (ECB, 1999-a).

The ECB Governing Council marked a quantitative benchmark value for money growth in order to build a coherent and credible guidance for EMU. This helps Governing Council to both, the monetary aggregate analysis, and the public information presentation.

The benchmark value for monetary growth (M3) has to be compatible with price stability over the medium term, helping to its achievement. So that, an important and sustained deviation of the monetary aggregate growth form the benchmarked value, will indicate a serious risk for long-term price stability.

Nevertheless, this does not obligate to Eurosystem to correct all the short-term deviations, because in this monetary policy strategy, the monetary aggregate is not an intermediate goal, but only an indicator. Subsequently, the monetary aggregate does not have to be controlled in the short-term.

M3 was chosen because there was a lot of empirical evidence of its stable demand and because it served as a good advanced indicator. The reference value marked for the annual growth of M3 was 4.5 %. The derivation of this reference value is based on the relationship between changes in monetary growth (ΔM), inflation (ΔP), real GDP growth (ΔYR) and velocity (ΔV), explained by the "quantity equation":

$$\Delta M = \Delta YR + \Delta P - \Delta V$$

As a result, the derivation of the M3 reference value is based in: (i) the definition of price stability as a HIPC increase below 2% per annum; (ii) the assumption of a medium-term annual growth trend of potential GDP for the euro-area of 2-2 ½ %; and (iii) the assumption of a decline of M3 velocity in the range of ½-1 % per annum.

2.4. Discretion in the European Monetary Policy

Some economists see this European single monetary framework as excessively discretionary and judgemental (see a discussion in Papademos, 2006). Monetary rules are the alternative.

Friedman (1956) proposed a simple k-percent rule to lead year-in-year the rising of the money stock. Critics explain that a pre-defined fixed rate for money growth does not permit central bankers to accommodate it to economy changing conditions, fluctuations of money demand or shocks.

More sophisticated monetary rules have been developed, the most well-known of which is Taylor's rule (Taylor, 1993). It explains the sort-term nominal interest rate as a function of the divergence between some variables (expected or actual inflation and output) and their targeted levels. The main focus of critics is centred in the fact that the rule is founded on macroeconomic indicators that are not observable, such us the output gap or the equilibrium interest rate. Moreover, two much information is loosening when decisions are based on so few variables.

Lately, optimising rules have been presented (Woodford, 2003). They are based on an empirical model that allows considering a wide range of variables describing the economy. The model will link monetary policy objectives with instruments and will offer a path for an optimal policy. This kind of models permit to surpass the limitation of precedent ones in the use of information. However monetary policy actuations will be as good as the model robust is.

On the other hand, "inflation targeting" is a framework developed over the optimising rules theories. Broadly defined, almost all central banks follow this framework, because they give importance to price stability. Nevertheless, in a more narrow sense, inflation targeting is a type of monetary policy rule, since changes in intervention interests rates are determined by the divergence between inflation forecast and the inflation objective in a sort-term horizon. Critics see this as a narrow strategy, too limited by an arbitrary pre-fixed horizon.

From the ECB point of view, all of these strategies have some drawbacks: monetary policy framework has to be flexible to react to different types of economic shocks; it cannot be strictly linked to a simple reaction function due to the imperfect knowledge of the state, structure and dynamics of economy. "*The "policy reaction function" of a central bank cannot be written down in stone, in a precise quantitative form. There is a need for judgement in the conduct of monetary policy. In other words, the central bank needs some flexibility or, to use a term, some "discretion", since it is not desirable to commit itself to a fully specified reaction function*" Papademos (2006: 31)

3. The Emu Fiscal Policy Framework

The debate about rules and discretion exists also in fiscal policy. In this case, European Union authorities have given a strong support for fiscal rules. They believe that fiscal rules are vital for a proper functioning of a monetary union, because it is very important to avoid that a member-state would join the sort-term benefits of a too expansive fiscal policy by sharing the negative consequences of such a policy between the resting members. Vicious circles of increasing deficit and debt have to be avoided. So that, a fiscal rule should block the negative consequences of the electoral cycle on growing deficits.

European Union has established in Amsterdam Treaty a framework for fiscal coordination through various mechanisms: the Excessive Deficit Procedure (Article 104), the Stability and Growth Pact (Council Regulation 1467/97), the Mutual Surveillance Procedure (Article 99-3) and the Broad Economic Policy Guidelines (Article 99). The Euro area policymakers have decided that a closer fiscal coordination among memer-states is needed, because the centralised monetary policy has as objective the price stability and decentralised fiscal policies have as objective each country outcome.

The Maastrich Treaty and the Stability and Growth Pact (see Box 1) compose the European Union fiscal framework. The Maastritch Treaty, from the economic point of view, is based on a strict budgetary stability, as a means to reach a path of non-inflationary sustainable growth. For this reason, among the requirements that the Treaty fixed for the countries that wanted to pass to the third phase of the process of economic and monetary integration, they were picked up two requisites relative to public deficit and public debt. (Carrasco y Pardo, 2006 and 2007)

The danger of this institutional framework is the inadequate stabilization of shocks whether there is a tendency that the overall policy mix becomes inappropriate. This possibility may arise since fiscal authorities do not fully consider how their actions affect inflation and therefore in turn the monetary policy stance which affects all members states of the EMU (ECB, 2001-b and Andersen, 2005). In this sense, some literature has analysed the possible policy mix problems in the EMU (Cangiano and Mottu, 1998, Beetsma and Bovenberg, 1998, Beetsma and Debrun, 2004, Catenaro and Tirelli, 2000, Dixit, 2000, Uhlig, 2002, Andersen, 2005).

Critics of the current European fiscal framework argue that in practice, it will suppose a severe limitation for the national governments to implement stabilization policies in recession times, because it establishes a limit for public deficits. As a result EU governments will be constraint to conduct effective counter-cyclical stabilisation policies, to provide public services in an adequate level and to maintain and improve public infrastructures.

BOX 1. THE STABILITY AND GROWTH PACT

The Stability and Growth Pact included the following elements:

- Countries have to pursue medium-term goals of budgetary positions close to balance or in surplus, respecting the 3 per cent ceiling even in economic downturns.
- The *exceptionality condition* can be declared in two circumstances
  - In case of harsh and persistent recession, with an annual fall of real GDP of 2 per cent or more, but also new SGP consider persistent recession with a negative growth rate or an accumulated loss of production during periods without growth.
  - In case of a severe economic downturn, with the annual fall of real GDP of at least 0.75 per cent.

  The Commission is in charge of watching over the fulfilment of the conditions, and of informing to the Council. The Governing Council decides by qualified majority and it declares the exceptionality situation, ordering to the Commission to take measures.
- The *temporariness condition*. Only while exceptional conditions, the deficit can overpass 3 per cent of GDP. The year following to the last one in this circumstances, the country has to adjust the budget to present a deficit into the limit of 3 per cent.
- New SGP considers the budgetary efforts to increase or to maintain at a high level the financial contributions to foment the international solidarity and to achieve the European political objectives, especially, Europe's unification, if it has a harmful effect on economic growth of a state member.
- New SGP considers special situations, in this situation it is possible that procedure of excessive deficit could not be applied. The efforts carried out in innovation and research investments, the application of Lisbon reforms, the contributions to the international solidarity and measures that ensure the long-term sustainability of public finances would be considered.
- Countries participating in euro-zone would have to evidence *stability programs*. Those not participating would have to present *convergence programs*. Both have to plan a medium-term national budgetary objective that will be examined regularly by de Council, who can made recommendations to the countries in order to encourage the reaching of the referred goals. Only EMU-member countries can be sanctioned.
- The country exceeding the deficit limit has to take decisions in the following year to its identification, in order to eliminate it in the two next years to de year of the excess, unless special conditions (that they are not specified by the Treaty).
- In case of sanction, the amount to be deposited (without interest) would be calculated by a fixed component of 0.2 per cent of GDP plus a variable component of one tenth of the difference between de deficit and the 3 per cent reference value, with a ceiling of 0.5 per cent of GDP.

SOURCE: CARRASCO, I. and PARDO, I. (2006 and 2007) and GALINDO and CASTAÑO (2006)

Nevertheless, ECB (2001-a, 2001-b and 2008-b) is against fiscal activism, i.e. fiscal policies aimed at fine-tuning the business cycle, is disappointing. There is ample evidence that the discretionary fiscal policies pursued in the 1970s in many European and other OECD countries did not stabilise their economies as intended, but rather led to a sustained increase in debt-to-GDP ratios. Often, fiscal policy measures turned out to be pro-cyclical (exacerbating the cycle) rather than countercyclical as originally intended. The failure of activist fiscal policies can be traced to a number of factors, among which the information, political, implementation and economic lags associated with discretionary fiscal policy measures figure prominently. For activist fiscal policies to be effective, policy-makers need to correctly identify the cyclical state of the economy and fiscal measures need to be implemented in a timely manner, well temporary targeted. In practice, these conditions are very difficult to meet. Moreover, if fluctuations in short-run economic growth are caused by supply-side rather than demand-side developments, activist fiscal policies aimed at smoothing short-run growth will be destabilising rather than stabilising. Against this background, a consensus view has emerged; it states that the best contribution that fiscal policy can make to short-term macroeconomic stabilisation is to avoid discretionary fiscal fine-tuning, while ensuring the free operation of automatic stabilisers (ECB, 2008-b: 75 -76).

However, ECB (2008-b: 76) defend to apply discretionary fiscal policy when the ensuring of long-term sustainability of public finances should be the overarching goal of fiscal policy. For countries with unsustainable fiscal positions, this implies the need to take structural consolidation measures to correct the fiscal imbalances. It is sometimes argued that during the transition period there will be a trade-off between the goals of sound public finances and macroeconomic stabilisation. However, there is evidence showing that consolidation measures which correct severe fiscal imbalances are likely to result in only small output costs, if any (Briotti, 2005). Second, discretionary fiscal policy action may be necessary to correct severe internal and/or external macroeconomic imbalances. Third, there may be a need for emergency fiscal policy action in the rare event of a major crisis.

4. Monetary and Fiscal Interactions: The European Union Case

In this section the relations between monetary and fiscal policies in the context of European Economic and Monetary Union (EMU) will be examined. Traditionally, literature has been worried about macroeconomic policy coordination within one country and cooperation across countries on the design of macroeconomic policies. However, the Maastricht Treaty began to debate these issues in reference to EMU.

According to Mundell (1961), the main element in a Monetary Union is the real convergence level existing among the countries that they have decided to form a monetary union. When such convergence exits, then the asymmetric shocks affect equally to all the economies. So, it is possible to consider that their business cycles are connected and when an external shock is produced, all the economies would be affected equally.

Moreover, Optimum Monetary Union theory states that it is necessary to consider two elements: wage flexibility and the level of factors mobility.

Taking into account these elements, when asymmetric shocks are produced or when different unemployment rates exit in countries of monetary union, theses countries only have three options to reduce unemployment, if they cannot use the monetary and exchange rate policies:

1. To use an active fiscal policy. This possibility is limited in EMU by SGP.
2. To use a stabilisation fund to help to those countries that could be affected negatively by the asymmetric shocks, trying to reduce the negative effects on employment. In EMU, this possibility is restricted by the community budget limit to growth.
3. The last mechanism is to get wages more flexible and to promote the geographical mobility. The emigration process from countries with high unemployment levels could help to get a more equally unemployment rates in the European Union (Bustillo and Bonete, 2000). The viability of this mechanism is questioned because the geographical mobility in the European Union is low due to differences of linguistic and cultural type.

Therefore, theory of optimum monetary unions applied to EMU, considers that it is desirable to reduce countries budgets and increase the European Union's budget. In this case, the countries that could be affected by asymmetric shocks will receive transfers that could help them to eliminate their problems. This idea was also considered by Werner Report (1970), in which it is proposed a great Community budget including a fiscal harmonization process and centralized control of national fiscal policies. Similar arguments were presented by MacDougall Report (1977). In this case, it was stated that in the own countries the regional stabilization is achieved in an automatic way through fiscal system benefits. The Report suggested that it would be necessary different transfers from countries through a central Community budget to counteract the shocks in each country. This Report also stated that a monetary union without a significant centralization of budget would be dangerous for Union survival.

These recommendations have not been introduced in its entirely. In the European Monetary Union's case, the governments design their fiscal policies to reduce the negative effects of the asymmetric shocks, but they have a limit in the public deficit creation (GDP 3%) and public debt (60%).

Therefore, euro area have chosen a institutional framework where monetary policy is centralised (decisions are taken by European Central Bank) and fiscal policy is a tool in national governments hands to resolve asymmetric shocks, as it is previously indicated.

In this context, the literature is focused on analysing the fiscal policy in the case of currency union, more concretely, on the debate about discretionary measures and automatic stabiliser, since more active fiscal policies pose the question of cross-border spillovers or externalities associated with decentralised actions on national fiscal instruments (Beetsma and Debrun, 2004: 110). So that, according to Hamada (1985) the existence of significant spill-over effects would justify certain degree of coordination or centralisation at supranational level in order to internalise the externalities and deliver collectively more efficient measures.

Externalities could appear when a change in a single country fiscal policy, via its effects on inflation, may release a monetary response affecting all member countries of the currency union. This monetary policy externality may tend to imply that non-cooperative fiscal policies are too expansionary, since single countries do not take the monetary policy response into account. On the other hand, there are interdependencies via trade links. A common interdependence is demand spillover effect that arises from a domestic fiscal expansion. It may benefit trading partners through an increase in foreign products demand. There is also a cost spillover effect since higher domestic activity tends to lead to higher domestic wage/price increase which in turn makes it possible for trading partners to increase insufficient expansionary fiscal policies, since single fiscal authorities do not take the positive the positive trade externalities for its trading partners into account (Cooper, 1985, Hamada, 1985, Andersen, 2002 y 2005).

In addition, if it is considered that the high-priority target of single monetary policy is inflation, and that policymakers consider that it is necessary a closer-coordination, fiscal policies have to contribute to achieve inflation target. Therefore, the previous announce of inflation target influence in design of fiscal policies.

In this institutional framework a credible monetary policy can contribute directly to a smooth conduct of fiscal policies by ensuring that low inflation expectations and low risk prima are incorporated in longer-term government bond yields. Because of these interdependencies, there is a need to embed the mandates of independent and stability-oriented central banks in broader-based institutional arrangements which also address the core responsibilities of fiscal policymakers. In particular, these responsibilities should include a credible fiscal commitment to respect the objective pursed by monetary policy (ECB, 2008: 73). Monetary policy is active while fiscal policies occupy a second position, since, the underlying idea is that inflation goal is the priority goal in EMU and if this target is achieved then output and employment goal could be achieved.

Since the EMU creation, a concern about fiscal policies coordination has increased, because, notwithstanding the existence of a credible no-bailout clause protecting the central bank, the excessive issuance of national government debt constitutes a widely acknowledged risk. Given the large number of independent fiscal policy-makers that share the benefits of a single currency and gain access to an enlarged pool of savings, a situation in which free-riding incentives for excessive government borrowing are created and needs to be avoided (Detken, Gaspar and Winkler, 2004 and ECB, 2008: 77). This fact could increase interest rate since international capital markets punish excessively expansive fiscal policy.

The problem of public finances sustainability could be formulated as a budgetary deficit that causes an increase of public debt that will originate a flow of future payments, as it will be seen in next section. If the interest rate of public debt exceeds a national economy GDP's growth, the process of debt accumulation will cause a continuous increment of public debt's weigh in GDP terms, until it becomes untenable. In this case it is necessary to take discretionary measures (De Grauwe, 1997).

This fact is confirmed by the last European countries experiences. Many of these countries have had high public deficit during 1970s, 1980s and principles of 1990s; it has taken it to problems of sustainability of public finances (De Grauwe, 1997 and ECB, 2002 and 2008). Therefore, it could be concluded that fiscal policy is not a flexible element (like defended by Optimum Monetary Union theory), since if fiscal policy are excessively expansive then it could generate problems of sustainability of public finances.

5. Empirical Analysis

In this section, we aim to analyse sustainability of public finances in the EMU case. Some basic budgetary identities will be considered (Anchuelo, 1998: 123-125). They include the factors that determine temporal evolution of public debt.

First, a budgetary identity is considered:

$$B_t - B_{t-1} = D_t \tag{1}$$

Where B is the stock of public debt and D is the total public deficit (this variable includes investment expenditure and payment of interest of debt).

On the other hand, prices growth and GDP growth are considered.

$$P_t = (1+\pi)P_{t-1} \tag{2}$$

$$Y_t = (1+g)Y_{t-1} \tag{3}$$

Operating (see Anchuelo, 1998)

$$b_t = \frac{1}{(1+\pi)(1+g)} b_{t-1} + d_t \tag{4}$$

where b is public debt and d is total public deficit in percentage of GDP, π is inflation rate and g is GDP rate of growth.

It is also possible to separate total public deficit between primary deficit and payment of interest of debt (see Anchuelo, 1998),

$$D_t = iB_{t-1} + PD_t \tag{5}$$

$$b_t = \frac{(1+i)}{(1+\pi)(1+g)} b_{t-1} + pd_t \tag{6}$$

where *i* is nominal interest rate of public debt, and *pd* is primary deficit in percentage of GDP.

The equation (6) allows identifying the factors of which the evolution of public debt in percentage of GDP depends. Given a previously accumulated debt stock, these factors are: nominal interest rate, inflation rate, GDP growth and primary deficit that excludes the payments of interests of public debt.

To simplify annotation:

$$\alpha = \frac{(1+i)}{(1+\pi)(1+g)}$$

$$b_t = \alpha b_{t-1} + pd_t \tag{7}$$

It is observed that α is smaller than 1 when nominal interest rates are behind the nominal GDP rate of growth (π+g). That is to say, when the real interest rate (i-π) is lower than the real GDP rate of growth, α is smaller than 1. In this case, public debt will decreased in terms of GDP if no primary deficits exist. With *pd*=0, the nominal debt (B) rate of growth is equal to the nominal interest rate, due to payments of interest. But public debt in percentage of GDP will diminish, since denominator grows more quickly, when prices and outcome increase.

But, if α>1, then public debt in percentage of GDP will become to get growing (in relation to GDP) unless public primary surplus would be big enough to impede it. (Anchuelo, 1998: 123-125).

By analysing EMU aggregating data, we could observe if these previous theoretical relationships are fulfilled. Next figures show the evolution of the following variables: public debt (*b*), nominal interest rate (*i*) Harmonised Index of Consumer Prices (HICP), real interest rate (*r*), GDP growth (*g*), total public deficit (*td*) and primary public deficit (*pd*).

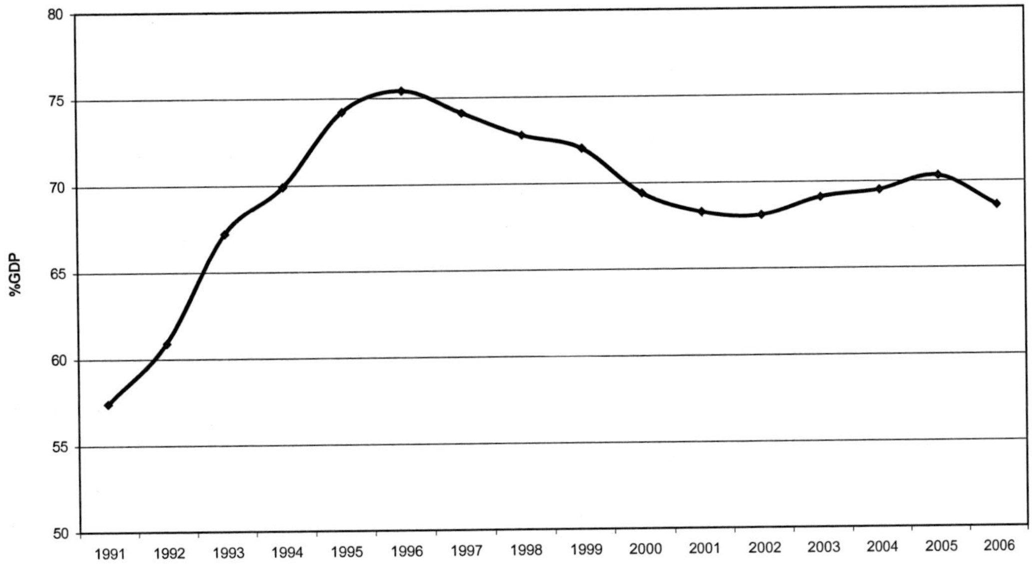

Source: ECB, Monthly Bulletin, several years and own elaboration.

Figure 1. Public Debt (b).

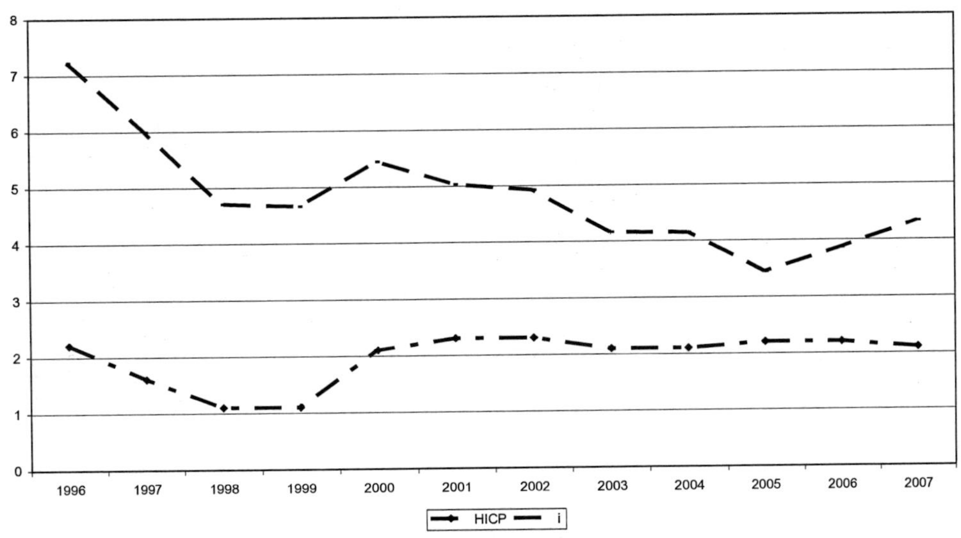

Source: ECB, Monthly Bulletin, several years and own elaboration.

Figure 2. Nominal interest rate and HICP.

From the analysis of the precedent charts, we can conclude that in the period 1996-2000 a decrease of real interest rate and a growing of primary surplus take place. Theses facts cause the reduction of public debt percentage of GDP that comes closer progressively to the limit imposed by SGP.

It is also observed that in the period of 2000-2003 there is a certain relaxation as regards fiscal discipline*, although the data show a favourable evolution. As real interest rate is above GDP growth rate, and primary surplus begins to decrease, the ratio between debt and GDP increases (due to interest payments). All of these factors lead to a fixed limit surpassing in 2003.

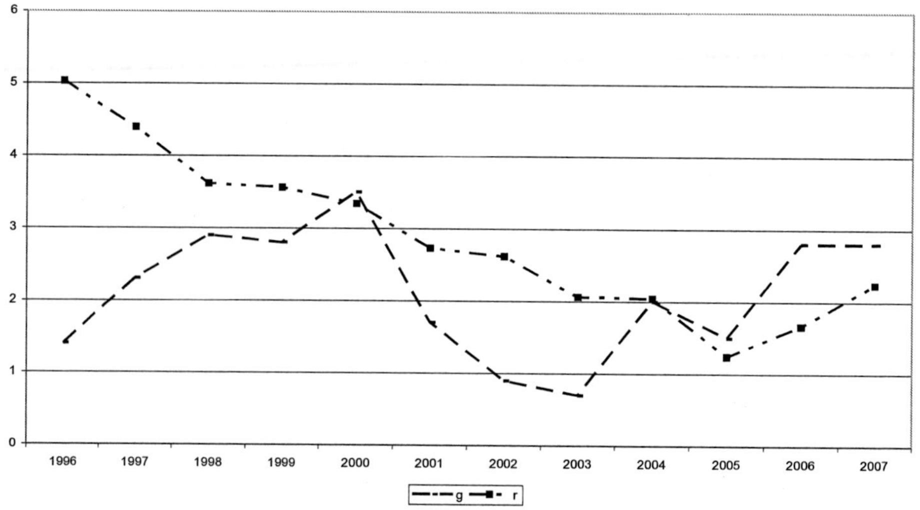

Source: ECB, Monthly Bulletin, several years and own elaboration.

Figure 3. Real interest rate and GDP growth.

Figure. 4. Total public deficit and primary public deficit

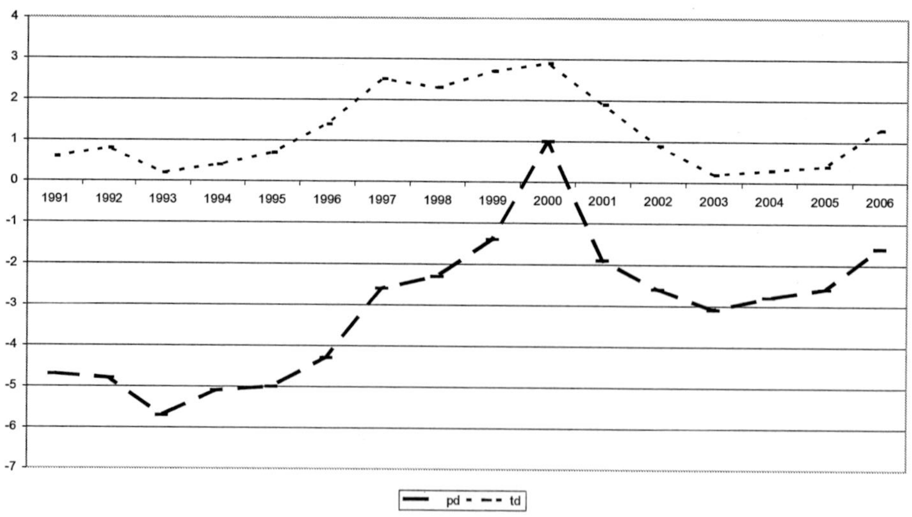

Source: ECB, Monthly Bulletin, several years and own elaboration.

Figure 4. Total public deficit and primary public deficit.

* The behaviour of different countries has been very different. For a detailed analysis by countries of euro-area countries see Galindo and Castaño (2006).

In general terms, it is observed that in the period 1996-2006, the inflation target has been achieved, and there has been an output growth that has made the unemployment[+] rate lowing. Since interest rates have been low, there has not been any sustainability problem; nevertheless public debt limit has been over-passed.

In spite of that, at this moment EMU is facing a great challenge, since the macroeconomic data such us inflation, GDP growth, employment, interest rate, public deficit, etc. have begun to get worse. So, due to the problems derived of economic crisis, European countries could use fiscal policy to resolve their economic problems. In this case it is possible that public finances sustainability problems could appeared. In this situation, certain doubts about the European Central Bank independence will be posing.

6. Conclusion

In this chapter a study of interactions between monetary and fiscal policies in EMU case has been reached, and an empirical analyse of the main EMU macroeconomic data has been realised.

First of all we have presented the singe monetary policy strategy that is characterised by three facts: the specification of prices stability as the main goal, and an implementation framework based on two pillars: the analysis of economic dynamics and shocks and the analysis of monetary trends. ECB has decided to apply a discretional monetary policy, even if the theoretical debate about the application of monetary rules is still alive and rules have a number of supporters.

Contrarily, European authorities have chosen the application of fiscal rules. It has been analysed how fiscal policies could affect the inflation target and sustainability problems of public finances, in it case of countries that carry out excessively expansive fiscal policies, since, these could increase public deficit, and this one could cause the increase of public debt, and this last one fact could increase interest rates.

Despite the theoretical uncertainties analysed, since EMU creation, policy mix has been well performed: the inflation target and output targets have been achieved, and there haven't been any sustainability problem of public finances. Fiscal policy has been more countercyclical than before EMU and monetary policy has get lower inflation rates. But the new crisis panorama has generated some shadows, especially on the sustainability on public finances.

References

[1] Anchuelo, A. (1998), "Aritmética presupuestaria y condiciones fiscales de la UME en España", *Las consecuencias económicas del euro*. Civitas, Madrid.

[2] Andersen, T. M. (2005). "Fiscal stabilization policy in a monetary union with inflation targeting", *ScienceDirect-Journal.*

[3] Andersen, TM, (2002), "Fiscal Policy Coordination", www.regeringe.se/propositioner/sou/pde/remiss.pdf.

1 See statistics of Eurostat

[4] Beetsma, R. and Debrun, X (2004). "The interactions between monetary and fiscal policies in monetary union: a review of recent literature", in Beetsma et al, *Monetary Policy, Fiscal Policies and Labour Markets, Cambridge University Press,* Cambridge, UK.

[5] Beetsma, R. and Bovenberg, A.L. (1999). "Monetary union without fiscal coordination may discipline policymakers", *Journal of International Economics* **45**, pp. 239-258.

[6] Briotii, G. (2005). "Economic reactions to public finance consolidation: a survey of the literature", *Occasional Paper* nº**38**, ECB.

[7] Bustillo, R and Bonete, R. (2000). *Introducción a la Unión Europea: Análisis desde la economía.* Alianza Editorial. Madrid.

[8] Cangiano, M. and Mottu, E. (1999). "Will Fiscal Policy be effective under EMU?. 1998. Working Paper. IFM.

[9] Carrasco, I and Pardo, I. (2007). "El Pacto de Estabilidad y Crecimiento. Implicaciones en una Europa ampliada" *ICE, Revista de Economía*. No. **835**. Pp. 63-77. ISSN: 0019-977 X

[10] Carrasco, I. and Pardo, I. (2006). "Stabilization Policies in the European Union Countries and the Effectiveness of the Stability and Growth Pact", *International Journal of Public Policy*, Vol. 1, Issue 3. pp. 297-308.

[11] Catenaro, M. and Tirelli, P. (2002). "Reconsidering the Pros and Cons of Fiscal Policy Coordination in a Monetary Union: Should we set Public Expenditure Targets?", mimeo, University of Milan-Bicocca.

[12] Cooper, R. (1985). "Economic interdependence and coordination of economic policies" in Jones R.W. and Kenen, P.B. (editors), *Handbook of International Economics,* vol. II. North-Holland, Amsterdam.

[13] De Grauwe, P. (1997). *The Economics of Monetary Integration*, Oxford University Press, New York.

[14] Detken, C. Gaspar, V. and Winkler, B. (2004), "On prosperity and posterity: the need for fiscal discipline in a monetary union", *ECB Working Paper*, nº **420**.

[15] Dixit, A. (2000). *Games of monetary and fiscal interations in the EMU*, Princeton University and UCLA.

[16] European Central Bank (1999-a). "Estrategia de política monetaria del Eurosistema orientada hacia la estabilidad". *Boletín Mensual del BCE*, January, pp. 45-57.

[17] European Central Bank (1999-b). "Estadísticas". *Boletín Mensual del BCE*, January.

[18] European Central Bank (2001a). "El marco de la política económica de la UE", *Boletín Mensual del BCE* , November , pp. 53- 66.

[19] European Central Bank (2001b). "La política fiscal y el crecimiento económico", Boletín Mensual del Banco Central Europeo, August, pp. 41-58

[20] European Central Bank (2002). "Funcionamiento de los estabilizadores fiscales automáticos en la zona euro", *Clm.economía,* nº **1**, pp. 147-172.

[21] European Central Bank (2003). "Estadísticas". *Boletín Mensual del BCE*, January.

[22] European Central Bank (2004). The Monetary Policy of the ECB (2nd edition)

[23] European Central Bank (2005). "Estadísticas". *Boletín Mensual del BCE*, January.

[24] European Central Bank (2008a). "Estadísticas". *Boletín Mensual del BCE*, January.

[25] European Central Bank (2008b). "One monetary policy and many fiscal policies: ensuring a smooth functioning of EMU" Monthly Bulletin, July, pp. 65-78.

[26] Friedman, M. (1956). *Studies in the quantity theory of money*. Chicago: University of Chicago Press

[27] Galindo, M.A and Castaño, M.S. (2006). "La política fiscal y el Pacto de Estabilidad y Crecimiento" in Saiz, J.M., *¿hacia dónde vas Europa?*, Ediciones FIEC, Madrid.

[28] Hamada, K. (1985). *The Political Economy of International Monetary Interdependence*, MIT Press, Cambridge.

[29] Mundell, R. (1961). "A Theory of Optimal Currency Areas", American *Economic Review*, **51**.

[30] Papademos, L. (2006). "Policy-making in EMU: strategies, rules and discretion" *Economic Theory* **27**, pp. 25-38

[31] Taylor, J. B. (1993), "Discretion versus policy rules in practice". *Carnegie-Rochester Conference Series on Public Policy*, **39**, pp. 195-214.

[32] Uhlig, H. (2002). One money, but many fiscal policies in Europe: What are the consequences?, *CEPR, Working Paper* **3296**.

[33] Woodford, M. (2003). *Interest and prices. Foundations of a theory of monetary policy*. Princeton: Princeton University Press.

In: Monetary Growth: Trends, Impacts and Policies
Editors: W.N. Squires et al, pp. 51-64

ISBN: 978-1-60692-305-4

Chapter 3

UNANTICIPATED MONEY GROWTH AND GDP: EVIDENCE FROM KOREA

Vladimir Hlasny
Michigan State Univ.

Abstract

The relationship between nominal and real macroeconomic variables is traditionally illustrated by the expectational Phillips curve. Empirically, there is evidence that short run changes in employment and output result from unanticipated changes in the stock of money and inflation. The problem is that expectations about the growth rates of money stock and prices are not observed. Previous literature estimates them using static models with a limited number of lagged variables. The possibility of omitting important factors or lags in these models is substantial. Furthermore, these models focus on mean expected growth rates and fail to explicitly account for the impact of the potential imprecision in these expectations. This study uses a state-space model where expectations about the money growth rate depend on the long history of macroeconomic variables and their distributions. Priors about the growth rate are updated using a Kalman filter method. Historic quarterly data on the Korean economy is used to infer the one-period-ahead expected growth rates in money stock, price level and price of oil, and to estimate the relationship between the unanticipated growth in money stock and growth of national output. The study controls for the determinants of aggregate supply and demand, money stock and inflation. The results show that a one-percent shock to Korea's money stock increases national demand by 0.02%. The study also confirms validity of the expectational Phillips curve between shocks to unemployment and the unexpected inflation rate.

1. Introduction

The relationship between nominal and real macroeconomic variables is traditionally shown by the Phillips curve (Phillips, 1958, and Lipsey, 1960). This curve has initially described a negative association between wages or price level on one side, and unemployment on the other side. Later, this curve was used to show the tradeoff between inflation and aggregate output. Empirical evidence validated the Phillips curve only in part. Exogenous supply shocks, changes in labor force, and changing institutions and expectations distorted the basic relationship over time. After the criticism by proponents of the natural-rate hypothesis (Friedman, 1968, and Phelps, 1968) and rational expectations (Lucas, 1976), the theoretical foundation of the tradeoff in question was reconsidered. The expectational Phillips curve was devised to answer some of the criticisms. Empirically, there is evidence that short run changes in employment and output result from unanticipated changes in the stock of money and prices. The problem is that usually expectations about the growth rates of money stock and prices are not observed. Tests of the expectational Phillips curve are thus based on imprecise estimates of individuals' expectations. Empirical literature has estimated them using simple static models and restrictive assumptions about individuals' rationality. A limited number of lagged variables has been assumed to capture individuals' full information set (for instance, Sargent, 1976, Fair, 1979, and Barro, 1981). The possibility of omitting important factors or lags in these models is substantial. Furthermore, these models are limited to evaluating the mean expected money growth rate. They ignore the full distribution of the a priori growth rate, and its impact on the evolution of individuals' future expectations.

This study uses a state-space model to relate the levels of actual national output, monetary stock and inflation in any time period, and to study their co-evolution over time. Recognizing the importance of individuals' expectations about the future, the model takes special care in relating actual and expected values of money growth and inflation. In this model, individuals' expectations about monetary growth rates depend on the long histories of the dependent and explanatory variables, their distributions, as well as the precision of past expectations. One-period-ahead priors about monetary growth rate are updated using the Kalman filter method (for example, Chapter 13 in Hamilton, 1994).

1987-2008 quarterly data on South Korean economy are used to estimate the relationship between the unanticipated growth in money stock and prices, and the change in Korea's gross domestic product. The main finding of this study is a confirmation of the relationship between unexpected growth of money stock in an economy and the economy's aggregate demand. A one-percent shock to Korea's money stock increases national demand by 0.02%. This study also confirms validity of the expectational Phillips curve relationship between shocks to unemployment and the unexpected inflation rate.

The next section describes the theoretical model relating money growth, inflation and national output. The following section introduces the estimable state-space model. Section IV describes the available variables and data, and the encountered empirical issues. Sections V and VI present the results and conclude.

2. Model

Using the Lucas supply curve, we can write the actual inflation π_t as a function of the core or underlying rate of inflation, and the difference between the actual and the natural rate of unemployment in a time period.

$$\pi_t = \pi_t^* + \alpha(u_t - \overline{u}_t) \tag{1}$$

π_t^* is the core inflation rate at time t. u_t is the actual unemployment rate and $\overline{u}_t$ the natural unemployment rate at time t. ε_{st} includes supply shocks in period t, such as shocks to input prices. Parameter α is expected to be negative, as unemployment rates below the natural rate create inflationary pressures in aggregate supply.* Core inflation rate is assumed to be a weighted average of the recent values of the actual inflation rate, and the expected inflation rate in time period t.

$$\pi_t^* = \beta_1 \cdot \pi_{t-1} + \beta_2 \cdot \pi_{t-2} + \beta_3 \cdot \pi_{t-3} + \beta_4 \cdot \pi_{t-4} + \beta_5 \cdot \pi_t^e(\cdot) \tag{2}$$

π_t^e is the expected inflation rate for t. $\beta_5 \neq 1$ implies the possibility of inertia, a reaction lag or stickiness of prices and wages, and presumably even risk aversion of price setters. All β_j are expected to be positive, less than one, and may or may not sum up to one depending on the dynamics in the core inflation rate over time. Expected inflation rate depends on the previous observed value of inflation, and on past and present (expected) economic conditions affecting prices. That includes the aggregate stock of money, interest rates, observed aggregate demand, and prices of raw materials in the economy.

$$\pi_t^e = \gamma_1 \cdot \pi_{t-1} + \gamma_2 \cdot \left(m_t^e - m_{t-1}\right) + \gamma_3 \cdot \left(r_{t-1} - r_{t-2}\right) + \gamma_4 \cdot \left(y_{t-1} - \overline{y}_{t-1}\right) + \gamma_5 \cdot \left(p_{oil\,t}^e - p_{oil\,t-1}\right) \tag{3}$$

Here $\left(m_t^e - m_{t-1}\right)$ denotes the change in the log of money supply expected in t, $\left(r_{t-1} - r_{t-2}\right)$ is the observed change in the real interest rate, lagged, $\left(y_{t-1} - \overline{y}_{t-1}\right)$ is the observed deviation in aggregate output from its natural rate, lagged, and $\left(p_{oil\,t}^e - p_{oil\,t-1}\right)$ is the change in the real price of oil expected in t. Aggregate output is in logarithmic form. The effects of money growth and oil prices are thus instantaneous, while the effects of interest rates and aggregate output operate with a lag. γ_3 is expected to be negative, while all other coefficients are expected to be positive.

Deviations in aggregate demand from the natural rate of output can be modeled as a function of the change in real interest rate and a distributed lag function of present and past shocks to the money supply (following Sargent and Wallace, 1975, and Barro and Rush, 1980), assuming prices are not completely flexible.

$$\left(y_t - \overline{y}_t\right) = \Phi(L) \cdot \left(m_t - m_t^e\right) + \varphi_{k+1}\left(r_t - r_{t-1}\right) + \varepsilon_{dt} \tag{4}$$

Both aggregate demand and money stock are in logarithmic form. The relationship between the changes in aggregate demand and the changes in money supply is thus thought to be of constant elasticity. $\Phi(L)$ is a polynomial lag operator of finite order k, whose k parameters φ_j must be estimated. Lag operator of order up to ten is considered (Barro and Rush, 1980). ε_{dt} are aggregate demand shocks in period t. Coefficient on the first lag of the money supply shock, φ_1, is expected to be positive. Previous lags may have positive or negative impacts, depending on the dominance of demand multipliers or rational expectations

* For simplicity, α is modeled as a constant, but more generally could depend on the variance of aggregate output.

regarding m_t at different lengths of displacement. The change in the real interest rate is expected to affect aggregate demand negatively, as the opportunity cost of expenditures increases.

The expected change in the real price of oil is a distributed lag function of the prices of oil observed in the past four quarters. In the following expression, signs of all coefficient are unclear a priori. They depend on the exact dynamics in the real price of oil.

$$\left(p^e_{oil\,t}-p_{oil\,t-1}\right)=\lambda_1\left(p_{oil\,t-1}-p_{oil\,t-2}\right)+\lambda_2\left(p_{oil\,t-2}-p_{oil\,t-3}\right)+\lambda_3\left(p_{oil\,t-3}-p_{oil\,t-4}\right)+\lambda_4\left(p_{oil\,t-4}-p_{oil\,t-5}\right) \quad (5)$$

Finally, the change in the log of money supply expected in t can be written as a distributed lag function of the changes in money supply, and a function of the deviation of lagged unemployment rate from its natural rate $\left(u_{t-1}-\overline{u}_{t-1}\right)$ and deviation of lagged aggregate output from its natural rate. Imprecision in the expectations comes from unobserved money supply shocks, such as the central bank's objectives, changing institutions and political climate, and innovations in the banking sector (Goldfeld, 1976). The lagged changes in money supply, $\left(m_t-m_{t-1}\right)$ are separated into the expected and unexpected parts, to reflect individuals' rational expectations given their previous misjudgment regarding the central bank's moves.

$$\left(m^e_t-m_{t-1}\right)=\Theta_1(L)\cdot\left(m^e_{t-1}-m_{t-2}\right)+\Theta_2(L)\cdot\left(m_{t-1}-m^e_{t-1}\right)+\theta_{2k+1}\cdot\left(u_{t-1}-\overline{u}_{t-1}\right)+\theta_{2k+2}\cdot\left(y_{t-1}-\overline{y}_{t-1}\right) \quad (6)$$

Here $\Theta(L)$ are polynomial lag operators of finite order k, whose $2k$ parameters θ_j must be estimated. Lag operators of order ten are used, for consistency with the assumption on $\Phi(L)$. m_t enters as the log of the M1 measure of aggregate money stock.* Coefficients within Θ_1 and Θ_2 are expected to be positive, while the last two coefficients are unclear, depending on the dominance of pro-cyclical or stabilizing monetary and fiscal policies.

Equation 6 is the main equation of the model that tracks the evolution of expected and unexpected changes to money supply as a function of recent economic trends, success of predicting changes to money supply in the past, and some white noise innovations. It is the state equation that dictates the progression of the system between individual states. Equations 1-4 are measurement equations identifying the diffusion of the changes in the money stock to the future values of other variables in the system. Changes in π_t, π^e_t and y_t are a function of the expected and unexpected money supply growth, other measurable factors and unpredictable innovations. Here ε_{st} and ε_{dt} are serially-uncorrelated white noise error terms,

* The nominal interest rate, following the Fisher identity, is the difference between the real interest rate and the expected inflation rate $i_t=r_t+\pi^e_t$. Variations in the money growth at t-1 affect the real interest rate at t through their impact on the expected aggregate demand (and thus on the expected aggregate stock of output goods) – the liquidity effect. Thus, monetary expansion has two effects – a negative effect on the real interest rate, and a positive effect on inflation. With slow adjustment of prices, we may observe the liquidity effect dominating in the short run, but the expected-inflation effect taking over in the long run (Friedman, 1969). The change in the real interest rate is a simple function of the change in aggregate log output expected at time t $\Delta r_t=-\chi\cdot\Delta y^e_t$. Here the relationship operates though the monetary policy. The Federal Reserve is assumed to

representing shocks to the aggregate supply and demand, as well as imprecision in the measurement of dependent and explanatory variables. They are independent of each other.

A final note should be made that the expected growth rates of money stock and prices should be related to the actually observed growth rates in a particular way. Assuming (1) rational expectations and perfect information regarding past values of relevant variables; and (2) constant underlying institutional and cognitive processes in the economy, the averages of the expected and actual growth rates should be the same in the long run. Within a particular sample period, this long-run property may not hold. With sufficiently long time-series, however, one may restrict the expected cumulative growth rates to equal the observed cumulative rates. For one, this assumes that individuals, learning from their previous forecasting mistakes, never choose to ignore mistakes made long time ago. Knowing *each* past value of aggregate output, inflation, money stock and unemployment, as well as the time-constant relationships among them, is always helpful to forecasting future growth rates, a rather strong but standard assumption.

3. Estimation

The dynamics of the expected growth of money stock in Korea is investigated using a linear state-space model, fitted using a maximum-likelihood method refined by the Kalman filter. This model allows for uncertainty over true inflation, aggregate output and the central bank's monetary policy. The estimates of uncertainty in the model are based on the likelihood function for the available data.

Because the effect of unanticipated money stock on aggregate output is the central theme of this paper, precision in estimation of the aggregate output is the main objective. The objective function for the model is thus the likelihood of observing the actual values for each y_t, conditional on the information set at time *t*.

$$L(\alpha,\beta,\gamma,\varphi,\lambda,\theta;m) = pr(y_1, y_2, \ldots, y_T) = \prod_{t=1}^{T} pr(y_t \mid y_{t-1}, y_{t-2}, \ldots, y_1) \qquad (7)$$

The likelihood for the entire sample is just the product of likelihoods of the *T* individual observations. The goal of our estimation is to find model parameters maximizing this joint likelihood. We can let $y_{t|t-1}$ denote the conditional expectation of y_t given all our knowledge as of time period *t*, which covers information on all y_s, m_s, π_s, u_s and $p_{oil\ s}$ up to and including $s=t-1$. Assuming the errors in the model are close to Gaussian, we can write the appropriate log-likelihood function as

$$\log(L) = \sum_{t=1}^{T} \log[pr(y_t)] = -\frac{1}{2}\log(2\pi) - \frac{1}{2}\sum_{t=1}^{T} \log[\text{var}(y_t)] - \frac{1}{2}\sum_{t=1}^{T} \frac{(y_t - \hat{y}_t)^2}{\text{var}(y_t)} \qquad (8)$$

conduct the open-market operations in an attempt to keep the federal funds rate as close as possible to its target (Meulendyke, 1990).

where the conditioning on $y_{t-1}, \ldots y_1$ is suppressed. Model parameters maximizing this log-likelihood can be found numerically with the help of a recursive Kalman filter. The Kalman filter has two steps, the prediction step and the update step. The prediction step uses information from the previous time period to produce an estimate in the current time period. The updating step then uses measurement information from the current time period to refine the prediction. In the prediction step, we note that

$$\hat{m}^e_{t|t-1} = \hat{m}_{t-1} + \Theta_1(L)\cdot\left(\hat{m}^e_{t-1|t-1} - \hat{m}_{t-2}\right) + \Theta_2(L)\cdot\left(\hat{m}_{t-1} - \hat{m}^e_{t-1|t-1}\right) + \theta_{2k+1}\cdot\left(u_{t-1} - \hat{\hat{u}}_{t-1}\right) + \theta_{2k+2}\cdot\left(y_{t-1} - \hat{\bar{y}}_{t-1}\right) \tag{9}$$

and

$$\mathrm{var}\left(m^e_{t|t-1}\right) = \left\{\left[\Theta_1(L) - \Theta_2(L)\right]^2 + \theta^2_{2k+1}\alpha^{-2}\beta_5^2\left[\gamma_2^2 + \gamma_4^2\Phi^2(L)L\right] + \theta^2_{2k+2}\Phi^2(L)\right\}\mathrm{var}\left(m^e_{t-1|t-1}\right) + z \tag{10}$$

In Equation 10, z is a simple function quadratic in coefficients and linear in variances of error terms from Equations 1-6 $(\beta_j, \gamma_j, \theta_j, \varphi_j; \sigma_d^2)$.* $\Phi^2(L)L\,\mathrm{var}\left(m^e_{t-1|t-1}\right)$ denotes the squared lag polynomial lagged by one period, or $\Phi^2(L)\mathrm{var}\left(m^e_{t-2|t-2}\right)$.

The updating step of the Kalman filter uses measurement information from a time period to refine the prediction in Equations 9 and 10 for the same time period. As a result, even more accurate estimates of m_t^e for the same time period can be obtained.

$$\hat{\pi}^e_{t|t-1} = \gamma_1\cdot\pi_{t-1} + \gamma_2\cdot\left(\hat{m}^e_{t|t-1} - m_{t-1}\right) + \gamma_3\cdot\left(r_{t-1} - r_{t-2}\right) + \gamma_4\cdot\left(y_{t-1} - \hat{\bar{y}}_{t-1|t-1}\right) + \gamma_5\cdot\left(\hat{p}^e_{oil\,t|t-1} - p_{oil\,t-1}\right) \tag{3b}$$

$$\left(\hat{y}_{t|t-1} - \hat{\bar{y}}_{t|t-1}\right) = \Phi(L)\cdot\left(m_t - \hat{m}^e_{t|t-1}\right) + \varphi_{k+1}\left(r_t - r_{t-1}\right) \tag{4b}$$

$$\mathrm{var}\left(\pi^e_{t|t-1}\right) = \gamma_2^2\cdot\mathrm{var}\left(m^e_{t|t-1}\right) + \gamma_4^2\cdot\mathrm{var}\left(\bar{y}_{t-1|t-1}\right) + \gamma_5^2\cdot\mathrm{var}\left(p^e_{oil\,t|t-1}\right) \tag{11}$$

$$\mathrm{var}\left(y_{t|t-1}\right) = \Phi^2(L)\mathrm{var}\left(m^e_{t|t-1}\right) + \sigma_d^2 \tag{12}$$

In the updating phase, the gain that minimizes the error between the desired response and the prediction in time period t – the stepping stone of Kalman filter – can be written as

$$K_{st} = \frac{\mathrm{var}\left(m^e_{t|t-1}\right)\cdot\left[\alpha^{-1}\beta_5\gamma_2 + \alpha^{-1}\beta_5\gamma_4\Phi(L)L\right]}{\mathrm{var}\left(m^e_{t|t-1}\right)\cdot\left[\alpha^{-2}\beta_5^2\gamma_2^2 + \alpha^{-2}\beta_5^2\gamma_4^2\Phi^2(L)L\right] + \left[\alpha^{-2}\sigma_s^2 + \alpha^{-2}\beta_5^2\gamma_4^2\sigma_d^2\right]} \tag{13}$$

and

$$K_{dt} = \frac{\mathrm{var}\left(m^e_{t|t-1}\right)\cdot\Phi(L)}{\mathrm{var}\left(m^e_{t|t-1}\right)\cdot\Phi^2(L) + \sigma_d^2} \tag{13b}$$

---

* $z = \theta^2_{2k+1}\cdot\alpha^{-2}\cdot\left[\sigma_s^2 + \beta_5^2\cdot\gamma_4^2\cdot\sigma_d^2\right] + \theta^2_{2k+2}\cdot\sigma_d^2$

where K_{st} is the gain in Equation 1, and K_{dt} is the gain in Equation 4. The updated estimate of $m^e{}_t$, using the measurement information from period t, becomes

$$\hat{m}^e_{t|t} = \hat{m}^e_{t|t-1} + K_{dt}\left[(y_t - \bar{y}_t) - \Phi(L)(m_t - \hat{m}^e_{t|t-1}) - \varphi_{k+1}(r_t - r_{t-1})\right] + K_{st}\left[\alpha(u_t - \bar{u}_t) - (\pi_t - \hat{\pi}^*_t(\hat{m}^e_{t|t-1}))\right] \quad (14)$$

where $\hat{\pi}^*_t\left(\hat{m}^e_{t|t-1}\right)$ is the core inflation rate computed using the prediction from the first phase of the Kalman filter. Finally, variance of this updated estimate of $m^e{}_{t+1}$ is

$$\mathrm{var}(m^e_{t|t}) = \mathrm{var}(m^e_{t|t-1}) \cdot \left\{1 - K_{dt}\left[\Phi(L)(m_t - \hat{m}^e_{t|t-1}) - \varphi_{k+1}(r_t - r_{t-1})\right] - K_{st}\alpha^{-1}\left[\pi_t - \pi^*_t(\hat{m}^e_{t|t-1})\right]\right\} \quad (15)$$

To implement the recursive model we need to specify the initial values of the mean and variance of the expected money stock ($\hat{m}^e_{1|1}$ and $\mathrm{var}(m^e_{1|1})$). For an initial year $t=1$, we may assume that prior expectations regarding money growth were precise. It is furthermore plausible that $u_0 = \bar{u}_0$ and $y_0 = \bar{y}_0$, and so we can write

$$\hat{m}^e_{1|0} = m_0 + \Theta_1(L)\cdot(m_0 - m_{-1}) \quad (16)$$

and

$$\mathrm{var}(m^e_{1|0}) = \Theta^2_1(L)\,\mathrm{var}(m_{0|0}) \quad (17)$$

In the absence of more information about individuals' expectations in the initial period (coming from a source other than the used dataset), or assuming that the system started at a steady state with perfectly predictable dynamics, we may use these expressions as reasonable approximations.* Note that expressions (16) and (17) allow for growth and uncertainty in the expected money stock due to the actual previous levels of the money stock, and Gaussian uncertainty. There is by assumption no contribution or noise due to shocks in the aggregate output or the unemployment rate, because these trends arose only in the modeled years. Equations (16) and (17) allow the recursive Kalman filter to derive the rationally expected money stock in all future years, and find the set of parameters that maximize the model log-likelihood.+

The system of Equations 1-15 is estimated in the General Algebraic Modeling System (GAMS), a flexible mathematical programming platform that allows one to impose arbitrary objective functions, restrictions and other model specifications, and model-solving algorithms. GAMS also allows the computation of various statistics and measures of fit.

* It turns out that the initial period of our empirical analysis, first quarter of 1987, occurred during a stable time period when oil prices (as well as prices of other raw materials), inflation, aggregate output and money stock grew at a relatively constant, sustainable and predictable pace. Refer to Figure 1 and discussion in Section IV.

\+ Standard errors of all parameters can be found using the inverse of the Hessian matrix at the maximum (the Fisher information matrix). Residuals from Equations 1-6 can be calculated and analyzed for any evidence of functional form misspecification.

4. Data and Empirical Issues

Our model is estimated for quarters starting with 1987:3 and ending with 2008:1. There are potentially several empirical problems with that time range, but also several advantages. This section discusses the potential pitfalls, and the arguments justifying our selection.

Our ability to estimate unbiased and efficient model parameters depends on the quality of the available data. Model estimating the dynamics of variables over time requires that the data follow the same underlying process and do not appreciably change in their structure during the analyzed years. This is usually a strong requirement from data, and particularly so for long time-series macroeconomic variables, and for countries undergoing economic transition.

Between 1987 and 2008, South Korea underwent several significant political and economic regime changes. Until 1993, military leadership exercised central planning and promoted the country's export expansion by backing industry financially and legally (against downturns, lack of expertise, competition, labor disputes etc.). During the 1990s, in pursuit of growth in high value-added and technology industries, leftist government continued working with major conglomerates (chaebol) hand in hand. The economy remained under command and control governance until 1997, when the financial crisis prompted oversight from abroad and brought about widespread restructuring (Hlasny, 2008a,b). The financial crisis itself represents a problem to estimation, because all relevant variables underwent large changes that were not generated within the model and could not be explained using past model dynamics. Since 1998, deregulation, corporate restructuring and privatization have continued in Korea at a varying pace until present. A related issue is that political and regulatory changes have presumably affected individuals' expectations about the relationships among macroeconomic variables. In spite of these regime changes, it is hoped that the performance of the Korean economy evolves according to a constant underlying process, and that our model can shed light on this process as well as on the role that individuals' rational expectations play in it.

Another empirical issue concerns the starting point of estimation. The Kalman filter method mandates that the initial year under analysis exhibit certain steady state properties. This would allow the model to unravel using only the dynamics observed within a sample of time periods. In macroeconomic setting, it is difficult to pinpoint the time when a set of variables started interacting. 1987 is obviously not the birth year of the Korean economy, but data on several variables are unavailable for prior years.[+] In any case, the true birth year of the country's economy is difficult to track down amid Korea's turbulent modern history (Cumings, 1997).[*]

+ 1987:1 allows inclusion of lagged explanatory variables in Equations 2-6 even in the first quarter under analysis.

* Korea, an agrarian and Confucian society, remained secluded from the outside world and closed to foreign trade until late 19th century. In the 1880s, following a government reform movement, ports were opened to foreign vessels, and industry opened to foreign technologies. Western powers were allowed to acquire interests in Korean gold and coal mines, operate public utilities and transportation, and open factories. Trade in raw resources, agricultural products with Japan and China exploded. During 1905-1945, as a Japanese protectorate, Korea became industrialized. Manufacturing and agricultural production soared. Labor was relocated by force to Japan's mainland. (The flow of resources and funds during the colonization period is difficult to track, as the boundaries within Japan's empire became unimportant.) In the aftermath of WWII, in the wake of the Cold War, the peninsula was tactically split in half. Soon it became engulfed in Korean War. Devastated, Korea became fiscally dependent on US postwar grants and the presence of US military (as it was an important bastion of the free world). Between 1945-1965 Korea received over $12 billion from US treasury, and at least into the late 1970s, assistance from the US and Japan accounted for more than half of Korea's fiscal revenues.

Of the possible candidates, 1987 is a good initial year for this analysis, because it sees relatively stable growth rates of GDP, prices, unemployment and money stock. Politically, late 1980s mark the end of long-standing military rule in Korea and the ascent of market competition (albeit still carefully watched by government stakeholders) – a point in time that can be considered steady-state. Table 1 describes the available data and the variables to be estimated in the model. Figure 1 shows time plots of the observable variables. Most notably, the recessions of 1980 and 1997 are clearly discernable in all the time series.

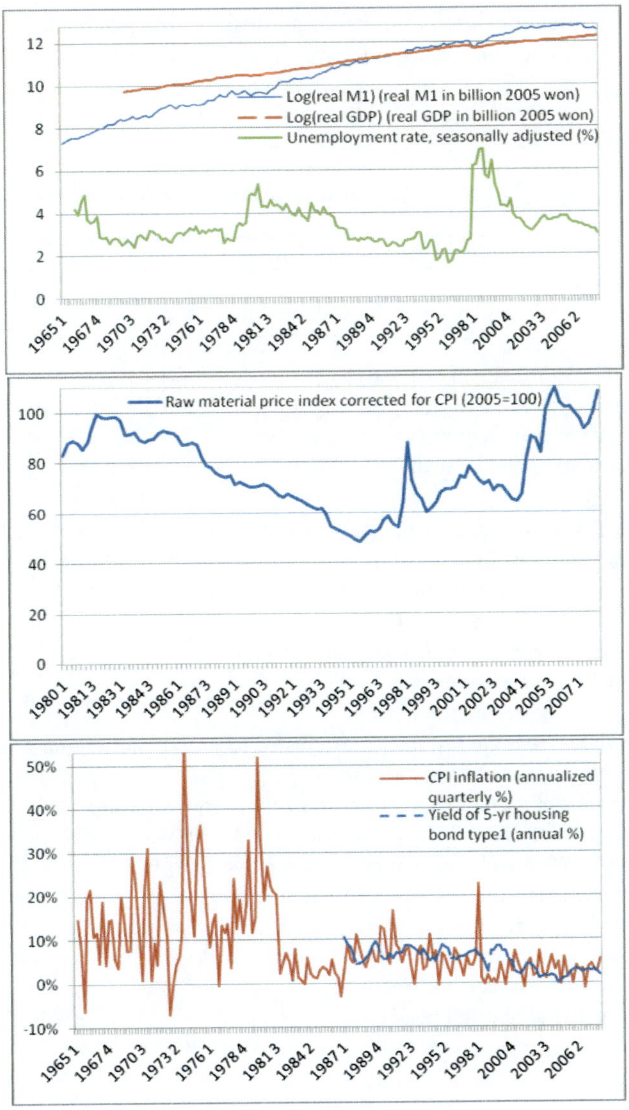

Figure 1. Observable Model Variables.

Servicing of US military represented another significant source of national income. From the 1950s into the 1970s, Korea's government-planned and US-assisted economic growth relied on imitating production processes in industrialized countries (import substitution industrialization). Current, conglomerate-dominated face of the Korean economy arguably dissociated from governmental management can be traced back to mid-1970s.

Finally, a comment is warranted regarding the relationship between actual and expected growth rates of money and prices. Average expected and actual growth rates of money are made exactly equal to one another. Average expected and actual inflation rates are also made equal to each other. These restrictions are made under the assumptions of long-run rational expectations and constant underlying institutional and cognitive processes. In particular, 84 quarters are assumed to represent a sufficiently long period when long-run properties may be thought to hold. Yet, 1987:3-2008:1 are also assumed to be homogenous in the underlying political processes, financial institutions, and individuals' understanding of the central bank's objectives, so that the intertemporal relationships underlying all model variables remain the same. This is plausible in Korea where the modern democratic and market principles, and market landscape have been in place since the late 1980s, and where the central bank operates under the same jurisdiction since 1962.

Table 1. Estimated and Explanatory Variables

Variable	Description (Units)	Availability
Estimated Variables		
m_t^e	Expected real M1 money stock in t (billion 2005 won)	
π_t^*	Core inflation rate in t (%·0.01)	
π_t^e	Expected inflation rate in t (%·0.01)	
$p^e_{oil\ t}$	Expected real price of oil in t (price index $p_{oil\ 2005} = 100$)	
$\check{y}_t$	Natural rate of real GDP in t (billion 2005 won)	
$\bar{u}_t$	Natural rate of unemployment in t (%·0.01)	
Explanatory Variables		
m_t	Actual real M1 money stock in t (billion 2005 won)	1960:1-2008:1
π_t	Actual inflation rate in t (%·0.01)[a]	1965:2-2008:1
$p_{oil\ t}$	Actual real price of oil in t (price index $p_{oil\ 2005} = 100$)[b]	1980:1-2008:1
y_t	Actual real GDP in t (billion 2005 won)	1970:2-2008:1
u_t	Actual unempl. rate in t, seasonally adjusted (%·0.01)[c]	1966:1-2008:1
r_t	Actual real rate of interest (%·0.01)[d]	1987:1-2008:1

Source: Bank of Korea, Economic Statistics System

Notes: Real monetary variables and interest rates are adjusted for inflation using up-to-date, annualized CPI.

[a] Quarterly CPI inflation rate converted to annual rate: $(1+\pi_{quarter})^4-1$.

[b] Price index of raw materials for crude fuel, divided by CPI and normalized so that $p_{oil\ 2005}=100$.

[c] Unemployment rate on quarterly basis is available for 1999:3-2008:1. Unemployment rate on annual basis is available for 1963-2007, and the number of employed workers is available for 1966:1-2008:1. Quarterly unemployment rate for 1987:2-1999:2 is interpolated using the annual unemployment rates, inversely weighted by the number of employed workers. This assumes that, within a year, movements in and out of labor force approximately offset each other. Constant seasonal effects as well as linear and quadratic growth in seasonal effects are removed.

[d] Annual yields of 5-year national housing bonds, type 1, adjusted for up-to-date annualized CPI inflation.

5. Results

The model in Sections II-III was estimated for quarters starting with 1987:3 and ending with 2008:1. Lagged explanatory variables in Equations 2-6 came from time range 1984:4 to 2008:1. Table 2 presents the main results. The first coefficient, in the Lucas supply curve (Equation 1), verifies that there is a negative trade-off between unemployment rate and unexpected inflation rate. One percentage point decrease in unemployment from its natural rate appears to increase annual inflation by 0.6 percentage points. Figure 2 illustrates this relationship in our sample. The next set of rows shows that core inflation is primarily determined by expected inflation, and to some degree by a two-quarter lag of actual inflation. One could say that the economy is able to implement 92.7% of the expected inflation within the coming quarter. This suggests that inertia, price stickiness and reaction lags are not very important in affecting the price level in the Korean economy. To the extent that there is reaction lag, it appears three quarters long. The five coefficients in Equation 2 sum up to 1.007 as one could expect under rational expectations.

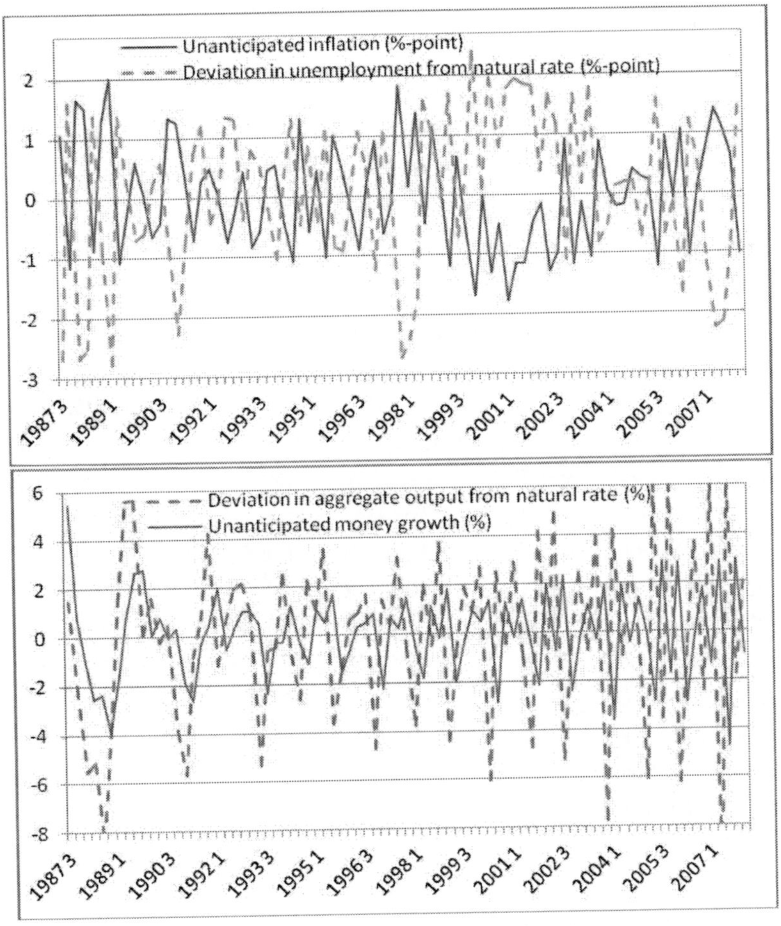

Figure 2. Unemployment v. Unanticipated Inflation, and Unanticipated Money Growth v. GDP

Coefficients in the expected inflation equation (Equation 3) show that the expected inflation is primarily determined by the expected changes in the money supply, and the change in national output in the preceding quarter. Surprisingly, the expected increase in the price of oil has essentially zero (but positive, as expected) effect on the expected inflation. This is perhaps due to individuals' imprecision in forecasting oil prices, or to delayed responses of the general price level in Korea to oil prices. This could also be due to our imprecise measure of the price of oil. Lagged changes in the interest rate have a small negative effect on inflation.

Coefficients in the expected oil price equation (Equation 5) show that the expected real price depends significantly on the recently observed oil prices (showing close to a unit-root in the equation). The coefficients sum up to 4.01 which is significantly higher than a naive expectation of unity. That indicates that the real price of oil is highly auto-correlated and exploding, and that individuals may take recent oil-price increases as evidence of further increases of greater magnitude in the future.

The second column, with coefficients for Equation 6, indicates that the growth rates in money supply expected in the past are positively correlated with the expectation of money growth today. This is expected, because monetary decisions are in part predictable, and possibly even a deterministic function of past decisions. The next group of coefficients, θ_{11}-θ_{20}, show that the expected money growth depends positively on individuals' forecasting errors in the past. This verifies that individuals use rational expectations, and adjust their forecasts according to the performance of their past forecasts. Coefficients θ_{21} and θ_{22} imply that the deviations of unemployment rate and aggregate output from their natural rates in the preceding period affect the expected money growth negatively. This combination of coefficients is difficult to explain and reconcile, and probably reflects a variety of pro-cyclical, stabilizing and stimulus programs by the Bank of Korea.

Table 2. Main Model Results

Coefficient	(Std. Error)	Coefficient	(Std. Error)	Coefficient	(Std. Error)
Aggregate Supply Equation		Expected Money Stock Equation		θ_{19}	0.0043‡ (0.0000)
α	-0.0060‡ (0.0000)	θ_1	0.0069‡ (0.0000)	θ_{20}	0.0000 (0.0000)
Core Inflation Equation		θ_2	0.0039‡ (0.0000)	θ_{21}	-0.0005‡ (0.0000)
β_1	0.0000‡ (0.0000)	θ_3	0.0000‡ (0.0000)	θ_{22}	-0.4693‡ (0.0000)
β_2	0.0004‡ (0.0000)	θ_4	0.0038‡ (0.0000)		
β_3	0.0799‡ (0.0000)	θ_5	0.0019‡ (0.0000)	Aggregate Demand Equation	
β_4	0.0000‡ (0.0000)	θ_6	0.0000 (0.0000)	φ_1	0.0177‡ (0.0000)
β_5	0.9269‡ (0.0000)	θ_7	0.0068‡ (0.0000)	φ_2	0.9776‡ (0.0000)
Expected Inflation Equation		θ_8	0.0007‡ (0.0000)	φ_3	-0.4167‡ (0.0000)
γ_1	0.0002‡ (0.0001)	θ_9	0.0035‡ (0.0000)	φ_4	-0.3607‡ (0.0000)
γ_2	85.4249‡ (0.0086)	θ_{10}	0.0001‡ (0.0000)	φ_5	0.9218‡ (0.0000)
γ_3	-0.0002 (0.0004)	θ_{11}	0.0047‡ (0.0000)	φ_6	-0.9975‡ (0.0000)
γ_4	40.1759‡ (0.0040)	θ_{12}	0.0037‡ (0.0000)	φ_7	-0.5775‡ (0.0000)
γ_5	0.0001 (0.0000)	θ_{13}	0.0023‡ (0.0000)	φ_8	-0.0610‡ (0.0000)
Expected Oil Price Equation		θ_{14}	0.0021‡ (0.0000)	φ_9	1.0000‡ (0.0000)
λ_1	0.8124‡ (0.0146)	θ_{15}	0.0008‡ (0.0000)	φ_{10}	0.1736‡ (0.0000)
λ_2	1.0609‡ (0.0147)	θ_{16}	0.0032‡ (0.0000)	φ_{11}	-0.4711‡ (0.0000)
λ_3	1.1922‡ (0.0148)	θ_{17}	0.0050‡ (0.0000)	φ_{12}	-0.2347‡ (0.0001)
λ_4	0.9431‡ (0.0148)	θ_{18}	0.0000 (0.0000)		
Observations	83				
Log likelihood	-0.979				
Quasi R-squared	0.999				

Standard errors are in parentheses. ‡ Significant at 1%, two-sided test.

The last column shows coefficients estimated for Equation 4. Coefficients φ_1-φ_{11} have varying signs and magnitudes. As expected, unanticipated money growth has a positive, stimulating effect (φ_1) on aggregate demand in the same time period. One percent shock to the money stock has a 0.02 percent effect on aggregate demand. Figure 2 shows this relationship as estimated for our sample. Unanticipated money growth in preceding quarters has mixed effects on aggregate demand. We have no clear interpretation for this without delving into the particular circumstances linking aggregate demand and money stock in Korea. These coefficients may also be an artifact of the particular sample used, and may change in a different sample. φ_{12} implies that the interest rate has a negative effect on aggregate demand. One percentage point increase in interest rates tends to retard aggregate demand by 0.002 percent.

Finally, we can note that standard errors, log likelihood ratio and quasi R-squared all confirm high measure of fit of the model to actual data. This provides some evidence that the model was well specified and that the qualitative as well as quantitative findings are not only interesting but also valid.

6. Conclusions

This study has used a state-space model where expectations about the money growth rate depend on the long history of macroeconomic variables and their distributions. Priors about the growth rate were updated using a Kalman filter method. Historic quarterly data on the Korean economy were used to infer the one-period-ahead expected growth rates in money stock, price level and price of oil, and to estimate the relationship between the unanticipated growth in money stock and growth of national output. The study has controlled for the determinants of aggregate supply and demand, money stock and inflation. The main contribution of this study is a confirmation of the relationship between unexpected growth of money stock in an economy and the economy's aggregate demand. A one-percent shock to Korea's money stock increases national demand by 0.02%. This study also confirms validity of the expectational Phillips curve relationship between shocks to unemployment and the unexpected inflation rate. More broadly, this study contributes to understanding of the intricate linkages among macroeconomic variables, and the workings of national economies. Taking modern Korea as its subject, the study has advanced understanding of data that have not yet received sufficient attention.

References

[1] Barro, Robert J., "Unanticipated Money Growth and Economic Activity in the U.S." In *Money, Expectations and Business Cycles*, Academic Press, p.137-169, 1981.

[2] Barro Robert J., and Mark Rush, "Unanticipated Money and Economic Activity." In *Rational Expectations and Economic Policy*. Ed. Stanley Fischer, NBER, 1980.

[3] Cumings, Bruce. *Korea's Place in the Sun: A Modern History*, W.W. Norton, 1st Edition, 1997.

[4] Fair, Ray C., "An Analysis of the Accuracy of Four Macroeconometric Models." *Journal of Political Economy* **87**(4):701-718, August 1979.

[5] Friedman, Milton, "The Role of Monetary Policy." *American Economic Review* **58**(1):1-17, March 1968.

[6] Friedman, Milton, "The Optimum Quantity of Money." In *The Optimum Quantity of Money and Other Essays*, p.1-50, Chicago: Aldine Publishing, 1969.

[7] Goldfeld, Stephen M., "The Case of the Missing Money." *Brookings Papers on Economic Activity*, **3**:683-730, 1976.

[8] Hamilton, James D., *Time Series Analysis*. Princeton University Press, Princeton, 1st Edition, 1994.

[9] Hlasny, Vladimir. "Regulatory Climate Change in Korea." *Korea Policy Review* **4**(1):55-58, January 2008a.

[10] Hlasny, Vladimir. "Competition and Competitiveness among Korean Firms." *Korea Herald* Feature & Analysis, p.4, 14-March 2008b.

[11] Kalman, Rudolf E. "A New Approach to Linear Filtering and Prediction Problems." *Transaction of the ASME—Journal of Basic Engineering* **82**(1):35-45, March 1960.

[12] Lipsey, R., "The Relation between Unemployment and the Rate of Change of Money Wage Rates in the United Kingdom, 1862-1957: A Further Analysis." *Economica* **27**(105):1-31, February 1960.

[13] Lucas, Robert E., Jr., "Econometric Policy Evaluation: A Critique," Carnegie-Rochester *Conference Series on Public Policy* **1**:19-46, Elsevier, 1976.

[14] Meulendyke, Ann-Marie, "U.S. Monetary Policy and Financial Markets," Federal Reserve Bank of New York, New York, 1990.

[15] Phillips, Alban W., "The Relation between Unemployment and the Rate of Change of Money Wage Rates in the United Kingdom, 1861-1959" *Economica* **25**:283-299, November 1958.

[16] Romer, David, *Advanced Macroeconomics*, McGraw-Hill Intl., 1996.

[17] Sargent, Thomas J., "A Classical Macroeconometric Model for the United States," *Journal of Political Economy*, April 1976.

[18] Sargent, Thomas J., and Neil Wallace, "'Rational' Expectations, the Optimal Monetary Instrument, and the Optimal Money Supply Rule," *Journal of Political Economy*, **83**(2), 1975.

Short Communications

In: Monetary Growth: Trends, Impacts and Policies
Editors: W.N. Squires et al, pp. 67-76

ISBN: 978-1-60692-305-4

Short Communication A

MONETARY POLICY AND ECONOMIC GROWTH

Miguel-Ángel Galindo
University of Castilla-la Mancha, Spain

Abstract

Traditionally different factors and variables have been considered in the economic growth models. Following Solow's model, economists considered physical capital and technology during 1950s-1980s as the main forces that promote economic growth. With the introduction of endogenous growth models, new forms of capital were introduced in the production function; human capital, public capital income distribution and more recently social capital.

The improvement of statistical information has favored the introduction of different kind of variables in the economic growth models. However, monetary policy has not been sufficiently analyzed in this literature. Except in the case of a few approaches, it is considered that monetary policy affects economic growth indirectly through other variables that directly have any influence on growth, for instnace, inflation. The main goal of this paper is to show the way monetary policy could have effects on economic growth process, considering some approaches, such as Tobin, Levhari and Patinkin, Schumpeter and Kaleckian models.

Introduction

During the last decades, economic growth and its causes have been considered as the most important questions in economics: "economic growth has become the secular religion of advancing industrial societies" (Bell, 1976, 237). The main reason of this relevance is due to the fact that economic growth implies higher prosperity (e.g. Layard, 1997). Therefore, from this point of view economic growth is considered as an ultimate measure of a country well-being, because it implies more employment and more products and services. Economic growth facilitates the achievement of other objectives (employment, income distribution…) that have a positive impact on individuals' happiness

For this reason political process is especially worried on this question. Countries rate the incompetence of the government activity in terms of economic growth. Higher economic growth rates imply an adequate economic policy and are cause of national pride. So, those countries that achieve lower economic growth must change their policy strategy and they have to follow and to copy the policies designed by the higher economic growth countries.

As it is well known two main economic growth models have been developed since 1950s: exogenous and endogenous growth models. Former assumes, among other questions, the existence of appropriate institutions for markets and they don't introduce any price distortions and there are no resources misallocations. All at all, exogenous growth models assume that the institutions operate in an appropriate way. There are not possibilities to create monopolies and the efficiency of the system prevents the existence of corruption.

The exogenous growth models are based on Solow (1956) approach that supposed the start of the modern era of the economic growth analysis. He developed an exogenous growth model that implies that the variables are exogenous determined. The exogenous technological changes are the necessary condition to improve growth. Economic policy would have effects at short term but not at long term. This conclusion and the fact that the economic situation of the countries in the 1950s and 1960s was positive in terms of employment and growth rates, explain the reasons because economists lost again interest to study economic growth process. Likewise this model predicted the existence the convergence among the nations.

However, the situation changed dramatically during the 1970s and 1980s. The stagflation and the ineffectiveness of the orthodox policies as well as the appearance of the endogenous growth models (Romer, 1986, 1987, Aghion and Howitt, 1998), favoured the return to the economic growth analysis. In opposition to exogenous growth models these models stated that the variables are endogenous determined and questioned the convergence hypothesis.

Endogenous growth models on the other way, introduces the factor accumulation from R&D expenditure, the spillovers from introduction of new technology, the development of human capital… that have relevant effects on productivity that enhances economic growth. In this sense, it is possible to incorporate the effects of governance on the capital-augmenting effects as well as on the efforts of individuals.

This return to economic growth analysis was also favored by the improvement of econometrician methods and empirical data. Since the 1990s a huge empirical literature has been developed, considering not only quantitative variables but also qualitative variables and new factors. The number of countries introduced in the test has also increased.

However, in these approaches money is not considered usually. The main factors consider are the real ones, and it is supposed that the inflation reduction has a positive effect on economic growth. And this target can be achieved with an independent central bank and with a restrictive monetary policy.

It is assumed that at short term it is possible that monetary policy would have some effects on income. But at long-term the most approaches consider that real variables are the main factors to alter economic growth path. The objective of this paper is to show some approaches in which monetary policy would have effects on economic growth. Before that, in the next section we will analyze the monetary mechanisms of transmissions and we will finish with the main conclusions of our analysis.

The Role Of Monetary Policy

From the theoretical point of view, economic growth models have not considered the role of money of money in the process. Since the 1960s the so-called superneutrality of money – that is permanent change of money has not long-term effects on the real interest rate, capital accumulation and output growth- has been the subject of a huge theoretical analysis.

There have been other kind of analysis that refute the supreneutrality of money, for example the Tobin (1965) model as we will see below. However, in general terms, it is defended that monetary policy would have some effects on income at short-term and depending on the authors, it would not have effects at long-term.

From this perspective, the monetary authority could be interested to improve the economic growth of a country and monetary policy could have some influence about economic activity and employment over short term. A restrictive or expansive monetary policy would have some influence on the cycle of the economy, mainly through variations of the aggregate demand, as we will see in the next section. If a monetary policy is bad designed could end up the expansionary stage of the economy. If the monetary policy is well designed could introduce stable conditions that would have positive effects on future economic activity. It would be a pro-growth policy achieving a stable basis for a long-term growth.

Considering the long-term economic growth, the main influence of the monetary policy it would be controlling inflation rate. Economic agents must understand that the main target of the monetary authority in the control of inflation. Therefore, in this case the focus is on the supply side, trying to know how to increase the productivity capacity of the economy. This is the main reason why the economic growth models have not considered traditionally the money in their analysis.

The main monetary transmission mechanisms are showed in figure- 1.

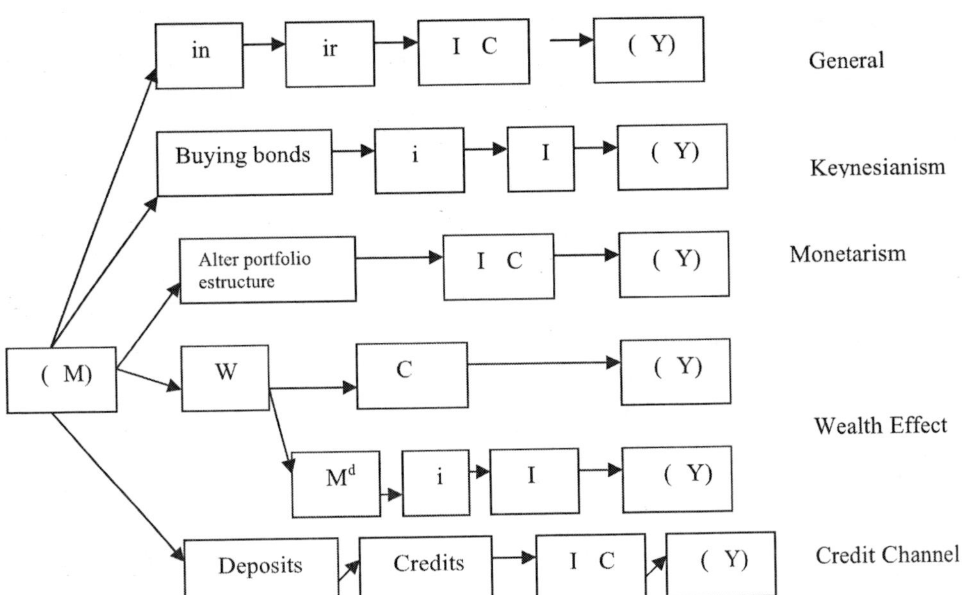

M: Money Supply; in, nominal interest rate; ir, real interest rate; I, investment; C, consumption; Y, income; W, wealth, M^d demand of money

Source: Own elaboration

Figure 1.

As we can see, there are several ways in which money supply alter income. We have supposed and increase of money supply. In all the cases, income increases except in the wealth effect that the final result would depend on elasticity of demand on money in relation to the consumption effect on income. That is, it must compare the income increase due to the higher consumption with the income reduction due to the increase of demand of money.

There is also another mechanism due to exchange rate that has also a no definitive conclusion on income. Currency depreciation due to a higher money supply would increase exports and reduce imports, so the income would be higher. However, the prices of raw materials will be higher, increasing the production costs that reduce income.

All in all, we can see that monetary policy can affect to income in different ways. However, it is interesting to analyze if it is possible to alter it at long-term.

Monetary Policy and Long-Term

As it is shown in a previous section, the main target of the monetary policy at long-term is to control inflation. Due to a low inflation, the economy would be more stable and a more sable basis is introduced for a long-term growth.

Economic growth models have stressed the influence of several factors on economic growth. Depending on the approach, different variables have been considered, being the most relevant, physical capital, human capital, social capital, income distribution, among others. Therefore, following some recent models, the behavior of such variables would have effects on economic growth.

Orphanides and Solow (1990, p. 228) state that the basic mechanism to analyze the relationship between money and growth is studying the effects of money on the real interest rate and thereby on capital accumulation. This possibility was showed by Metzler (1951) when he tried to explain the reason why the real interest rate is a monetary variable, pointed out that the central bank can affect such variable through money market operations, adding that the central bank with his behavior could increase the propensity to save and to carry out to a new equilibrium with a permanent lower interest rate and higher rate of capital accumulation.

However, in the analysis of the effects of monetary policy on economic growth, the most known contribution is the Tobin´s (1965) model. He refuted the superneutrality of money, considering that money is an asset and a store of value. Therefore, an increase of money growth leads to a higher rate of inflation that reduces the rate of return of money and produces a portfolio shift in favor of real capital, increasing the capital stock generating a higher level of output per capita in the long run. Therefore, accepting this explanation inflation can lead to higher rates of growth, and this statement is called the "Tobin effect". Several models have been developed to test the Tobin effect and the results depend mainly on the assumptions considered. About these developments see, Orphanides and Solow (1990).

In this sense, one development to be considered is the Levhari and Patinkin (1968) approach. They consider two assumptions in their model:

1. National income must include the utility that the economic agents obtained derived from the maintenance of real balances.
2. Real balance can be also consider as a productive factor.

Considering the first assumption, national income must include the cost of opportunity derived from the maintenance of such balances. So, the equation is:

$$Yb = Y + \frac{M}{P}(\mu - \pi) + \frac{M}{P}(r + \pi) = Y + \frac{M}{P}(r + \mu) \qquad [1]$$

Being Yb the disposable income, Y income, M money supply, P prices, μ growth money supply rate, π growth prices rate and r return rate of assets.

The total consumption (Ct) depends on the disposable income:

$$Ct = (1 - s)\left[Y + \frac{M}{P}(r + \mu)\right] \qquad [2]$$

Being s the ratio saving/disposable income

The consumption of material goods (Cm) is the difference between the total consumption and the part due to the demand of real balances (M^d/P) , that is:

$$Cm = (1 - s)\left[Y + \frac{M}{P}(r + \mu)\right] - \frac{M^d}{P}(r + \pi) \qquad [3]$$

Thus, the capital accumulation would be the part of the income that is not consumed in material goods:

$$\frac{dK}{dt} = Y - \left\{ (1 - s)\left[Y + \frac{M}{P}(r + \mu)\right] - \frac{M^d}{P}(r + \pi) \right\} \qquad [4]$$

This equation suggests that the economic agents' behavior would affect on prices through the real balances. If the design of monetary policy has a positive effect on real balance it would increase the capital accumulation and indirectly would have a positive effect on economic growth.

However, these models are not the only approaches on the relationship between inflation and economic growth. Theoretical of economic growth have paid special attention to this relationship and for this reason it has been a relevant literature on this issue (See Hossain and Chowdhury, 1996, for a survey) considering at least two aspects: first if this relationship exist and second the causality. For example, Tun Wain (1959) didn't obtain a meaningful relationship between inflation and economic growth and Paul, Kearney and Chowdhury (1997) found different causal direction depending on the countries. And negative relationship was found by Levine and Renelt (1992), Fischer (1993), Barro (1996) and Bruno and Easterly (1998) Kormendi and Li and Zou (2002).

So, following these analyses the main conclusion achieved is that an expansive monetary policy that provokes a higher inflation would have a negative effect on economic growth, except if we accept the Tobin effect.

On the other hand, the Levhari and Patinkin model has considered the role of capital accumulation in the process. This is another possibility to analyze the relationship between monetary policy and economic growth including also the role of the technology. The main reason is that the empirical studies conclude that capital accumulation is growth enhancing. So, it is interesting to know if there is a relationship between monetary policy and capital accumulation considering the role of innovations and the entrepreneurs. In general terms, if an expansionary monetary policy creates more facilities to accumulate capital, then it would have an indirect effect on economic growth.

Recently, Schumpeter (1934) model developed in his book *The Theory of Economic Development* is used to analyze the relationship between capital accumulation and economic growth. His model is based on a production function that includes labor, capital stock, resources and technology. In his model, innovation process (technological progress or/and discovery of new resources) plays a relevant role that depends on entrepreneur behavior. In this case, if the entrepreneur has enough facilities to introduce innovations in the production process he will introduce them enhancing economic growth. And in this process monetary policy could have a positive effect. If this policy is not restrictive, a higher money supply would reduce interest rate and there would be more credit facilities and the entrepreneurs would have the opportunity to innovate or to introduce new technologies in their production process.

From empirical point of view, this possibility can be tested considering the following equation to be estimated (Galindo and Mendez, 2008):

$$TEA = \beta_1 + \beta_2 y + \beta_3 t + \beta_3 ms$$

being TEA the Total Entrepreneurship Activity, that is the index estimated by the GEM (Global Entrepreneurship Monitor) for several countries, that captures individuals who are involved in either the startup phase or managing a business that is less than 42 months old; y is the income (GDP), τ taxes and ms the money supply (representative variable of monetary policy). The expected sign is positive in all the variables except in the case of taxes.

The period considered is 2000-2006 and for the following countries: Argentina, Australia, Belgium, Brazil, Canada, Denmark, Finland, France, Germany, Ireland, Italy, Japan, Netherland, New Zealand, Norway, Singapore, Spain, South Africa, Sweden, United Kingdom, and United States. The results obtained are shown in table-1*.

Table 1.

Dependent Variable: TEA

Variable	Coefficient	Std. Error	t-Statistic	Prob.
Constant	0,625022	27,5512	44,0804	0.0000
Y	5,04365E-7	0,00000151313	3,00008	0.0081
T	0,0000035147	-0,000009748	-2,77361	0.0130
Ms	6,61003E-7	0,00000118739	1,79635	0.0902
	Unweighted Statistics			
R^2	0,600925	Sum squared resid		0.0011
R^2 Adjusted	0,5305	Durbin-Watson stat		2,2195

Sources: World Bank and GEM (2005)

* We acknowledge the help supplied by Professor José Luis Alfaro Navarro to develop this estimation.

The table shows that the signs are the expected. Therefore an expansive monetary policy that increases the money supply will have a positive effect on entrepreneurial activity that would be economic growth enhancing.

Finally, a third possibility to analyze the effect of monetary policy on economic growth is considering the income distribution. Economists have not had a unanimous position on the sign of the relationship between income distribution and economic growth. In the literature of the 1950s and 1960s it was accepted that higher inequality would enhance economic growth (e.g. Kaldor, 1956; Kelly and Williamson, 1968; Cook, 1995). They considered the hypothesis that the savings is related to income and play a relevant role in the economic growth process. This implied to use a redistribute fiscal policy that shifts income from poorer to richer, who have a higher propensity to save.

This view has been criticized and changed during the last decades. The empirical literature showed from this new position that could be a negative relationship between inequality and economic growth (Kuznets, 1955, Galor and Zeira, 1993, Persson and Tabellini, 1994, Bénabou, 1996, Alesina and Perotti, 1996, Aghion et al., 1999, Zou. and Li, 2000, Alfranca and Galindo, 2006). Different channels could explain this new view (Perotti, 1996, pp. 150-154; Aghion, Caroli and García-Peñalosa, 1999, pp. 1621-1630). First, the fiscal channel. In an unequal society, poor voter will vote for those fiscal programs that promise a better income distribution through taxation or public expenditure that would have a negative effect on economic growth (Alesina and Rodrick, 1994; Bertola, 1993. On the public capital effects, see Alfranca and Galindo, 2003); Socio-political problem. Second, some literature (Alesina and Perotti, 1996; Benabou, 1996a, b) has stressed the impact of income inequality on political instability and social tensions. Third, creates economic volatility (Alesina and Perotti, 1996; Aghion, Banerjee and Piketty, 1997), and so on.

Therefore, if monetary policy alters the income distribution, would have also effects on economic growth. In this sense, Fry (1995, p. 125) states that following the work of Michael Kalecki (1939, 1971) could be showed that changes in the interest rate can alter the income distribution, as Akyüz (1991) demonstrates. From this perspective, a restrictive monetary policy that increases interest rate would increase household incomes at expense of firms and government. In this case, the firms would have fewer resources to accumulate capital and it would have a negative effect on economic growth. If the government tries to compensate to the firms, this public activity could create economic volatility and social tensions that would have also negative effects on economic growth.

Conclusion

The literature has paid especial attention to the effects of monetary policy on income at short-term. Several monetary mechanisms of transmission have been considered by the economists. From this perspective, monetary authority could alter the path of the cycle if it is considered that the results are not adequate. However, when economic growth is analyzed monetary variables are not included considering that real factors are the most important to enhance it. Only through the effects on inflation, the effects of monetary variables on economic growth are analyzed. The causality is easy to see. Inflation has a negative effect on economic growth, so an expansionary monetary policy would be harmful. On the other hand, it is necessary that the monetary authority must be independent, because in this case she could fight more efficiently against inflation and, indirectly, improve economic growth.

In this paper we have seen four approaches that connect monetary policy with economic growth. The first two ones, Tobin and Levhari and Patinkin, show the role of inflation and real balances, respectively, in the process. Schumpeterian model stresses the relevance of the capital accumulation and innovation as economic growth promoting factors. A lower interest rate and credit facilities enhance to entrepreneurs to innovate and accumulate capital that would have positive effect on growth. The empirical analysis developed confirms this statement. And, finally, the Kaleckian model states that interest rate alter income distribution that would have also effects on economic growth.

References

[1] Aghion, P., Banerjee, A. & Piketty, T. (1997). "Dualism and macroeconomic volatility". University College, London, mimeo.

[2] Aghion, P., Caroli, E. & Garcia-Peñalosa, C. (1999). "Inequality and economic growth: The perspective of the new growth theories". *Journal of Economic Literature*, Vol. XXXVII, December, pp. 1615-1660.

[3] Aghin, P. & Howitt, P. (1998). *Endogenous Growth Theory*, Cambridge, Mass.: The MIT Press.

[4] Akyüz, Y. (1991). "Financial liberalization in developing countries: A Neo-Keynesian Approach". Geneva: United Nations Conference on Trade and Development, *Discussion Paper*, n. **36**, March.

[5] Alesina, A. & Perotti, R. (1996). "Income distribution, political instability, and investment". *European Economic Review*, **40**, 1996, pp. 1203-1228.

[6] Alesina, A. & Rodrik, D. (1994). "Distribution policies and economic growth?. *Quarterly Journal of Economics*, **109**, pp. 465-490.

[7] Alfranca, O. & Galindo, M. A. (2003). "Public capital, income distribution, and growth in OECD countries". *International Advances in Economic Research*, **9**, May, pp. 133-139.

[8] Alfranca, O. & Galindo, M. A. (2006). "Income distribution and economic growth with environmental restrictions", in Bahmani-Oskooee, M. & Galindo, M. A. (Eds.). *Next Economic Growth*. New York: Nova science Publisher, pp. 67-80.

[9] Barro, R., (1996). "Inflation and growth". *Federal Reserve Bank of St. Louis Review,* vol. 78, pp. 153-169.

[10] Bell, D. (1976). *The Cultural Contradictions of Capitalism*. New York: Basic Books.

[11] Bénabou, R. (1996a). "Unequal societies". *NBER Working Paper* **5583**.

[12] Bénabou, R. (1996b). "Inequality and growth". *NBER Macroeconomic Annual 1996.*

[13] Cambridge, MA.: The MIT Press , pp. 11-74.

[14] Bertola, G. (1993). "Factor shares and savings in endogenous growth?". *American Economic Review*, **83**, pp. 1184-1198.

[15] Bruno, M. & Easterly, W. (1998). "Inflation crises and long-run growth". *Journal of Monetary Economics*. vol. 41, pp. 3-26.

[16] Cook, C. J. (1995). "Saving rates and income distribution: further evidence from LDCs". *Applied Economics*, **27**, pp. 71-82.

[17] Fischer, S., 1993. “The role of macroeconomic factors in economic growth”, *Journal of Monetary Economics,* vol. 32, pp. 485-512.

[18] Fry, M. (1995). *Money, Interest, and Banking in Economic Development.* Baltimore: The Johns Hopkins University Press.

[19] Galindo, M. A. &Mendez, M. T. (2008), “Entrepreneurship and economic policy objectives”. New York: Nova Press (forthcoming).

[20] Galor, O. & Zeira, J. (1993). “Income distribution and macroeconomics”. *Review of Economic Studies*, **60**: 1, pp. 35-52.

[21] Hossain, A. & Chowdhury, A. (1996). *Monetary and Financial Policies in Developing Countries.* London: Routledge.

[22] Kaldor, N. (1956). “Alternative theories of distribution”. *Review of Economic Studies*, **23** (2), pp. 83-100.

[23] Kalecki, M (1939). *Essays in the Theory of Economic Fluctuations.* London: Allen and Unwin

[24] Kalecki, M (1971). *Selected Essays on the Dynamics of the Capitalist Economy: 1933-1970.* Cambridge: Cambridge University Press.

[25] Kelly, A. C. & Williamson, J. G. (1968). “Household savings behaviour in developing country: The Indonesian case”. *Economic Development and Cultural Change*, **16**(3), pp. 385-403.

[26] Kuznets, S. (1955). “Economic growth and income inequality”. *The American Economic Review*, **73** (5), pp. 1132-1136.

[27] Layard, R. (1997). “Foreward”, in R. Barro (1997). *Determinants of Economic Growth.* Cambridge, Mass: The MIT Press.

[28] Levhari, D. & Patinkin, D. (1968). “The role of Money in a monetary economy”. *American Economic Review*, vol. 68, pp. 713-753.

[29] Levine, R. & Renelt, D. (1992). “A sensitivity analysis of cross-country growth regressions”. *American Economic Review*, **82**(4), pp. 426-430.

[30] Li, H. & Zou, H. F. (2002). “Inflation, growth, and income distribution. A cross country study”. *Annuals of Economic and Finance*, **3** (1), pp. 85-101.

[31] Metzler, L. (1951). “Wealth, saving and the interest rate”. *Journal of Political Economy*, **59**, pp. 93-116.

[32] Orphanides, A. & Solow, R. M. (1990). "Money, Inflation and Growth" in B. M. Friedman and F. H. Hahn (eds.), *Handbook of Monetary Economics.* Amsterdam: Elsevier Science Publishers B. V., pp. 223-261.

[33] Paul, S., Kearney, C. & Chowdhury, K. (1997). “Inflation and economic growth: a multi-country empirical analysis”. *Applied Economics,* vol. 29, pp. 1387-1301.

[34] Perotti, R. (1996). “Growth, income distribution and democracy: What the data say”. *Journal of Economic Growth*, vol. 1, pp. 149-187.

[35] Persson, T. & Tabellini, G. (1994). “Is inequality harmful for growth?”. *American Economic Review*, **84**, pp. 600-621.

[36] Romer, P. M. (1986). “Increasing returns and long-run growth”. *Journal of Political Economy*, **94**, Octuber, pp. 1002-1037.

[37] Romer, P. M. (1987). “Growth based on increasing returns due to specialization”. *American Economic Review*, **77**, May, pp. 56-62.

[38] Solow, R. M. (1956). "A contribution to the theory of economic growth". *Quarterly Journal of Economics*, **70**, pp. 65-94.

[39] Tobin, J. (1965). "Money and Economic Growth". *Econometrica,* Vol. 33, pp. 671-684.

[40] Tun Wai, U. (1959). "The relation between inflation and economic development: a statistical inductive study". *IMF Staff Papers,* vol. 7, pp. 302-317.

[41] Zou, H. & Li, H. (2000). "Income inequality is not harmful for growth: theory and evidence". *Journal of Development Economics*, **2** (3), 1998, pp. 318-334.

In: Monetary Growth: Trends, Impacts and Policies
Editors: W.N. Squires et al, pp. 77-86
ISBN: 978-1-60692-305-4

Short Communication B

Discount Rate Requests and the Federal Funds Target Rate

*Jerry H. Tempelman**
New York, NY

Abstract

Discount rate requests by the 12 district Federal Reserve Banks are highly reliable indicators of subsequent FOMC federal funds target rate decisions. In recent years, the correlation between the two has been approximately 90 percent. Because discount rate requests are submitted prior to FOMC meetings, monetary policy appears to flow from the district level to Washington rather than vice versa, or from the bottom up rather than top-down.

Introduction

Of the Federal Reserve's three main tools of monetary policy—the federal funds target rate, the discount rate, and reserve requirements—the discount rate is generally considered less significant than the federal funds target rate. The amount of reserve balances traded in the federal funds markets on any given day tends to vastly outweigh the amount borrowed at the discount window. The federal funds target rate is the one that is decided by the Federal Open Market Committee (FOMC) in the periodic meetings in which it sets monetary policy. Market participants study the minutes of these meetings to pick up clues on the future direction of monetary policy, and tend to pay less attention to the minutes of the meetings in which the Board of Governors of the Federal Reserve System makes its discount rate decisions.

In this paper I will present evidence that suggests that the discount rate is far more influential as a tool of monetary policy than is often thought. Discount rate requests by the 12 district banks turn out to be highly reliable indicators of subsequent federal funds target rate decisions by the FOMC, of whose members some of the district bank presidents form a subset. In recent years, the modal values of discount rate requests by the 12 district banks have been highly correlated to subsequent FOMC federal funds target rate decisions. Furthermore, discount rate requests by individual district banks have been highly correlated to subsequent FOMC votes on the federal funds target rate cast by their presidents. Because discount rate requests are submitted prior to FOMC meetings, it would appear that monetary policy in the United States emanates from the district level rather than from Washington. Monetary policy decisions are shaped "from the bottom up" rather than "top-down."

I will first make some general statements about the discount rate, specifically about the way in which the process of requests for changes in the discount rate is intertwined with FOMC meetings. I will then present evidence drawn from the minutes of the meetings in which the Board considers requests by the district banks to change the discount rate, and from statements by the FOMC released after its meetings in which it announces changes in the monetary policy stance. Finally, I will draw some conclusions and implications.

Discount Rate Changes

Changes in the discount rate are initiated by the 12 district Federal Reserve Banks that, along with the Board of Governors located in Washington, D.C., make up the Federal Reserve System. Every 14 days, the boards of directors of the 12 district banks review the discount rate, and independently of each other submit requests for changes in the rate to the Board of Governors, which considers the requests and either approves or denies them. Because each board of each district bank consists of 9 directors, discount rate requests submitted to the Board at any given time are based on as many as 108 (12 times 9) observations of economic conditions around the country. Thus, discount rate requests by the district banks function as an important barometer for the FOMC in its assessment of economic conditions. As Federal Reserve Vice Chairman Donald L. Kohn (2006) has noted on the role of the district banks: "What they tell the Committee about what they are hearing from their contacts helps us recognize shifting economic conditions before they are evident in the data. Their reports often illuminate the reasons for the data we are receiving, thereby helping us anticipate what will come next."

The Board of Governors meets periodically to consider discount rate requests submitted by the district banks. These meetings tend to take place more frequently than FOMC meetings, which are scheduled to occur 8 times a year. If none of the 12 boards of directors vote to request a change in the discount rate, the Board still meets but does not consider discount rate changes. In the past, the discount rate has tended to change less frequently than the federal funds target rate,[+] but since August 1999 the two rates have moved in virtual lock-

* Jerry H. Tempelman, CFA, is a financial analyst in New York City. Contact information: P.O. Box 230116, New York, NY 10023-002, j48t@yahoo.com

+ For historical changes in the two interest rates, please see http://www.newyorkfed.org/markets/statistics/dlyrates/fedrate.html

step of each other: on days when the federal funds target rate changed, the discount rate usually did as well, in the same direction and by the same magnitude.±

There is no fixed pattern as to the timing of discount rate requests relative to the timing of FOMC meetings. Usually, the Board meets to review the most recent discount rate requests by the district banks one or two days prior to an upcoming FOMC meeting, and then again on the (closing) day of the FOMC meeting, right after the FOMC meeting but prior to the release of the FOMC statement. Even if all 12 district banks have submitted identical requests for a change in the discount rate, since at least August 1999 the Board has denied those discount rate requests prior to the FOMC meeting, and has approved any discount rate changes in the Board meeting that immediately followed the FOMC meeting. Both changes (in the federal funds target rate and in the discount rate) are announced in the FOMC statement. Even district banks that did not request a change in the discount rate adopt the new rate, sometimes after a lag of a day or two. If there are no changes in the federal funds target rate or the discount rate, there is no Board meeting immediately following the FOMC meeting.

Presentation of the Data

To gain insight into the blending of discount rate decisions and federal funds target rate decisions, I reviewed all such decisions from August 1999, when the two rates began moving in lockstep, through December 2007.* The analysis was intended to determine two factors: (i.) the extent to which discount rate requests by all district banks provide an indication as to subsequent federal funds target rate decision, and (ii.) the extent to which discount rate requests submitted by individual district banks provide an indication as to the subsequent FOMC votes cast by their presidents while serving on the voting rotation.+

I will first present some of the data in narrative form (a full tabulation may be found in the Appendix to this paper). I will then attempt to aggregate the data and draw some conclusions.

In August 1999, the federal funds target rate and the discount rate were each increased by 25 basis points. Only 3 of the 5 district banks whose presidents then served on the voting rotation requested the discount rate increase, but of the two banks that did not, one cast a

± There have been two main exceptions. From August 1999 to January 2003, the discount rate was priced 50 basis points below the federal funds target rate. On January 6, 2003, the Federal Reserve made some changes in its discount window policy, and priced the discount rate 100 basis points above the federal funds target rate while stating explicitly that this "[did] not represent a change in the stance of monetary policy." On August 17, 2007, the difference between the discount rate and the federal funds target rate was reduced to 50 basis points, which was a change that was not said to be implemented at the request of any of the district banks as a reflection of regional economic conditions. Thus, these two changes in the discount rate have been left out of the analysis in this paper. Since January 2003, the discount window distinguishes between a primary and a secondary credit rate. The former is the equivalent of the discount rate. FOMC statements still refer to the primary rate as the discount rate, and this paper follows that terminology.

* Minutes of discount rate meetings may be found at http://www.federalreserve.gov/monetarypolicy/discountrate.htm. Minutes and statements of FOMC meetings may be found at http://www.federalreserve.gov/monetarypolicy/fomc.htm.

+ The FOMC, whose 12 members vote on changes in the federal funds target rate, consists of the 7 members of the Board of Governors of the Federal Reserve System, and 5 of the 12 district bank presidents, who serve as FOMC members on a rotating basis.

dissenting FOMC vote favoring no change in the federal funds target rate. Thus, in 4 of the 5 votes, the discount rate request by the district bank matched the subsequent FOMC vote by its president.

In October 1999 there were neither rate changes nor requests for changes. In November 1999, the federal funds target rate and the discount rate were each increased by 25 basis points, even though 8 district banks, including all 5 whose presidents served on the voting rotation, had requested no change in the discount rate (4 had requested an increase of 25 basis points). Thus, the rate requests and votes of this meeting do not exhibit the pattern found for most other meetings during the sample period. In December 1999 there were neither rate changes nor requests for changes.

In February and March 2000, most discount rate requests were for a 25 basis point increase. In both meetings, the federal funds target rate and the discount rate were each increased by that amount. Before May 2000, 8 district banks requested a discount rate increase of 25 basis points while only 4 requested a 50 basis point increase. But the presidents of all 4 of those district banks happened to serve on the rotation for that FOMC meeting, and the federal funds target rate and the discount rate were each increased by 50 basis points.

For most of the rest of 2000, there were neither rate changes nor requests for changes. In December, however, 4 district banks requested a discount rate reduction of 25 basis points. Eight, including 3 whose presidents served on the voting rotation, requested no changes, and none were adopted in the December 2000 FOMC meeting.

By early January 2001, as many as 7 district banks had requested a discount rate reduction of 25 basis points. The FOMC conducted an unscheduled meeting via conference call, in which it unanimously voted for a reduction in the federal funds target rate of 50 basis points. Because at that point no district banks had requested that large a discount rate reduction, the Board approved only a 25 basis point reduction in the discount rate, but in its announcement stated that it stood ready to act if requests for a larger reduction were submitted. Those followed promptly, and the next day the Board announced another 25 basis point reduction in the discount rate. Thus, the total discount rate reduction ended up matching the federal funds target rate reduction.

On the days of the next 10 FOMC meetings, the federal funds target rate and the discount rate were both reduced by either 25 or 50 basis points. For 7 of these changes, the size of the reduction reflected the mode of the discount rate requests by the 12 district banks. In one of the other 3 meetings, in May 2001, 6 banks had requested a 50 basis point decrease, 5 a 25 basis point decrease, and one (Kansas City) no change. The presidents of 3 of the banks that had requested a 50 basis point reduction served on the FOMC voting rotation, and that is the change that was adopted (the Kansas City president cast a dissenting vote favoring a tighter policy stance than the consensus vote). In June 2001, the St. Louis district bank requested no discount rate change, and its president cast a dissenting vote against the 25 basis point reduction of the federal funds target rate adopted during the FOMC meeting.

In September 2001, the 50 basis point discount rate reduction reflected the mode of the requests by the district banks, even though 3 presidents of the district banks that had requested a 25 basis point reduction served on the voting rotation. November 2001 deviates from the usual pattern in that the federal funds target rate and the discount rate were both reduced by 50 basis points, even though 7 banks, including 3 whose presidents served on the voting rotation, had requested a discount rate reduction of only 25 basis points. Arguably, deviations from the usual pattern during the months after the September 11, 2001 terrorist attacks may not be entirely unexpected. In December 2001, the federal funds target rate and the discount rate were each reduced by 25 basis points. Although 6 district banks had requested no change in the discount rate, 5—including 3 whose presidents served on the FOMC voting rotation—had requested a reduction of 25 basis points and one had requested a reduction of 50 basis points.

During the first 6 FOMC meetings of 2002, no rate changes were adopted, in spite of an occasional request for a reduction in the discount rate. According to the minutes of the Board meeting just before the September 2002 FOMC meeting, Governor Edward M. Gramlich "was strongly leaning toward a reduction in the discount rate." Indeed, he cast a dissenting vote in that FOMC meeting, in which monetary policy was left unchanged, favoring a reduction in the federal funds target rate. On the day of the following FOMC meeting, in November 2002, the federal funds target rate and the discount rate were each reduced by 50 basis points, even though 7 district banks had requested no change in the discount rate. At the next 4 FOMC meetings, no rate changes were adopted in spite of an occasional request for a discount rate reduction. In March 2003 there were 2 such requests, in May there were 3, and in June 2003 there were 8, and the federal funds target rate and the discount rate were then each reduced by 25 basis points, to 1 percent and 2 percent, respectively. From August 2003 through May 2004, both rates remained at those levels, and there were no requests for changes in the discount rate during this time frame.

From June 2004 through June 2006, the federal funds target rate and the discount rate each moved up by 25 basis point increments during each meeting. During this period, there were on occasion one or two deviations from the usual pattern in the discount rate requests. In the September 2005 FOMC meeting, there were as many as five deviations. One of the governors dissented on the federal funds target rate vote, preferring to leave it unchanged. But, with one exception, during this time frame none of the presidents whose district banks submitted discount rate requests that deviated from the majority happened to serve on the voting rotation.

From August 2006 through December 2006, the federal funds target rate and the discount rate remained unchanged. In the 4 FOMC meetings during this time frame, the president of the Richmond district bank dissented in favor of a higher federal funds rate. Prior to 3 of these 4 meetings, the board of the Richmond district bank had requested an increase in the discount rate. Prior to the first 2 of the FOMC meetings during this time frame, the board of the Philadelphia district bank also requested an increase in the discount rate, but its president did not serve on the FOMC voting rotation and so was not in a position to cast either an assenting or dissenting FOMC vote. From January 2007 through the August 2007 FOMC meeting, there were no changes in the federal funds target rate and no requests for changes in the discount rate. Neither president of the Philadelphia or Richmond district banks served on the FOMC voting rotation during this time.

Prior to the September 2007 FOMC meeting, 7 district banks requested a decrease in the discount rate of 50 basis points, while 4 requested a decrease of 25 basis points and one (Philadelphia) requested no change.* Although following the credit turmoil of August 2007

* As was pointed out in the press, the board of the Philadelphia district bank had last met one day before the September 7 release of an unexpectedly weak employment report for August 2007. Its president would

financial markets were clearly expecting a decrease in the federal funds target rate in the September meeting, there was substantially less clarity as to the likely magnitude of the decrease. In retrospect, however, considering the fact that 7 district banks had requested a 50 basis point decrease in the discount rate, 4 of whose presidents served on the FOMC voting rotation for that meeting, the 50 basis point reduction in the federal funds target rate may have been less of a surprise to those aware of the discount rate requests.

In October 2007, the federal funds target rate and the discount rate were both reduced by another 25 basis points. These reductions were by no means a foregone conclusion.* Six of the 12 district banks had requested the reduction in the discount rate, and 6 had requested no change. Indeed, the minutes of the FOMC meeting characterized the federal funds target rate decision as "a close call," but the presidents of 3 of the district banks that had requested the discount rate reduction happened to serve on the FOMC voting rotation. The Kansas City district bank had requested no change in the discount rate, and its president cast a dissenting FOMC vote favoring an unchanged federal funds target rate. It was subsequently reported in the press that the president of the Philadelphia district bank, who did not serve on the voting rotation in the October meeting, "disagreed" with the reduction in the federal funds target rate (Andrews, 2007). Indeed, the board of the Philadelphia district bank had not requested a reduction in the discount rate prior to the FOMC meeting.

In December 2007, the federal funds target rate and the discount rate were both reduced by another 25 basis points. The reduction in the discount rate had been requested by 7 of the 12 district banks, the presidents of 3 of which served on the FOMC voting rotation. Three district banks had requested a 50 basis points reduction in the discount rate. The president of only one of these 3 district banks (Boston) served on the FOMC voting rotation, and cast a dissenting vote on the federal funds target rate, favoring a larger reduction than 25 basis points. Thus, for 4 of the 5 votes, the discount rate request by the district bank matched the subsequent FOMC vote by its president.

Analysis of the Data

During the sample period, there were 71 FOMC meetings, 56 of which were presided over by Alan Greenspan and 15 by current Federal Reserve Chairman Ben S. Bernanke. Of the 71 FOMC monetary policy decisions, 33 constituted no change in the policy stance while 38 were a change. Of the 38 changes, 22 were a tightening of monetary policy while 16 were an easing. Of the 22 tightening moves, 21 were 25 basis points in size while one was 50 basis points (total of 575 basis points). Of the 16 easing moves, 10 were 50 basis points in size while 6 were 25 basis points (total of 650 basis points). All in all, monetary policy does not appear to have been heavily skewed in any particular direction during the 8-year sample period.

For the analysis, I considered the most recent discount rate requests prior to all FOMC meetings. During the sample period there were a total of 852 such observations (71 times 12) of discount rate requests by individual district banks. Because in any given FOMC meeting 5

---

subsequently characterize the September reduction in the federal funds target rate as "appropriate" (Sudeep Reddy, "Some at Fed Favored A Smaller Rate Cut", *Wall Street Journal*, October 17, 2007, p. A2).

* Cf. Greg Ip, "Why Rate Cut Isn't a Sure Thing", *Wall Street Journal*, October 30, 2007, p. A2

district bank presidents serve as voting FOMC members, 355 (71 times 5) of the 852 discount rate requests can be compared to the votes cast by these presidents.

Because changes in both the discount rate and the federal funds target rate take place in increments of 25 basis points, I used mode as the metric for the central tendency of the discount rate requests. For each FOMC meeting during the sample period, I compared the mode of each group of 12 individual discount rate requests submitted most recently prior to the meeting with the federal funds target rate decision made in that meeting. For 64 of the 71 meetings, or 90.1 percent, the mode of the 12 discount rate requests and the change in the federal funds target rate were identical in both direction and magnitude. In other words, *9 out of 10 times, the mode of the discount rate requests submitted by the 12 district banks most recently prior to an FOMC meeting formed an accurate predictor of the FOMC decision on the federal funds target rate in that meeting.*

Of the 355 discount rate requests by district banks whose presidents served on the FOMC voting rotation, 309, or 87.0 percent, matched the subsequent FOMC votes on the federal funds target rate cast by those presidents in both direction and magnitude.* There were 24 inconsistencies in direction between the FOMC votes and the discount rate requests (for example, 25 basis points of easing vs. no change), and 19 inconsistencies in magnitude (for example, 25 basis points of easing vs. 50 basis points of easing). In addition, there were 3 occasions on which there was a match between the discount rate request and the consensus FOMC vote, but the president somehow decided to cast a dissenting vote. Thus, *almost 9 out of 10 times, discount rate requests by individual district banks formed an accurate predictor of the subsequent FOMC votes on the federal funds target rate cast by their presidents.*

Conclusion

As noted, the federal funds target rate is arguably the Federal Reserve's most important monetary policy tool. It is the interest rate that is debated vigorously by the FOMC. Financial markets often await its announcements with great anticipation. Discount rate changes included in the same announcement are usually considered as an afterthought. The evidence in this paper, however, suggests that, if anything, the decision making process takes place in the opposite direction. This is not just a chicken-or-egg thing. There is a clear temporal sequence: discount rate requests come first, and the federal funds target rate decision comes after. This can be observed even more clearly on occasions when discount rate requests formed a leading indicator of new future changes in the federal funds target rate. For example, the monetary policy easing cycle that began at the unscheduled FOMC meeting in early January 2001 was preceded by 4 requests for a reduction in the discount rate prior to the December 2000 FOMC meeting, after no such requests had been submitted prior to the previous 4 FOMC meetings. The final move in that easing cycle, in June 2003, was also preceded by an increase in the number of requests to reduce the discount rate.

* Of the 309 votes, 300 were in assent of the FOMC decision while 9 were in dissent (for example, a request for no change in the discount rate along with a dissenting vote in favor of no easing of monetary policy at a time when the Committee lowered the federal funds target rate by 25 basis points).

Changes in the monetary policy stance appear to originate at the district level in the form of discount rate requests made by the boards of directors of the individual district banks, some of whose presidents form a subset of the FOMC members who subsequently vote on the level of the federal funds target rate. These discount rate requests are considered and discussed by the Board, which constitutes the remaining subset of voting FOMC members, in the days leading up to the FOMC decision. If you knew the discount rate requests, you could predict the outcome of the FOMC meeting with a high (90 percent) degree of accuracy. If you knew the discount rate requests by individual district banks, you could predict the individual FOMC votes of their presidents, when serving on the voting rotation, with an almost equally high degree of accuracy.

Two implications come to mind. The first relates to the way in which the Federal Reserve was originally structured, with a board that is a federal government agency in Washington presiding over 12 district reserve banks set up as separate corporations. This structure, unusual for central banks, reflects a concern at the time of the founding of the Federal Reserve that concentrating too much power in a central government institution is undesirable. The evidence presented in this paper suggests that in spite of many years and reorganizations of the structure of the Federal Reserve System, which are generally thought to have shifted decision making authority from the district banks to Washington, the original provision remains firmly intact. Monetary policy decisions made by the FOMC still largely find their origin in the individual reserve banks that are spread out over the various districts.

The second implication concerns an undue degree of influence that the FOMC chairman is sometimes thought to have in determining the outcome of FOMC decisions. Former governor Laurence H. Meyer (2004, pp. 216-217) complains about this in his memoir:

> To be truthful, I was…frustrated by the disproportionate power the Chairman wielded over the FOMC. While I respected his judgment and leadership, I had envisioned a greater opportunity to make a difference than I believe I had. I'm not suggesting that I was ignored or that the rich discussions inside the Committee room of which I was part did not influence policy. But the Chairman exercised such disproportionate power that unless you could sway him over to your point of view, your view was not going to prevail.

Similar sentiments occur from time to time in the financial press. According to Ip (2006), for example, "[a]t Federal Reserve meetings under Alan Greenspan, the chairman would state his recommendations for interest rates. Then the 18 other policy makers would say if they agreed. They usually did." Ip characterizes this as Mr. Greenspan's "dominance of the Fed," and believes that market participants "could safely assume only Mr. Greenspan's opinion really mattered." Furthermore, "Mr. Greenspan's views usually preordained the outcome" of FOMC meetings. But the evidence presented in this paper suggests that such concerns are much overstated. If there is anything that "preordains" the outcome of FOMC decisions, it is not the chairman's views but rather the discount rate requests by the 12 district banks.[*]

* Mr. Greenspan, in response to an earlier draft of this paper, replies that he "believe[s monetary] policy comes out of the perceptions of the thrust of economic developments which equally informs all members of the FOMC" (personal correspondence, 27 December 2007).

The overall conclusion is inescapable that monetary policy decisions flow from the district level to Washington rather than vice versa. Monetary policy takes shape in a "bottom-up" direction rather than a "top-down" one.

Appendix

		Federal funds rate		Discount rate		Most recently requested discount rate changes												FOMC	Mode	5 voting presidents				
		Change	Level	Change	Level	BOS	NY	PHI	CLE	RICH	ATL	CHI	STL	MINN	KC	DAL	SF	dissents	of all 12	A.	B.	C.	D.	E.
1999	Aug 24	0.25	5.25	0.25	4.75	0.25	0.25	0.25	0.25	0.25	0.25	0.25	0.25	-	0.25	-	0.25	DAL (E)	0.25	3	1		1	
	Oct 5	-	5.25	-	4.75	-	-	-	-	-	-	-	-	-	-	-	-		-	5				
	Nov 16	0.25	5.50	0.25	5.00	0.25	-	-	0.25	0.25	-	-	-	-	0.25	-	-		-	5				
	Dec 21	-	5.50	-	5.00	-	-	-	-	-	-	-	-	-	-	-	-		-	5				
2000	Feb 1-2	0.25	5.75	0.25	5.25	0.25	0.25	0.25	0.25	0.25	0.25	0.25	0.25	-	0.25	-	0.25		0.25	5				
	Mar 21	0.25	6.00	0.25	5.50	0.25	0.25	0.25	0.25	0.25	0.25	0.25	0.25	0.25	0.25	-	0.25		0.25	5				
	May 16	0.50	6.50	0.50	6.00	0.50	0.25	0.25	0.50	0.50	0.25	0.25	0.25	0.25	0.25	0.25	0.50		0.25	3			2	
	Jun 27-28	-	6.50	-	6.00	0.25	-	-	-	-	-	-	-	-	-	-	-		-	5				
	Aug 22	-	6.50	-	6.00	-	-	-	-	-	-	-	-	-	-	-	-		-	5				
	Oct 3	-	6.50	-	6.00	-	-	-	-	-	-	-	-	-	-	-	-		-	5				
	Nov 15	-	6.50	-	6.00	-	-	-	-				-	-	-	-	-		-	5				
	Dec 19	-	6.50	-	6.00	-	-	-	-0.25	-	-	-	-0.25	-	-	-0.25	-0.25		-	3		2		
2001	Jan 3-4	-0.50	6.00	-0.50	5.50	-	-0.25	-	-0.25	-	-0.25	-	-0.25	-	-0.25	-0.25	-0.25		-0.25			2	3	
	Jan 30-31	-0.50	5.50	-0.50	5.00	-0.25	-0.50	-0.50	-0.50	-0.25	-0.50	-0.50	-0.50	-0.50	-0.25	-0.50	-0.50		-0.50	3			2	
	Mar 20	-0.50	5.00	-0.50	4.50	-0.50	-0.50	-0.50	-0.50	-0.50	-0.50	-0.50	-0.50	-0.50	-0.50	-0.50	-0.50		-0.50	5				
	Apr 18	-0.50	4.50	-0.50	4.00	-0.50	-0.50	-0.50	-0.50	-	-0.50	-	-	-0.50	-	-0.50	-0.50		-0.50	2		3		
	May 15	-0.50	4.00	-0.50	3.50	-0.25	-0.50	-0.25	-0.25	-0.50	-0.25	-0.50	-0.50	-	-0.25	-0.25	-0.50	KC (T)	-0.25	3	1		1	
	Jun 26-27	-0.25	3.75	-0.25	3.25	-0.25	-0.25	-0.25	-	-	-0.25	-0.25	-	-0.50	-	-0.25	-0.25	STL (T)	-0.25	3	1	1		
	Aug 21	-0.25	3.50	-0.25	3.00	-0.25	-0.25	-0.25	-	-0.25	-	-0.25		-	-0.25	-0.25	-		-0.25	4		1		
	Sep 17	-0.50	3.00	-0.50	2.50	-0.25	-0.25	-	-	-0.50	-0.25	-0.50	-0.25	-0.50	-	-0.50	-0.50		-0.50	1		1	3	
	Oct 2	-0.50	2.50	-0.50	2.00	-0.50	-0.50	-0.25	-0.50	-0.50	-0.50	-0.25	-0.50	-0.25	-0.50	-0.25	-0.50		-0.50	4			1	
	Nov 6	-0.50	2.00	-0.50	1.50	-0.25	-0.25	-0.25	-	-0.50	-	-0.25	-	-0.25	-	-0.25	-0.25		-0.25			2	3	
	Dec 11	-0.25	1.75	-0.25	1.25	-0.25	-0.25	-0.25	-	-0.50	-	-0.25	-	-	-	-	-0.25	KC (T)	-	3	1	1		
2002	Jan 29-30	-	1.75	-	1.25	-	-0.25	-	-	-	-	-	-	-	-	-	-		-	4		1		
	Mar 19	-	1.75	-	1.25	-	-	-	-	-	-	-	-	-	-	-	-		-	5				
	May 7	-	1.75	-	1.25	-	-	-	-	-	-	-	-	-	0.25	-	-		-	5				
	Jun 25-26	-	1.75	-	1.25	-	-	-	-	-	-	-	-	-	0.25	-	-		-	5				
	Aug 13	-	1.75	-	1.25	-0.25	-	-	-	-	-	-	-	-	-	-	-		-	5				
	Sep 24	-	1.75	-	1.25	-	-	-	-	-	-	-	-	-	-	-	-	DAL, Brd (E)	-	4				1
	Nov 6	-0.50	1.25	-0.50	0.75	-0.25	-0.50	-0.25	-	-	-	-	-	-	-	-0.50	-		-	2		2	1	
	Dec 10	-	1.25	-	0.75	-	-	-	-	-	-	-	-	-	-	-	-		-	5				
2003	Jan 28-29	-	1.25	-	2.25	-	-	-	-	-	-	-	-	-	-	-	-		-	5				
	Mar 18	-	1.25	-	2.25	-	-	-	-	-	-	-	-0.50	-	-	-	-0.50		-	4		1		
	May 6	-	1.25	-	2.25	-0.25	-0.50	-	-	-	-	-	-	-	-	-	-0.25		-	3		2		
	Jun 24-25	-0.25	1.00	-0.25	2.00	-0.25	-0.25	-0.50	-	-0.50	-	-	-0.25	-0.50	-0.25	-	-0.25	SF (E)	-0.25	1		2	1	1
	Aug 12	-	1.00	-	2.00	-	-	-	-	-	-	-	-	-	-	-	-		-	5				
	Sep 16	-	1.00	-	2.00	-	-	-	-	-	-	-	-	-	-	-	-		-	5				
	Oct 28	-	1.00	-	2.00	-	-	-	-	-	-	-	-	-	-	-	-		-	5				
	Dec 9	-	1.00	-	2.00	-	-	-	-	-	-	-	-	-	-	-	-		-	5				
2004	Jan 27-28	-	1.00	-	2.00	-	-	-	-	-	-	-	-	-	-	-	-		-	5				
	Mar 16	-	1.00	-	2.00	-	-	-	-	-	-	-	-	-	-	-	-		-	5				
	May 4	-	1.00	-	2.00	-	-	-	-	-	-	-	-	-	-	-	-		-	5				
	Jun 29-30	0.25	1.25	0.25	2.25	0.25	0.25	0.25	0.25	0.25	0.25	0.25	0.25	0.25	0.25	0.25	0.25		0.25	5				
	Aug 10	0.25	1.50	0.25	2.50	0.25	0.25	0.25	0.25	0.25	0.25	0.25	0.25	0.25	0.25	0.25	0.25		0.25	5				
	Sep 21	0.25	1.75	0.25	2.75	0.25	0.25	0.25	0.25	0.25	0.25	0.25	0.25	0.25	0.25	0.25	0.25		0.25	5				
	Nov 10	0.25	2.00	0.25	3.00	0.25	0.25	0.25	0.25	0.25	0.25	0.25	0.25	0.25	0.25	-	-		0.25	5				
	Dec 14	0.25	2.25	0.25	3.25	0.25	0.25	0.25	0.25	0.25	0.25	0.25	0.25	0.25	0.25	0.25	0.25		0.25	5				
2005	Feb 1-2	0.25	2.50	0.25	3.50	0.25	0.25	0.25	0.25	0.25	0.25	0.25	0.25	0.25	0.25	0.25	0.25		0.25	5				
	Mar 22	0.25	2.75	0.25	3.75	0.25	0.25	0.25	0.25	0.25	0.25	0.25	0.25	0.25	0.50	-	0.25		0.25	5				
	May 3	0.25	3.00	0.25	4.00	0.25	0.25	0.25	0.25	0.25	0.25	0.25	0.25	0.25	0.25	0.25	0.25		0.25	5				
	Jun 29-30	0.25	3.25	0.25	4.25	0.25	0.25	0.25	0.25	0.25	0.25	0.25	0.25	0.25	0.25	0.25	0.25		0.25	5				
	Aug 9	0.25	3.50	0.25	4.50	0.25	0.25	0.25	0.25	0.25	0.25	0.25	0.25	0.25	0.25	0.25	0.25		0.25	5				
	Sep 20	0.25	3.75	0.25	4.75	0.25	0.25	0.25	-	0.25	-	0.25	-	0.25	0.25	-	-	Brd (E)	0.25	5				
	Nov 1	0.25	4.00	0.25	5.00	0.25	0.25	0.25	0.25	0.25	0.25	0.25	0.25	0.25	0.25	0.25	0.25		0.25	5				
	Dec 13	0.25	4.25	0.25	5.25	0.25	0.25	0.25	0.25	0.25	0.25	0.25	0.25	0.25	0.25	0.25	0.25		0.25	5				
2006	Jan 31	0.25	4.50	0.25	5.50	0.25	0.25	0.25	0.25	0.25	0.25	0.25	0.25	-	0.25	0.25	0.25		0.25	5				
	Mar 27-28	0.25	4.75	0.25	5.75	0.25	0.25	0.25	0.25	0.25	0.25	0.25	0.25	0.25	-	0.25	0.25		0.25	5				
	May 10	0.25	5.00	0.25	6.00	0.25	0.25	0.25	0.25	0.25	0.25	0.25	0.25	0.25	-	0.25	0.25		0.25	5				
	Jun 28-29	0.25	5.25	0.25	6.25	0.25	0.25	0.25	0.25	0.25	0.25	0.25	0.25	0.25	-	0.25	-		0.25	4		1		
	Aug 8	-	5.25	-	6.25	-	-	0.25	-	0.25	-	-	-	-	-	-	-	RICH (T)	-	4	1			
	Sep 20	-	5.25	-	6.25	-	-	0.25	-	-	-	-	-	-	-	-	-	RICH (T)	-	4				1
	Oct 24-25	-	5.25	-	6.25	-	-	-	-	0.25	-	-	-	-	-	-	-	RICH (T)	-	4	1			
	Dec 12	-	5.25	-	6.25	-	-	-	-	0.25	-	-	-	-	-	-	-	RICH (T)	-	4	1			
2007	Jan 30-31	-	5.25	-	6.25	-	-	-	-	-	-	-	-	-	-	-	-		-	5				
	Mar 20-21	-	5.25	-	6.25	-	-	-	-	-	-	-	-	-	-	-	-		-	5				
	May 9	-	5.25	-	6.25	-	-	-	-	-	-	-	-	-	-	-	-		-	5				
	Jun 27-28	-	5.25	-	6.25	-	-	-	-	-	-	-	-	-	-	-	-		-	5				
	Aug 7	-	5.25	-	6.25	-	-	-	-	-	-	-	-	-	-	-	-		-	5				
	Sep 18	-0.50	4.75	-0.50	5.25	-0.50	-0.50	-	-0.50	-0.25	-0.25	-0.25	-0.50	-0.50	-0.50	-0.25	-0.50		-0.50	4			1	
	Oct 30-31	-0.25	4.50	-0.25	5.00	-	-0.25	-	-	-0.25	-0.25	-0.25	-0.25	-	-	-	-0.25	KC (T)	-0.25, -	3	1	1		
	Dec 11	-0.25	4.25	-0.25	4.75	-0.50	-0.25	-0.25	-0.25	-0.25	-0.25	-0.25	-0.25	-0.50	-	-	-0.50	BOS (E)	-0.25	3	1	1		
																			Totals:	300	9	24	19	3

A. Matches between FOMC vote and discount rate request
B. Matches between FOMC dissent vote and discount rate request
C. Inconsistencies between FOMC vote and discount rate request in direction
D. Inconsistencies between FOMC vote and discount rate request in magnitude
E. Inconsistencies between FOMC dissent vote and discount rate request

Light shading indicates discount rate requests while also an FOMC voting member.
Dark shading indicates no match between mode of discount rate requests and federal funds target rate change.

References

[1] Andrews, Edmund L. (2007) "Within the Fed, Resistance to Further Rate Cuts", *New York Times*, November 7: C1

[2] Ip, Greg (2006) " 'Transparent Vision': New Fed Chairman Hopes to Downplay Impact of his Words", *Wall Street Journal*, September 8: A1

[3] Kohn, Donald L. (2006) "The Evolving Role of the Federal Reserve Banks", Washington: Board of Governors of the Federal Reserve System, November 3, available at http://www.federalreserve.gov/newsevents/speech/kohn20061103a.htm

[4] Meyer, Laurence H. (2004) *A Term at the Fed: An Insider's View: The People and Policies of the World's Most Powerful Institution*, New York: HarperCollins

In: Monetary Growth: Trends, Impacts and Policies
Editors: W.N. Squires et al, pp. 87-108
ISBN 978-1-60692-305-4

Short Communication C

Monetary and Education Policies in the Uzawa-Lucas Cash-in-Advance Economy: Closed Form Solution

Jana Hromcová*
Universitat de Girona, Departament d'Economia i Empresa
Campus de Montilivi, 17071 Girona, Spain

Abstract

We analyze the effects of monetary and education policies in the Uzawa-Lucas model without externality and with a general cash-in-advance constraint. We present the analytical solution. In the setup with the cash-in-advance constraint on consumption purchases only, money is super neutral and the monetary policy has no effect on the behavior of the economy. When also a fraction of investment into physical capital must be bought using cash, inflation has negative growth effects in the short run, but not in the long run. We study in detail the transition of the economy from a high inflation equilibrium towards a low inflation equilibrium. We find that a monetary intervention produces an overshooting in the inflation rate. If the disinflation is performed via an education policy, inflation rate converges smoothly towards its new balanced growth path value. A combination of both policies enables to avoid transition and may induce a direct switch from high to low inflation balanced growth path.

Keywords: monetary policy, education policy, two sector growth model; human capital accumulation; cash-in-advance; welfare effects

JEL classification: O41, O42

1. Introduction

We analyze the effects of monetary and education policies in the Uzawa-Lucas model without externality and with a general cash-in-advance constraint. We show that welfare losses of inflation can be offset by an increase in the productivity of the education sector.

*E-mail address: jana.hromcova@udg.edu. tel: +34-972418236. fax: +34-972418032

In a one sector growth model with cash-in-advance constraint on consumption purchases only, money may be super neutral and the monetary policy has no effect on the behavior of the economy, neither in the short, nor in the long run.[1] Therefore, higher inflation would not imply any welfare loss. Under the assumption that all consumption and some capital must be bough using money, an increase in the inflation rate has usually negative growth effects both in the short and the long run, as in Stockman (1981).

Human capital growth expands future possibilities. Hence the importance of its accumulation for the human development and economic growth. Building on Uzawa (1965) and Lucas (1988), a lot of research has been devoted to developing of the dynamics of two sector real models with agents that have to decide on the optimal allocation of human capital across the production and education sectors, for example Benhabib and Perli (1994), Caballé and Santos (1993), etc. Less attention has been devoted to monetary versions of these models.

Gomme (1993) analyzes a two sector growth model with cash-in-advance constraint. In his economy both production and education sectors use both physical and human capitals, all consumption goods are cash goods, but investment goods are credit goods.[2] Using a numerical solution he evaluates welfare effects of inflation. He concludes that if a public policy affects the long run growth rate of the economy, welfare losses tend to be of more importance. Einarsson and Marquis (1999) study the transitional dynamics and welfare effects of decreasing inflation tax in a model with similar characteristics to Gomme (1993). They present a numerical exercise of the disinflation of the economy, from high to moderate, and from moderate to optimal. Their analysis takes as given and constant the productivity of the education sector.

As we show here, a monetary version of the two sector model can provide interesting insights about interactions of monetary and education policies. In the present work we assume that all consumption and also some fraction of investment into physical capital is subject to cash-in-advance constraint. The assumption that a fraction of investment must be acquired by cash may not be of much importance for rich countries. However, in poor countries where the financial system is less developed this characteristic might matter. In poor countries purchases are small compared to rich countries. According to empirical studies, for example Hancock and Humphrey (1998), smaller purchases tend to be done by cash. Also, it is found for example in Dutta and Weale (2001), that the development influences the acceptability of credit. A decrease in the fraction of investment that must be bough using money means an increase in the income velocity of money. As shown for example in Ireland (1994) or in Hromcová (2008), velocity increases with the level of output per worker and development.

We will use a simple version of the two sector Uzawa-Lucas model. Both types of capital will be used in the production sector, but the education sector will use only human capital. The long run growth rate of output per worker is determined by the characteristics of the education sector and is not affected by the monetary side of the economy. Therefore,

[1] Policy functions for an AK model with cash-in-advance constraint on consumption are stated for example in Hromcová (1998). As the AK model has no transition, short run and long run effects are not distinguished.

[2] As defined in Lucas (1984), we can recognize different types of goods according to the way they are acquired for. Cash goods are the goods bought using government issued money, credit goods are the goods bought using privately issued securities.

inflation will affect the real variables only in the short run. We solve the model analytically assuming the logarithmic utility function and total depreciation of both capitals. The solution of an analogous real economy model of Bethmann (2007) serves us as a starting point. We apply the guess and verify method. The analytical solution allows for easy illustrations of the behavior of the model and quick comparisons of policy effects. Monetary policy will be executed by setting a nominal interest rate aiming at certain long run inflation target. Education policy will be viewed as a change in the productivity of the studying sector. We understand that the government can equip schools, train teachers or motivate parents to send their children to school. Such actions may lead to an improvement in the efficiency of studying and higher development. We analyze in detail the reaction of the inflation rate to policy changes. We compare the transition from a high inflation regime to a low inflation regime under three scenarios: (i) a decrease in the nominal interest rate, (ii) an increase in the productivity of the education system, (iii) a combination of both policies. Transitional dynamics of the inflation rate varies according to which instrument is used to disinflate the economy. The combination of both policies may lead to an immediate adjustment of the economy to the low inflation balanced growth path with no transition.

We also devote some attention to welfare effects of changes in monetary and education policies. If all physical capital is a credit good, inflation causes no welfare losses. When a positive fraction of capital is a cash good, only Friedman rule is optimal. Welfare gains of disinflation via an increase in the productivity of the education sector can be substantial due to the change in the long run growth rate of the economy.

The remainder of the chapter is organized as follows. The model and its main properties are stated in section 2.. In section 3. we describe the balanced growth path behavior. In section 4. we discuss the behavior in the transition and analyze the effects of both policies. In section 5. we develop the welfare analysis. Final conclusions are summarized in section 6.

2. Model Description

2.1. The Household Problem

We consider a representative agent economy. There is one consumption good which must be paid using currency. The economy has an infinitely lived representative household with preferences represented by the logarithmic utility function

$$\sum_{t=0}^{\infty} \beta^t \ln c_t \tag{1}$$

where c_t is the consumption in period t.[3]

[3] A more general utility function used in macroeconomics and public finance applications is an isoelastic one

$$u(c_t) = \frac{c_t^{1-\theta} - 1}{1-\theta}$$

where θ is the inverse of the elasticity of intertemporal substitution. As commented in Lucas (2003), the logarithmic utility, $\theta = 1$, is employed by many researchers, because the estimates of the parameter are close to unity.

At the beginning of the economy the government fixes the gross nominal interest rate constant, $R > 1$.[4] Agents enter the period t with certain amount of monetary balances M_t, and the debt B_t, carried over from the previous period, and the physical and human capital stocks k_t and h_t. A representative worker produces via the production function

$$y_t = Ak_t^{\alpha} (h_t u_t)^{1-\alpha} \tag{2}$$

where u_t is the amount of time spent working and α is the share of physical capital in output, $0 < \alpha < 1$. Human capital accumulation depends on the productivity of the education sector, on the time spent studying, on the present level of human capital and on the depreciation rate according to

$$h_{t+1} = \phi (1 - u_t) h_t + (1 - \delta_h) h_t \tag{3}$$

where ϕ is the efficiency of learning parameter (or the productivity of the education sector) and δ_h is the depreciation rate of human capital. We interpret ϕ as an instrument of the education policy. Government can increase the productivity of human capital by, for example, providing more finances, better teaching material, better trained teachers, promote school assistance, etc.

First, the goods market opens and consumption takes place. Agents acquire consumption and investment goods carrying the necessary monetary balances which are determined by the following liquidity constraint

$$c_t + \psi [k_{t+1} - (1 - \delta_k) k_t] \leq \frac{M_t}{p_t} \tag{4}$$

where $\psi \in [0, 1]$ is a fraction of investment into physical capital that must be bought using nominal monetary balances M_t.[5] Later on the monetary transfer

$$X_t = (\mu_{t+1} - 1) M_t \tag{5}$$

from the government is endogenously determined in the system according to the given nominal interest rate, so that the money demand is totally satisfied. We denote μ_{t+1} as the gross growth rate of money supply between periods t and $t+1$. At the end of the period, during the securities trading session, households choose their currency holdings M_{t+1}. They also purchase (or issue) one-period nominally denominated pure discount bonds paying B_{t+1} units of money at period $t+1$ while they cost $\frac{B_{t+1}}{R}$ units of money at period t. Bonds are in zero net supply. The budget constraint agents are facing can be written

$$c_t + k_{t+1} - (1 - \delta_k) k_t + \frac{M_{t+1}}{p_t} + \frac{B_{t+1}}{Rp_t} \leq Ak_t^{\alpha} (h_t u_t)^{1-\alpha} + \frac{M_t}{p_t} + \frac{B_t}{p_t} + \frac{X_t}{p_t}. \tag{6}$$

[4] As a policy instrument the government can target either monetary aggregates or interest rates. In this work the second approach will be used. This is because recently central banks have reoriented their operating procedures focusing on interest rates rather than regulating monetary aggregates. Using a fixed growth rate of money supply as a monetary policy can be easily done, too. It must be checked, however, that the given growth rate of money supply leads to the nominal interest factor bigger than unity.

[5] We should expect the value of ψ be higher in poor countries where the financial system is less developed.

2.2. Equilibrium

Definition: Given the set of initial conditions k_1, h_1, M_1, B_1, the nominal interest rate R and the efficiency of studying ϕ, the equilibrium consists of sequences $\{c_t, u_t, k_{t+1}, h_{t+1}, M_{t+1}, B_{t+1}, X_t, p_t\}_{t=1}^{\infty}$ such that

(a) a representative household is maximizing the discounted utility (1) subject to the budget constraint (6), the cash-in-advance constraint (4) and the condition for the accumulation of human capital (3), choosing the sequences $\{c_t, u_t, k_{t+1}, h_{t+1}, M_{t+1}, B_{t+1}\}_{t=1}^{\infty}$,

(b) markets for goods, money and bonds clear in every period,

$$c_t + k_{t+1} - (1-\delta_k) k_t = A k_t^{\alpha} (h_t u_t)^{1-\alpha}, \tag{7}$$

$$M_{t+1} = M_t + X_t, \tag{8}$$

$$B_{t+1} = 0. \tag{9}$$

Let λ_t, η_t and ε_t be the non-negative Lagrange multipliers associated with the budget constraint (6), the cash-in-advance constraints (4), and the condition for the accumulation of human capital (3), respectively. The equations that characterize the equilibrium are the above mentioned market clearing conditions (7), (8), (9), the first order conditions on consumption, physical capital, human capital, labor, nominal balances and nominal bonds, respectively,

$$\frac{1}{c_t} = \lambda_t + \eta_t, \tag{10}$$

$$\lambda_t + \psi\eta_t = \beta\lambda_{t+1}\left[\alpha\frac{y_{t+1}}{k_{t+1}} + 1 - \delta_k\right] + \beta\psi\eta_{t+1}(1-\delta_h), \tag{11}$$

$$\varepsilon_t = \beta\lambda_{t+1}\left[(1-\alpha)\frac{y_{t+1}}{h_{t+1}}\right] + \beta\varepsilon_{t+1}\left[\phi(1-u_{t+1}) + (1-\delta_h)\right], \tag{12}$$

$$\varepsilon_t\phi h_t = \lambda_t(1-\alpha)\frac{y_t}{u_t}, \tag{13}$$

$$\frac{\lambda_t}{p_t} = \beta\frac{\lambda_{t+1}+\eta_{t+1}}{p_{t+1}}, \tag{14}$$

$$\frac{\lambda_t}{p_t} = \beta R\frac{\lambda_{t+1}}{p_{t+1}}, \tag{15}$$

and the transversality conditions

$$\lim_{t\to\infty}\beta^t\lambda_t k_{t+1} = 0,$$

$$\lim_{t\to\infty}\beta^t\varepsilon_t h_{t+1} = 0,$$

$$\lim_{t\to\infty}\beta^t\lambda_t\frac{M_{t+1}}{p_t} = 0,$$

$$\lim_{t\to\infty}\beta^t\lambda_t\frac{B_{t+1}}{Rp_t} = 0.$$

The Lagrange multipliers associated with the budget constraint, cash-in-advance constraint and constraint on human capital accumulation, λ_t, η_t and ε_t can be interpreted as the marginal utility of wealth, the marginal utility of real balances and the shadow price of human capital, respectively. The first order condition on consumption (10) indicates that the existence of binding liquidity constraint drives a wedge between the marginal utility of wealth and the marginal utility of consumption since the wealth cannot be used instantaneously to buy consumption. The first order conditions on physical capital (11), human capital (12) and bonds (15) embody the costs and profits associated with investing one marginal unit of wealth in either capital and bonds, respectively. The first order condition on working time (13) sets the optimal allocation of human capital between the two sectors. The first order condition on nominal balances (14) is the equation for pricing money. Money is priced like other assets, once its return has been appropriately defined in terms of the liquidity services it provides.

Using (10), (14) and (15), we can rewrite the first order condition on consumption as follows:

$$\frac{1}{c_t} = R\lambda_t. \tag{16}$$

It also implies that

$$\eta_t = (R-1)\,\lambda_t. \tag{17}$$

Plugging (17) into (11) we get the evolution of the marginal utility of consumption

$$\frac{\lambda_t}{\lambda_{t+1}} = \frac{\beta\left[\alpha\frac{y_{t+1}}{k_{t+1}} + 1 - \delta_k + \psi\,(R-1)\,(1-\delta_h)\right]}{1+\psi\,(R-1)}.$$

From (12) and (13) we get the growth rate of the shadow price of human capital

$$\frac{\varepsilon_t}{\varepsilon_{t+1}} = \beta\,(\phi + 1 - \delta_h)\,, \tag{18}$$

which is constant in all periods. Defining π_{t+1} as the inflation rate between periods t and $t+1$, we can rewrite (15) as

$$\pi_{t+1} = \frac{p_{t+1}}{p_t} = \beta R\frac{\lambda_{t+1}}{\lambda_t}. \tag{19}$$

The gross growth rate of money supply can be written as

$$\mu_{t+1} = \frac{M_{t+1}}{M_t} = \pi_t\frac{m_{t+1}}{m_t} = \beta R\frac{\lambda_{t+1}}{\lambda_t}\frac{m_{t+1}}{m_t} \tag{20}$$

where

$$m_t = \frac{M_t}{p_t} \tag{21}$$

are real balances.

3. Long Run Solution

On the balanced growth path all variables grow at a constant rate. Working time is constant,

$$\lim_{t\to\infty} u_t = u^*,$$

and the goods market equilibrium (7)

$$\left(\frac{c_t}{h_t}\right) + \left(\frac{k_{t+1}}{h_{t+1}}\right)\left(\frac{h_{t+1}}{h_t}\right) - (1-\delta_k)\left(\frac{k_t}{h_t}\right) = A\left(\frac{k_t}{h_t}\right)^{\alpha} u_t^{1-\alpha}$$

implies that the consumption, output and physical capital must grow like human capital, equation (3)

$$\lim_{t\to\infty}\frac{h_{t+1}}{h_t} = \lim_{t\to\infty}\frac{y_{t+1}}{y_t} = \lim_{t\to\infty}\frac{k_{t+1}}{k_t} = \lim_{t\to\infty}\frac{c_{t+1}}{c_t} = \gamma^* = \phi(1-u^*) + 1 - \delta_h. \quad (22)$$

That also means that the ratio between physical and human capital is constant. If we define a new variable $x_t = \frac{k_t}{h_t}$, using equations (11) and (18), we get

$$\lim_{t\to\infty} x_t = x^* = \left\{\frac{\alpha A}{(\phi+1-\delta_h)[1+\psi(R-1)] - (1-\delta_k) - \psi(R-1)(1-\delta_h)}\right\}^{\frac{1}{1-\alpha}} u^*.$$

Conditions (17) and (13) imply that all Lagrange multipliers λ_t, η_t and ε_t grow at the same rate, too

$$\frac{\eta_t}{\lambda_t} = R-1, \quad (23)$$

$$\lim_{t\to\infty}\frac{\varepsilon_t}{\lambda_t} = \frac{(1-\alpha)A}{\phi}(x^*)^{\alpha} u^*. \quad (24)$$

Using (23), the relationship between consumption c_t and the marginal utility of wealth λ_t, equation (16), and the fact that the shadow price of human capital ε_t grows at the constant rate in all periods, we can write

$$\gamma^* = \lim_{t\to\infty}\frac{c_{t+1}}{c_t} = \lim_{t\to\infty}\frac{\lambda_t}{\lambda_{t+1}} = \lim_{t\to\infty}\frac{\eta_t}{\eta_{t+1}} = \frac{\varepsilon_t}{\varepsilon_{t+1}} = \beta(\phi+1-\delta_h). \quad (25)$$

Combining (22) and (25) we get the long run value of the working time u^*. Dividing the cash-in-advance constraint (4) with human capital at period t we can see that in order to achieve the balanced growth path, real balances must also grow at the same rate as the human capital

$$\left(\frac{c_t}{h_t}\right) + \psi\left[x_{t+1}\left(\frac{h_{t+1}}{h_t}\right) - (1-\delta_k)x_t\right] \leq \left(\frac{m_t}{h_t}\right).$$

Proposition 1 *On the balance growth path, consumption, real balances, physical capital, human capital and output grow at the rate*

$$\gamma^* = \beta(\phi + 1 - \delta_h),$$

physical to human capital ratio is

$$x^* = \left\{ \frac{\alpha A}{\phi[1+\psi(R-1)] + (1-\delta_h) - (1-\delta_k)} \right\}^{\frac{1}{1-\alpha}} (1-\beta)\left(1 + \frac{1-\delta_h}{\phi}\right), \tag{26}$$

the working time is

$$u^* = (1-\beta)\left(1 + \frac{1-\delta_h}{\phi}\right),$$

inflation rate is

$$\pi^* = \frac{R}{\phi + 1 - \delta_h} \tag{27}$$

and the growth rate of money supply is

$$\mu^* = \beta R.$$

We can see that the long run growth rate is not affected by the monetary policy, neither by a fraction of investment into physical capital that must be bought using money

$$\frac{d\gamma^*}{dR} = 0, \text{ for } 0 \leq \psi \leq 1.$$

The long run growth rate of the economy depends on the accumulation of human capital which is independent of the monetary policy. It is affected by the education policy, however,

$$\frac{d\gamma^*}{d\phi} > 0.$$

The efficiency of the education system influences directly the balanced growth path behavior of output, both capitals and consumption. The physical to human capital ratio can be altered by both monetary and education characteristics

$$\begin{aligned} \frac{dx^*}{dR} &= 0, \text{ for } \psi = 0, \text{ and } \frac{dx^*}{dR} < 0, \text{ for } 0 < \psi \leq 1, \\ \frac{dx^*}{d\phi} &< 0. \end{aligned}$$

For $0 < \psi \leq 1$ the balanced growth path ratio of both capitals x^* decreases with increasing interest rate, because more money in the economy slows down the accumulation of physical capital. Higher efficiency of studying speeds up the accumulation of human capital relative to physical one and decreases their mutual ratio.

Higher inflation rate, due to higher interest rate and higher growth rate of money supply, can be partially offset by a more productive education sector, see equation (27).

4. Transitional Dynamics

In the following we consider that both capitals depreciate totally, $\delta_k = \delta_h = 1$.

We begin by assuming that the policy functions for the following variables have a form like found in Bethmann (2004)

$$u_t = 1 - \beta, \tag{28}$$

$$k_{t+1} = \theta_k\, y_t,\ c_t = (1-\theta_k)\, y_t, \tag{29}$$

$$\lambda_t = \frac{\theta_\lambda}{y_t},\ \eta_t = \frac{\theta_\eta}{y_t},\ \varepsilon_t = \frac{\theta_\varepsilon}{h_t} \tag{30}$$

where θ_i, $i = k, \lambda, \eta, \varepsilon$ are constants.[6] Plugging into the first order conditions (10)-(15) and the goods market equilibrium condition (7) we find that the policy functions are

$$k_{t+1} = \frac{\alpha\beta}{1+\psi(R-1)} y_t,\ c_t = \left[1 - \frac{\alpha\beta}{1+\psi(R-1)}\right] y_t, \tag{31}$$

$$\lambda_t = \frac{1}{R\left(1-\frac{\alpha\beta}{1+\psi(R-1)}\right)}\frac{1}{y_t},\ \eta_t = \frac{R-1}{R\left(1-\frac{\alpha\beta}{1+\psi(R-1)}\right)}\frac{1}{y_t}, \tag{32}$$

$$\varepsilon_t = \frac{1-\alpha}{\phi R\left(1-\frac{\alpha\beta}{1+\psi(R-1)}\right)(1-\beta)}\frac{1}{h_t}. \tag{33}$$

Cash-in-advance constraint implies that the real balances are

$$m_t = \left[1 - \frac{\alpha\beta(1-\psi)}{1+\psi(R-1)}\right] y_t. \tag{34}$$

We can write for the evolution of the physical to human capital ratio

$$x_{t+1} = \frac{\alpha A (1-\beta)^{1-\alpha}}{\phi\left[1+\psi(R-1)\right]} x_t^\alpha. \tag{35}$$

In the transition, when the physical capital grows at a different rate than the human capital, growth rate of output will determine the growth rate of consumption and real balances. Under the present parametrization human capital grows at a constant rate. When the initial ratio $x_0 < x^*$, physical capital grows faster than human capital, converging towards the growth rate of human capital as approaching the level of x^*. We can see that the ratio of both capitals is affected by the monetary and education policies in the same way in the transition as in the short run. The monetary policy has an effect on real variables of the economy when $\psi \neq 0$. When the cash in advance constraint only applies for consumption, $\psi = 0$, the monetary policy does not affect neither the levels, nor the growth rates of the variables of the model.

Plugging (32) and (2) into (19), and using (35), we come up with the evolution of the inflation rate over time

$$\pi_{t+1} = \frac{R\left[1+\psi(R-1)\right]^\alpha}{\phi^{1-\alpha}(\alpha A)^\alpha (1-\beta)^{\alpha(1-\alpha)}} x_t^{\alpha(1-\alpha)}. \tag{36}$$

[6] Policy functions in the standard cash-in-advance models are usually very similar or identical to real models, and it helps us to guess.

Across the transition towards the balanced growth path, inflation rate is an increasing function of x_t. When the ratio $\frac{k_t}{h_t}$ increases, higher growth rate of physical capital is an impulse for higher growth and it translates into higher inflation rate.[7]

Substituting the policy function for the real balances (34) and the policy function for the marginal utility of consumption (32) into (20) we obtain that the growth rate of money supply will be constant over time

$$\mu_{t+1} = \beta R = \mu. \tag{37}$$

It is analogous to set the monetary policy in terms of constant nominal interest rate or constant growth rate of money supply.[8]

4.1. Numerical Example

In order to illustrate the behavior of the economy we present an example choosing values for the parameters. It is not a calibration exercise. We just want to make an intuitive exposition of the analytical solution of the model.

Both capitals totally depreciate, $\delta_k = \delta_h = 1$. The participation of the physical capital in output is set to $\alpha = 0.36$. This parameter value implies very rapid convergence towards the balanced growth path. We set the long run growth rate to $\gamma^* = 1.015$. The discount factor in the utility function $\beta = 0.9$, which implies that 10% of the available time is devoted to working, $u^* = 0.1$. The previous parametrization implies the baseline value for the education policy $\phi = 1.128$. The baseline monetary policy is $R = 1.173$, a nominal interest rate that leads to 4% inflation on the balanced growth path, $\pi^* = 1.04$.

4.1.1. Monetary Policy Changes

We begin by plotting the gross growth rate of the ratio of physical to human capital, $\frac{x_{t+1}}{x_t}$, as a function of x_t. In Figure 1 we show this relationship for four different monetary policies, one that corresponds to the Friedman rule, and others that lead to 4%, 20% and 50% inflation rate on the balanced growth path ($R = 1$, 1.173, 1.35 and 1.69), for $\psi = 0.5$. We can observe the effect of inflation over the steady state level of physical to human capital ratio commented before. When $\psi = 0$, physical capital is a credit good and the Friedman rule solution applies for any R. For $\psi \neq 0$, the behavior is analogous to the one in Figure 1.

In Figure 2 we plot the behavior of consumption and physical capital for $\psi = 0.5$, for 4 economies with the same initial condition, but different monetary policies (the economy on the left begins at $x_0 < x^*$, the one on the right begins at $x_0 > x^*$). We can see the

[7]Einarsson and Marquis (1999) also find positive correlation between physical to human capital ratio and inflation rate in the transition. For the steady state correlations they find $\frac{dx^*}{d\pi^*} > 0$, if the education sector is more human capital intensive than the production sector. Their result is different from ours, because in their model inflation affects the decisions about the distribution of the available time between working, studying and leisure.

[8]To write the policy functions when the monetary aggregates are set instead of nominal interest rate, just plug (37) into (28)-(30).

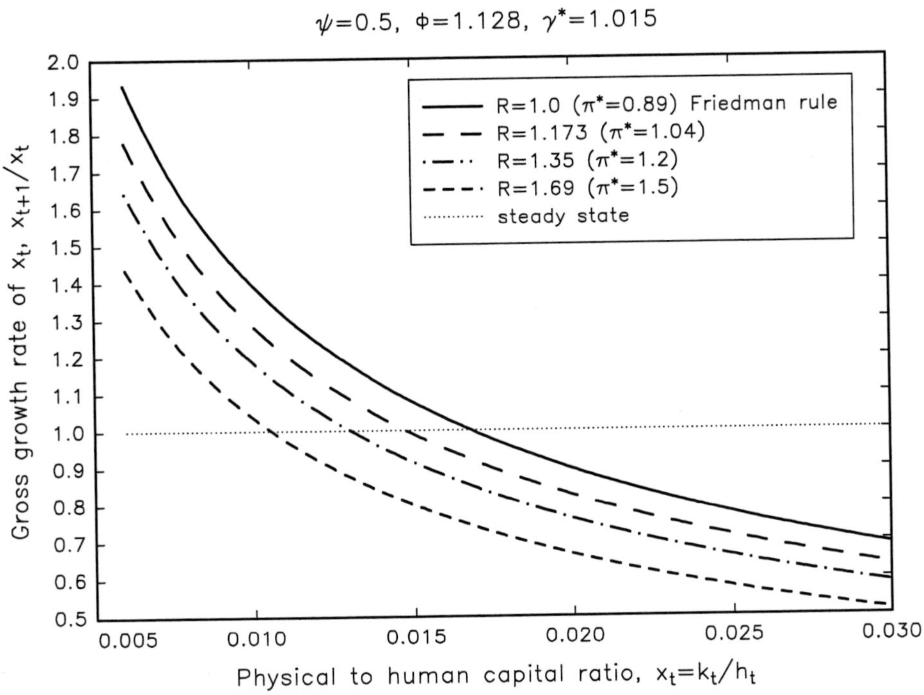

Figure 1. Gross growth rate of the physical to human capital ratio, $\frac{x_{t+1}}{x_t}$, as a function of x_t, for 4 different monetary policies, $R = 1$, 1.17, 1.35 and 1.67, for baseline parameters and for $\psi = 0.5$.

inflation taxing the future consumption. Agents in a high inflation regime consume more in early periods and less in later periods compared to a low inflation regime. Higher nominal interest rate affects negatively the physical capital accumulation, see the policy function (31).

Disinflation 1: In this experiment we begin at the balanced growth path where R is set such that the inflation rate is 20%, $\pi^* = 1.2$ (corresponding $R = 1.35$). The objective is to decrease the nominal interest rate to $R = 1.17$ and let the economy arrive to a new balanced growth path where the inflation reaches 4%, $\pi^* = 1.04$. We keep the economy on the high inflation balanced growth path until the period $t = 5$. At $t = 6$ a decrease in the nominal interest rate is applied. In Figures 3 and 4 we can observe the transition towards the low inflation balanced growth path for the growth rates of physical capital, $\frac{k_{t+1}}{k_t}$, consumption, $\frac{c_{t+1}}{c_t}$, real balances, $\frac{m_{t+1}}{m_t}$, output, $\frac{y_{t+1}}{y_t}$ and inflation rate π_{t+1}, and the evolution of k_t, c_t, m_t, y_t and p_t, respectively. From Figure 1 we see that a decrease in R implies a transition towards a higher physical to human capital ratio x^*. Given that the human capital grows at the same rate for all periods, it means that a drop in the nominal interest rate causes an increase in the physical capital accumulation. Due to the timing issues (real balances necessary for the next period purchases are acquired before the change in the monetary policy), there is a temporary increase in the inflation rate when the disinflation policy is applied. The inflation rate and the physical to human capital ratio are positively related,

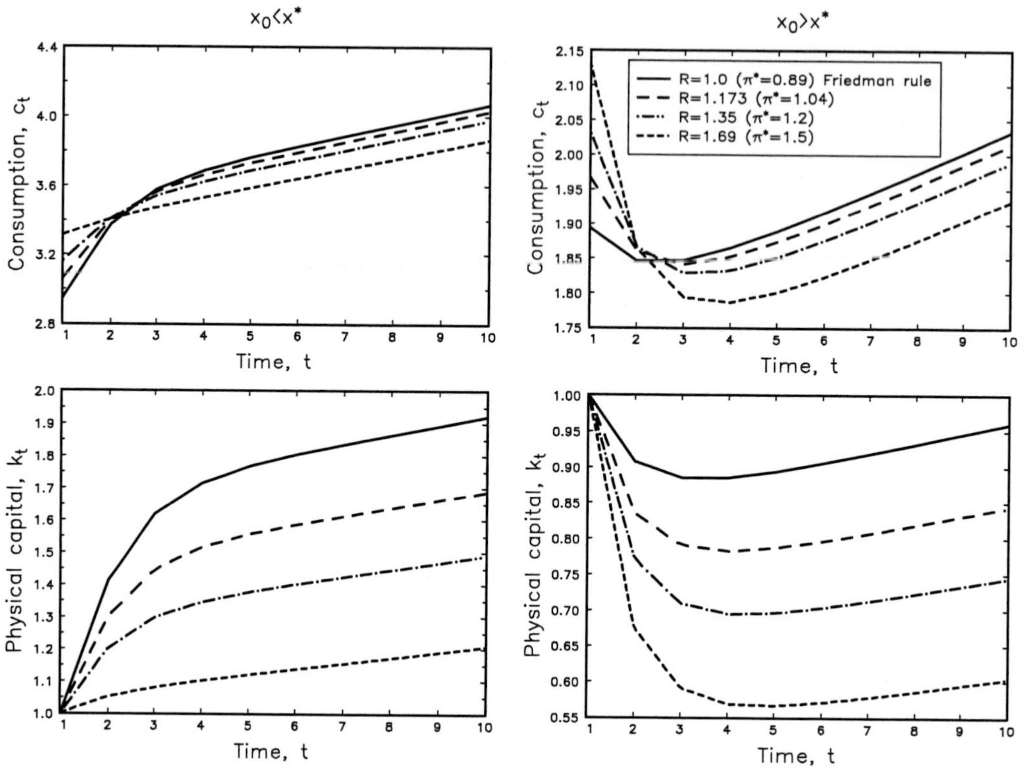

Figure 2. Evolution of consumption and physical capital from a common initial condition, for 4 different monetary policies, $R = 1,\ 1.17,\ 1.35$ and 1.67, for baseline parameters, $\phi = 1.128$ and for $\psi = 0.5$. Left column: initial value of physical to human capital ratio is below the balanced growth path value; right column: initial value of physical to human capital ratio is above the balanced growth path value.

see equation (36). For the inflation rate to increase later on, it must initially fall below its new balanced growth path value. We observe an overshooting in the inflation rate. The drop in the growth rate of consumption is related to the fact that after the decrease in the interest rate, the physical capital accumulation is enhanced. In later periods the increase in the physical capital accumulation translates into the increase in consumption. Once this adjustment happens, the growth rates of all variables converge to the one that corresponds to the balanced growth path.

4.1.2. Education Policy Changes

Concerning the education policy, an increase in the productivity of the education sector increases the growth rate of human capital. That increases the level of human capital and decreases relatively the ratio $\frac{k_t}{h_t}$. In Figure 5 we plot the gross growth rate of the ratio of physical to human capital, $\frac{x_{t+1}}{x_t}$, as a function of x_t, for four different education policies which lead to 0.5%, 1.5%, 5% and 10% balanced growth per period ($\phi = 1.117,\ 1.128,\ 1.167$ and 1.222), for $\psi = 0.5$.

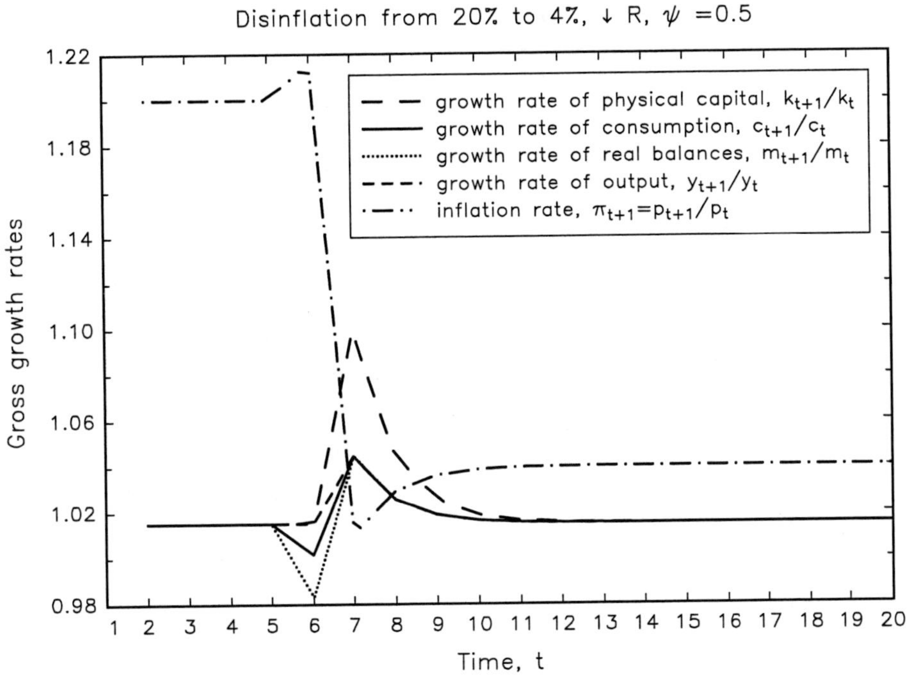

Figure 3. Transition of the economy from a high inflation balanced growth path, $\pi^* = 1.2$ $(R = 1.35)$ towards a low inflation balanced growth path, $\pi^* = 1.04$ $(R = 1.117)$: gross growth rates of physical capital, consumption, real balances, output and prices for $\psi = 0.5$ and $\phi = 1.128$.

The evolution of consumption and physical capital, for $\psi = 0.5$, for four economies that begin from the same initial level of output per worker but differ in the efficiency of learning is illustrated in Figure 6. The higher the productivity of the education sector, the higher the accumulation of human capital, the higher the level of consumption. Physical capital accumulation does not depend on ϕ, but it depends on the level of output that is higher for more efficient education sector. Therefore, between periods 1 and 2, physical capital level is the same in all four economies, but later on, its growth rate approaches the one of human capital, which is different for each of the four economies under comparison. Because the inflation tax acts through the monetary policy, in Figure 6 we no longer observe the inflation tax effect that was present in Figure 2. We should have in mind however, that even if the nominal interest rate and money growth rate are common, the balanced growth path inflation rate that corresponds to each education policy is different, see equation (27). Therefore, from now on we will refer to the inflation tax as to the monetary tax. It is the growth rate of money supply and the level of real balances that act as a tax on consumption.

Disinflation 2: In the following, our goal is to decrease the inflation rate from 20% to 4%, as before, but now we induce the change via the education sector. For $R = 1.35$, $\phi = 1.127$ leads to $\pi^* = 1.2$, and $\phi = 1.3$ leads to $\pi^* = 1.04$. The transition from a high inflation balanced growth path to a low inflation balanced growth path is plotted in Figures

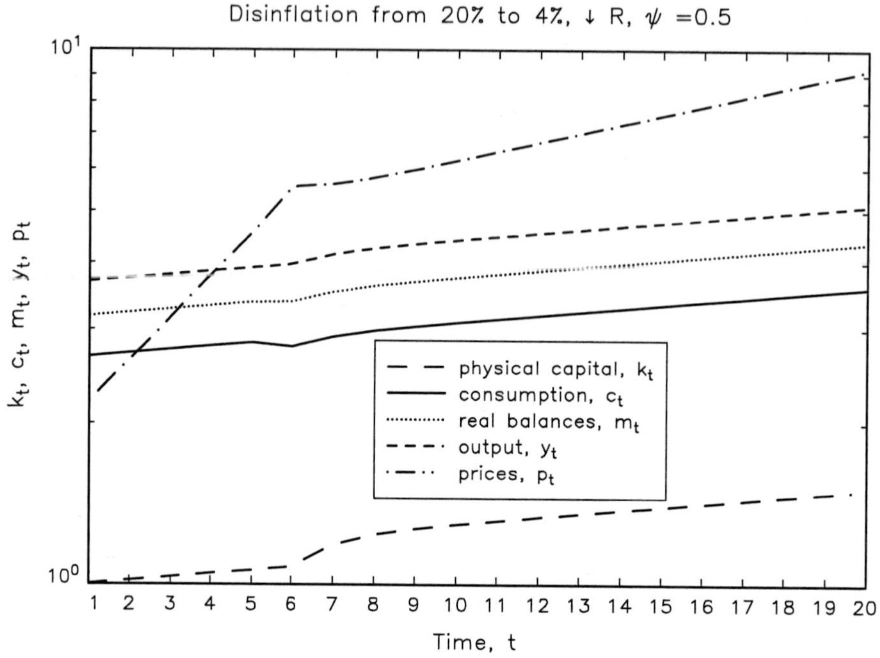

Figure 4. Transition of the economy from a high inflation balanced growth path, $\pi^* = 1.2$ ($R = 1.35$) towards a low inflation balanced growth path, $\pi^* = 1.04$ ($R = 1.117$): evolution of physical capital, consumption, real balances, output and prices for $\psi = 0.5$ and $\phi = 1.128$.

7 and 8, respectively. As the efficiency of studying increases, growth rate of accumulating human capital jumps up. Higher levels of human capital imply higher levels of output, more resources devoted to consumption and investment into physical capital, and more real balances. We thus deal with an economy with the same nominal balances as in the high inflation case, but higher demand for real balances. That implies lower price level. Inflation rate in the transition is higher than the one that corresponds to the balanced growth path. As can be seen from Figures 7 and 8, the consumption, physical capital and output all converge smoothly towards the new balanced growth path with higher growth rate.[9]

4.1.3. Simultaneous Change in Monetary and Education Policies

In this section we focus on the cases in which the combination of monetary and education policies lead to the same long run ratio of physical to human capital x^*. This means that the policy function for x_t, equation (35), will be identical for various pairs of R and ϕ.[10] To observe the effect of the monetary tax and higher productivity of the education sector on the

[9] There is a shift in the growth rate of physical capital and other variables, because $\frac{k_{t+1}}{k_t} = \mathcal{K}(y_t, y_{t-1})$, and $\frac{c_{t+1}}{c_t} = \mathcal{C}(y_{t+1}, y_t)$ and $\frac{m_{t+1}}{m_t} = \mathcal{M}(y_{t+1}, y_t)$.

[10] For $\psi = 0$, for any R there exists a unique ϕ that can lead to a given x^*. It is the same value as for the Friedman rule solution, $R = 1$.

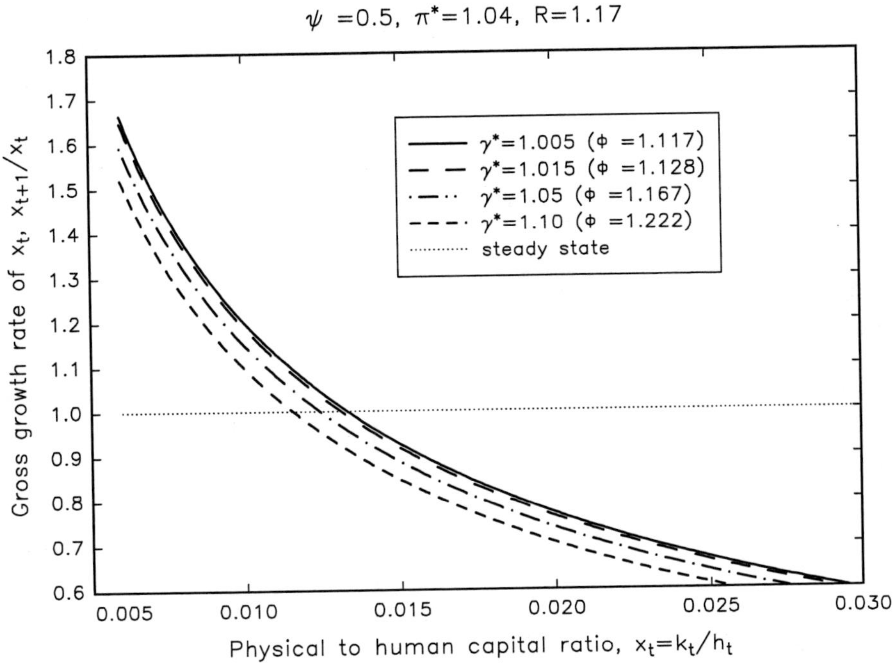

Figure 5. Gross growth rate of the physical to human capital ratio, $\frac{x_{t+1}}{x_t}$, as a function of x_t, for 4 different education policies, $\phi = 1.117$, 1.128, 1.167 and 1.222, for baseline parameters and for $\psi = 0.5$.

economy, we plot the evolution of consumption and physical capital in Figure 9. Different levels of R mean that the accumulation of physical capital is distorted by the monetary tax, and initially we observe higher consumption for higher R. In later periods higher efficiency of studying offsets the negative effect of the monetary tax.

Disinflation 3: In this experiment we change both monetary and education policies. Our goal is to reduce inflation from 20% to 4% but keep the ratio of physical to human capital unchanged. To set the proper values for R and ϕ we have to solve simultaneously the equations (26) and (27). In the high inflation balanced growth path the monetary policy is set to $R = 1.353$ and the education policy to $\phi = 1.128$. The low inflation balance growth path can be obtained by setting $R = 1.235$ and $\phi = 1.187$. The resulting growth rate of the economy will jump to $\gamma^* = 1.069$. Effects of both policies mix. We observe an initial jump in the inflation rate after lowering R, but the overshooting effect disappears because the physical to human capital ratio is constant over time. Compared to disinflation 1 and 2, the inflation rate immediately takes its new balanced growth path value. The evolution of the physical capital, consumption, output and prices, and the corresponding growth rates is illustrated in Figures 10 and 11.

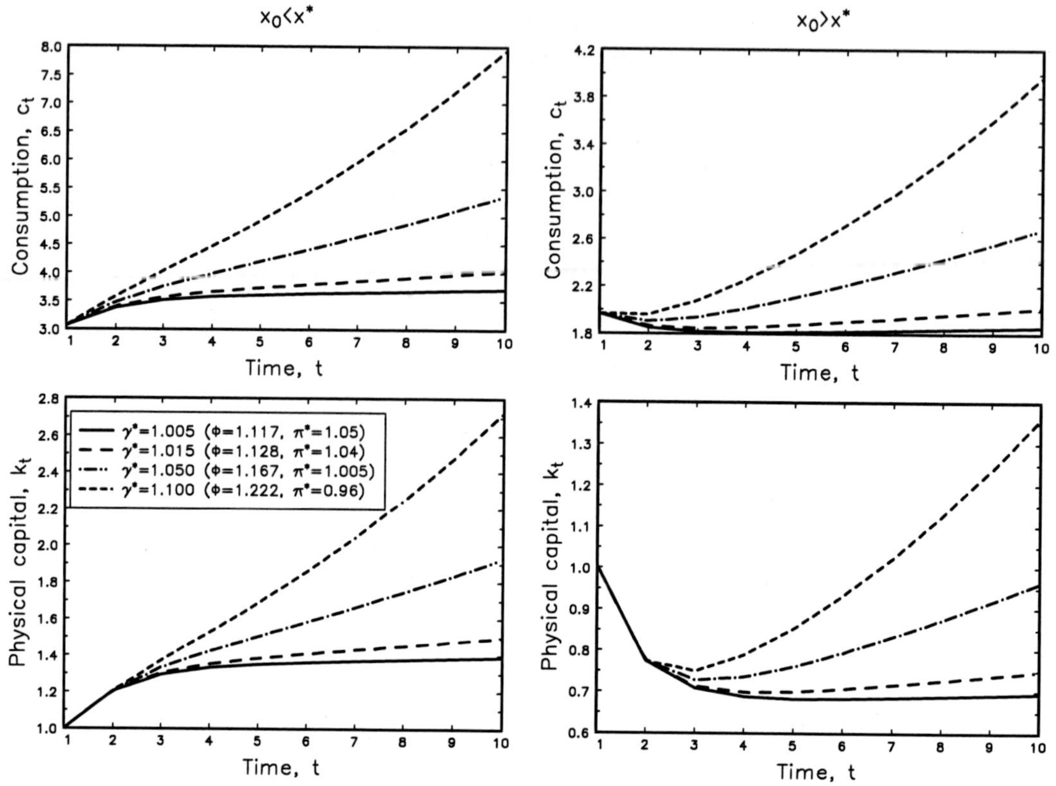

Figure 6. Evolution of consumption and physical capital from a common initial condition, for 4 different education policies, $\phi = 1.117$, 1.128, 1.167 and 1.222, for baseline parameters, $R = 1.173$ and for $\psi = 0.5$. Left column: initial value of physical to human capital ratio is below the balanced growth path value; right column: initial value of physical to human capital ratio is above the balanced growth path value.

5. Welfare Analysis

We want to evaluate the welfare losses of inflation and welfare gains of reducing inflation. The measure of welfare used is the one generally employed in the literature, as defined for example in Lucas (2003)

$$U\left[(1+\sigma)\,c^{A}\right] = U\left(c^{REF}\right).$$

Number σ, in units of a percentage of consumption goods, gives us welfare gain or loss of following a policy A with respect to a reference case REF. Taking into account our specification of the utility function we find σ that satisfies the equality

$$\sum_{t=0}^{\infty} \beta^{t} \ln\left[(1+\sigma)\,c_{t}^{A}\right] = \sum_{t=0}^{\infty} \beta^{t} \ln\left[c_{t}^{REF}\right].$$

The result

$$\sigma = \exp\left\{\frac{\sum_{t=0}^{\infty} \beta^{t} \ln\left[c_{t}^{REF}\right] - \sum_{t=0}^{\infty} \beta^{t} \ln\left[c_{t}^{A}\right]}{\sum_{t=0}^{\infty} \beta^{t}}\right\} - 1$$

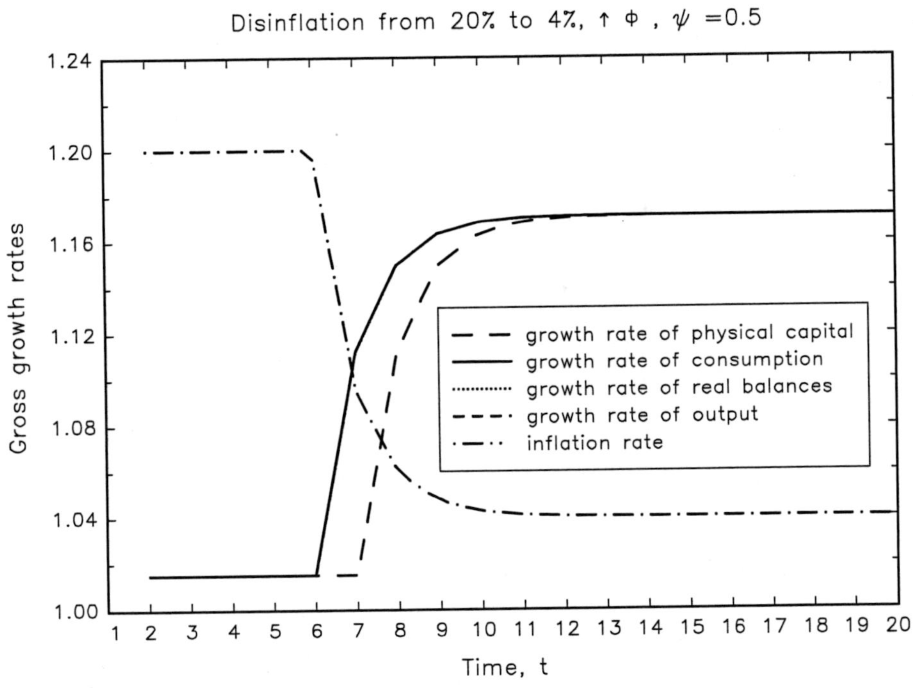

Figure 7. Transition of the economy from a high inflation balanced growth path, $\pi^* = 1.2$ ($\phi = 1.127$) towards a low inflation balanced growth path, $\pi^* = 1.04$ ($\phi = 1.3$): gross growth rates of physical capital, consumption, real balances, output and prices for $\psi = 0.5$ and $R = 1.35$.

will be positive (negative) if the policy A delivers lower (higher) lifetime utility than the reference policy REF.

In our economy, the Friedman rule is always optimal. If the investment into physical capital is a credit good ($\psi = 0$), inflation has no welfare effects. Table 1 shows the welfare loss of following a non-optimal monetary policy for different values of ψ.

Concerning the disinflation objective, we compare the welfare changes under 3 cases analyzed in the previous section. In the case 1, we reduce the nominal interest rate from $R = 1.35$ to $R = 1.17$, and keep the efficiency of studying fixed at $\phi = 1.13$. The long run growth rate of the economy remains unchanged. A partial elimination of the monetary tax implies welfare gains that amount up to 1% of consumption. In the case 2, we do not change the nominal interest rate, $R = 1.35$. Instead, we change the productivity of the education sector from $\phi = 1.13$ to $\phi = 1.30$. This change in the education policy does not affect the accumulation of physical capital, see equation (32), for a given ψ. However, it increases the growth rate of human capital, therefore the growth rate of all variables in the economy. It causes a huge welfare gain of the same magnitude for all ψ's. In the case 3, we simultaneously decrease the nominal interest rate and increase the efficiency of the education sector, from $R = 1.35$ and $\phi = 1.13$ to $R = 1.24$ and $\phi = 1.19$. In this case lower nominal interest rate also means lower monetary tax and higher physical capital accumulation, but the substantial welfare gains are due to the increase in the growth rate of

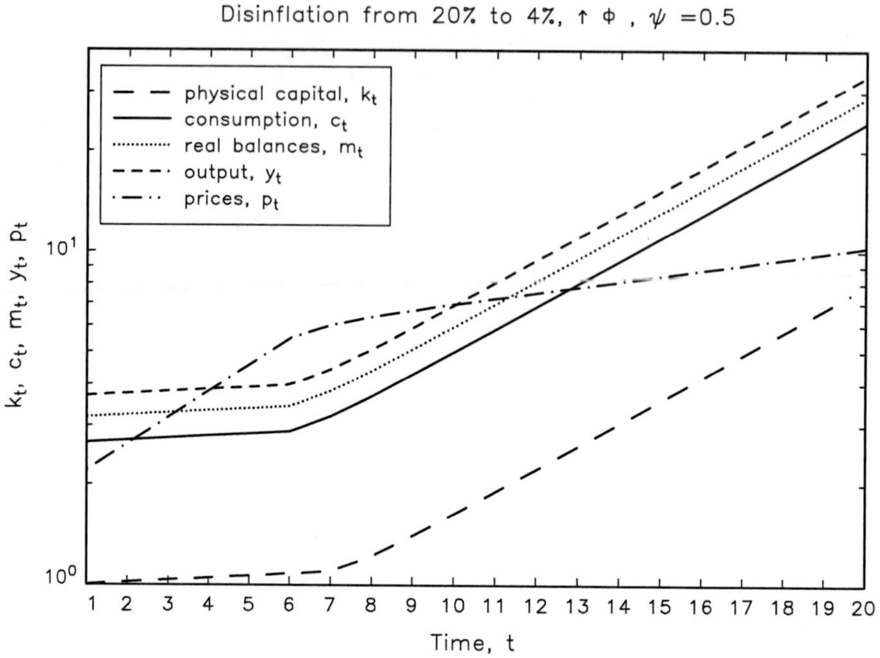

Figure 8. Transition of the economy from a high inflation balanced growth path, $\pi^* = 1.2$ ($\phi = 1.127$) towards a low inflation balanced growth path, $\pi^* = 1.04$ ($\phi = 1.3$): evolution of physical capital, consumption, real balances, output and prices for $\psi = 0.5$ and $R = 1.35$.

Table 1. Welfare loss of inflation for different fractions of investment subject to cash-in-advance constraint and different levels of balanced growth path inflation. Friedman rule and $\psi = 0$ are optimal here.

	$\sigma[\%]$				
$\psi \diagdown \pi^*$	0.89	1.04	1.2	1.5	2
0	0	0	0	0	0
0.01	0	0.0001	0.0004	0.0017	0.0055
0.2	0	0.04	0.158	0.55	1.56
0.5	0	0.23	0.85	2.6	6.6
0.8	0	0.55	1.9	5.5	12
1	0	0.82	2.7	7.5	16

the economy. Notice that when $\psi = 0$, we cannot simultaneously change both policies and maintain the physical to human capital ratio unchanged. Equation (26) implies, that there exists a single value of ϕ which delivers a given x^*. To reduce inflation rate we would keep ϕ fixed and lower the nominal interest rate. This would correspond to the case 1, changing R in an arbitrary way, the welfare is always the same. All results are reported in Table 2.

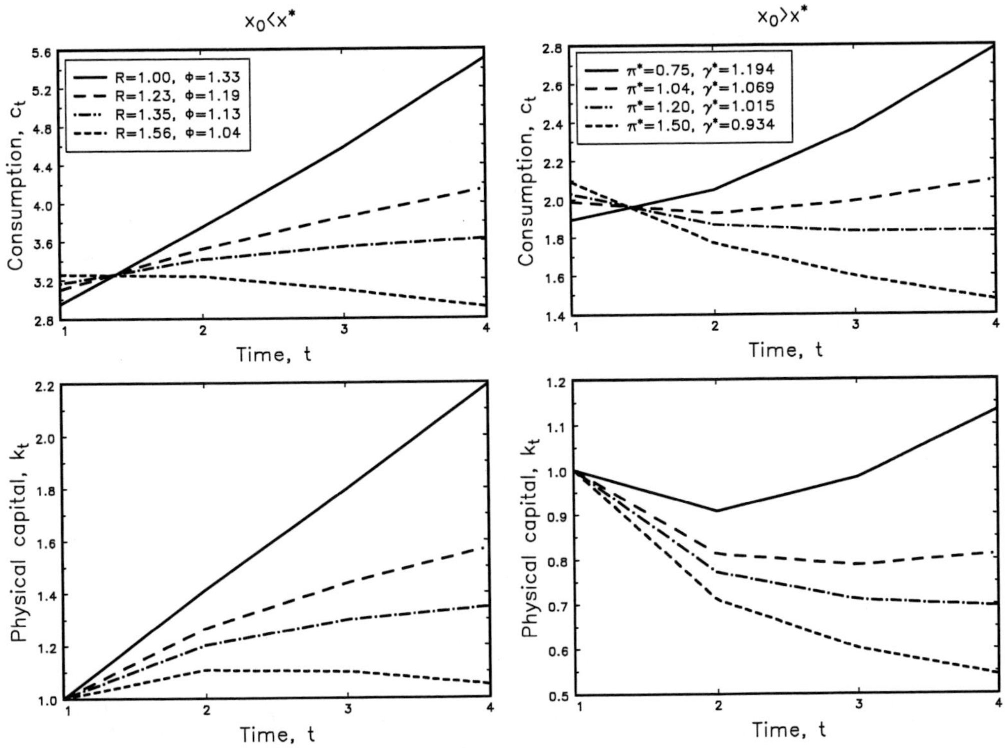

Figure 9. Evolution of consumption and physical capital from a common initial condition, for 4 different scenarios with the same x^*, $R = 1$ and $\phi = 1.33$ ($\pi^* = 0.75, \gamma^* = 1.194$), $R = 1.23$ and $\phi = 1.19$ ($\pi^* = 1.04, \gamma^* = 1.064$), $R = 1.35$ and $\phi = 1.13$ ($\pi^* = 1.2$, $\gamma^* = 1.015$), $R = 1.56$ and $\phi = 1.04$ ($\pi^* = 1.5, \gamma^* = 0.934$), for $\psi = 0.5$. Left column: initial value of physical to human capital ratio is below the balanced growth path value; right column: initial value of physical to human capital ratio is above the balanced growth path value.

6. Conclusion

We have shown the effects of monetary and education policies over the equilibrium behavior of the Uzawa-Lucas type two sector endogenous growth model with generalized cash-in-advance constraint. A closed form solution of the model has been presented.

A close attention is paid to the reaction of the inflation rate to policy changes which aim at lowering inflation. We show that the transitional dynamics of the inflation rate depends on the way the economy is disinflated. If a monetary policy is used, after a disinflation policy is executed, inflation exhibits an overshooting. If an education policy is used, inflation smoothly decreases from its high inflation equilibrium to the low one. If a certain combination of both policies is chosen, the inflation may adjust very quickly and the switch towards the balance growth path with low inflation can be accomplished immediately. Welfare effects can be huge if a policy alters the long run growth rate of the economy, a fact observed by Lucas (1987), or Gomme (1993).

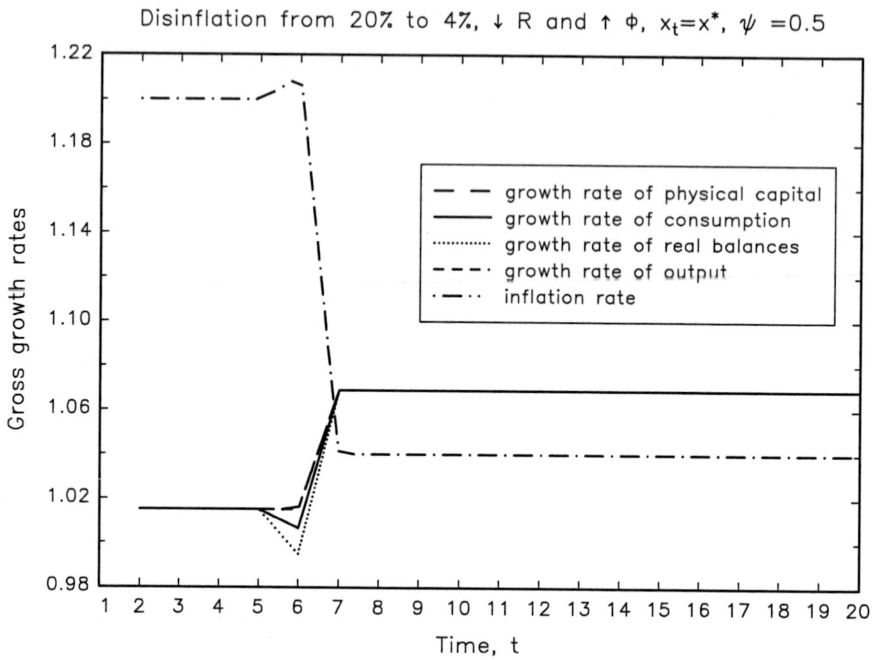

Figure 10. Transition of the economy from a high inflation balanced growth path $\pi^* = 1.2$ ($R = 1.35$ and $\phi = 1.13$) towards a low inflation balanced growth path $\pi^* = 1.04$ ($R = 1.23$ and $\phi = 1.19$): gross growth rates of physical capital, consumption, real balances, output and prices for $\psi = 0.5$.

Table 2. Welfare gain (therefore negative numbers) from disinflation from 20% to 4%: case 1 – a decrease in the nominal interest rate from $R = 1.35$ to $R = 1.17$, and $\phi = 1.13$; case 2 – an increase in the productivity of the education sector from $\phi = 1.13$ to $\phi = 1.30$, and $R = 1.35$; case 3 – simultaneous decrease in the nominal interest rate and increase in the productivity of the education sector, from $R = 1.35$ and $\phi = 1.13$ to $R = 1.24$ and $\phi = 1.19$.

	$\sigma[\%]$		
ψ	case 1 $\downarrow R$	case 2 $\uparrow \phi$	case 3 $\downarrow R$ and $\uparrow \phi$
0	0	-51.3	NA
0.01	-0.0002	-51.3	-0.9
0.2	-0.07	-51.3	-13
0.5	-0.36	-51.3	-23
0.8	-0.79	-51.3	-28.3
1	-1.11	-51.3	-30.6

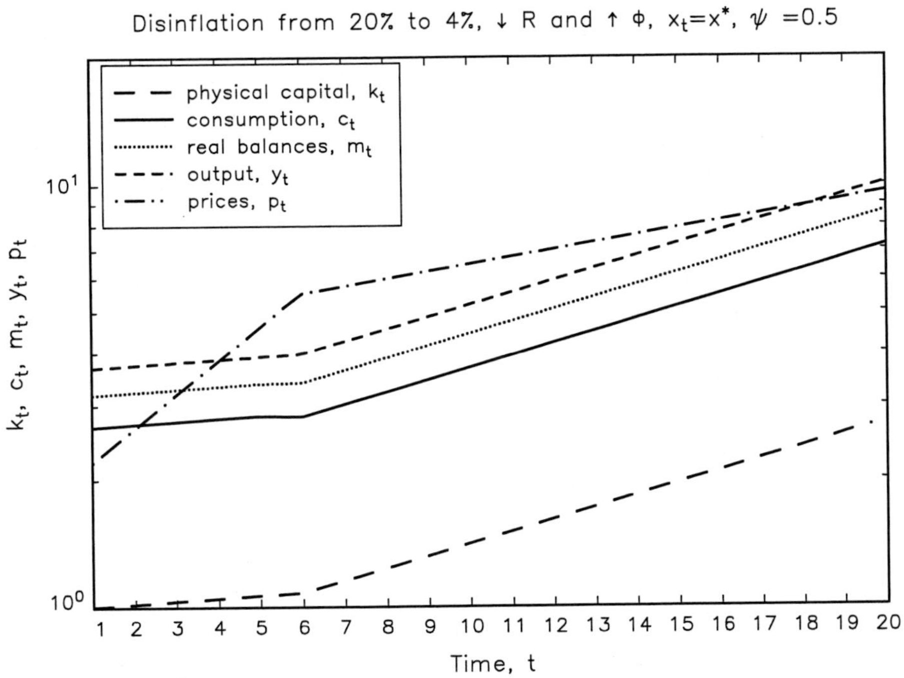

Figure 11. Transition of the economy from a high inflation balanced growth path $\pi^* = 1.2$ ($R = 1.35$ and $\phi = 1.13$) towards a low inflation balanced growth path $\pi^* = 1.04$ ($R = 1.23$ and $\phi = 1.19$): evolution of physical capital, consumption, real balances, output and prices for $\psi = 0.5$.

References

[1] Benhabib, J., and Perli, R. (1994). Uniqueness and Indeterminacy: On the Dynamics of Endogenous Growth, *Journal of Economic Theory,* **63**, 113-142.

[2] Bethmann, D. (2007). A Closed-form Solution of the Uzawa-Lucas Model of Endogenous Growth, *Journal of Economics,* **90**, 87-107.

[3] Caballé, J., and Santos, M. (1993). On Endogenous Growth with Physical and Human Capital, *Journal of Political Economy,* **101**, 1042-1067.

[4] Dutta, J., and Weale, M. (2001). Consumption and the Means of Payment: An Empirical Analysis for the United Kingdom, *Economica*, **68**, 293-316.

[5] Einarsson, T., and Marquis, M. H. (1999). *Transitional and Steady-state Costs of Disinflation when Growth is Endogenous, Economica,* **66**, 489-508.

[6] Gomme, P. (1993). Money and Growth Revisited: Measuring the Costs of Inflation in an Endogenous Growth Model, *Journal of Monetary Economics*, **31**, 97-115.

[7] Hromcová, J. (1998). A Note on Income Velocity of Money in a Cash-in-Advance Economy with Capital, *Economics Letters,* **60**, 91-96.

[8] Hromcová, J. (2008). Learning-or-doing in a Cash-in-Advance Economy with Costly Credit, *Journal of Economic Dynamics and Control,* doi: 10.1016/j.jedc.2007.11.001.

[9] Hancock, D., and Humphrey, D. B. (1998). Payment Transactions, Instruments, and Systems: A Survey, *Journal of Banking and Finance*, **21**, 1573-1624.

[10] Ireland, P. N, (1994). Money and Growth: An Alternative Approach, *American Economic Review,* **84**, 47-65.

[11] Lucas, R. E., Jr. (1984). Money in a Theory of Finance, *Carnegie-Rochester Conference Series on Public Policy,* **21**, 9-46.

[12] Lucas, R. E., Jr. (1987). *Models of business cycles.* Basil Blackwell, Oxford.

[13] Lucas, R. E., Jr. (1988). On the Mechanics of Economic Development, *Journal of Monetary Economics*, **22**, 3-42.

[14] Lucas, R. E., Jr. (2003). Macroeconomic Priorities, *American Economic Review*, **93**, 1-14.

[15] Stockman, A. C. (1981). Anticipated Inflation and the Capital Stock in a Cash-in-Advance Economy, *Journal of Monetary Economics,* **8**, 387-393.

[16] Uzawa, H. (1965). Optimum Technical Change in an Aggregative Model of Economic Growth, *International Economic Review,* **6**, 18-31.

In: Monetary Growth: Trends, Impacts and Policies
Editors: W.N. Squires et al, pp. 109-127
ISBN 978-1-60692-305-4

Short Communication D

EXCHANGE RATE BUBBLES WITH HETEROGENEOUS AGENTS AND STOCHASTIC POLICY SWITCHES

Gregory Gagnon*
Department of Economics
University of Toronto
150 St. George Street, Toronto, Ontario, M5S 3G7

Abstract

This paper analyzes the stability of the exchange rate with an irrational bubble. The fundamentalists pricing foreign exchange hold rational expectations. Monetary policy is affected by the bubble and in turn affects the fundamental exchange rate as well as speculation. When monetary policy experiences random changes the bubble and exchange rate are metastable. This means the bubble and exchange rate remain in one equilibrium for a long time and then abruptly break away to a new equilibrium. Large bubbles can be eliminated by a specific random policy for money growth.

Key words: Speculative bubble, Metastability

JEL Classifications: C62, F31, G12

1. Introduction

A typical heterogeneity found in financial economics is the distinction between noise traders who use technical trading rules and fundamentalists who are concerned with discounted expected future returns. In this paper, we analyze speculative bubbles in the foreign exchange market. This involves building bridges between Brock and Hommes (1997,1998) and a model of the exchange rate presented in Flood and Garber (1983). The model formalizes a proposal made in Brock and Hommes (1997) to analyze price dynamics when there are two time scales of trading.

*E-mail address: gregory.gagnon@utoronto.ca

It involves a modified Brock-Hommes model where the interest rate is random and the asset price (exchange rate) evolves in continuous time. The speculative bubble $(w_n, n \in Z^+)$, where Z^+ is the set of nonnegative integers, is a discrete time process determined endogenously by profit seeking investors. The fundamental exchange rate $(x_t, t \geq 0)$ is determined by sophisticated investors who hold rational expectations. The actual exchange rate, y_t, is affected by the bubble. It satisfies $y_t = x_t + w_n, n \leq t < n+1$ and therefore experiences endogenous jumps at discrete times.

To model the exchange rate we alter Brock-Hommes (1997,1998) so that the money supply affects speculation. Policy changes by the Federal Reserve can trigger large fluctuations in financial markets. Part of the fluctuation may be due to changes in speculation. LeBaron (1999) finds empirical evidence that technical trading rules are profitable only during periods of high Federal Reserve intervention. However, he does not present a theoretical model to support his findings. Our model demonstrates the validity of his empirical finding in the sense that there exist monetary policies which discourage speculation and drive the bubble toward zero over time. De Grauwe and Grimaldi (2005) present a discrete time model of exchange rate bubbles with Brock-Hommes dynamics. However, they focus on explaining empirical puzzles in exchange rate data, not the ability of policy to control bubbles.

In the model, monetary policy is also affected by the bubble. The central bank maintains a particular monetary policy up to a random time. The random time will be the first exit time of the money supply from a critical set. At the first exit time, the central bank makes a policy switch. Under the old policy the money supply is a stochastic differential equation. The new money supply will have no random shocks over a large interval. After a long time policy again changes to a stochastic differential equation. The result of this policy switch is metastability i.e. the exchange rate and speculative bubble will tend to stay in the vicinity of one equilibrium for a long time then abruptly break away and switch to a new equilibrium. The bubble will begin at a positive value and due to the policy switch drift toward zero at large times.

A related model is presented in Gagnon (2004); however there are many important differences between that paper and this study. In Gagnon (2004) the Brock-Hommes dynamics are in the stock market, not the foreign exchange market. Speculation is confined to the the stock market; the foreign exchange market is populated by rational agents. It is assumed that the market is segmented so that investors holding domestic assets and foreign exchange investors are distinct. This permits the bond interest rate to be deterministic as in Brock-Hommes. The theorems of Gagnon (2004) look at how monetary policy which is designed to affect the stock market bubble affects the exchange rate. It also shows that when the exchange rate is fixed at a random time the stock market bubble can converge to zero over time. Fixing the exchange rate involves freezing the money supply at some random time. One important difference of building Brock-Hommes speculation into the exchange rate is that the interest rate must be random to satify interest parity. The fresh random evolutions of monetary policy provide greater insight into how policy can affect speculative bubbles.

Flood and Garber (1983) as well as Froot and Obstfeld (1991) incorporated policy switches into money supply dynamics. They analyzed the case where the money supply and hence exchange rate are held constant after some random time which is itself linked to money supply dynamics. Mundaca and Øksendal (1998) as well as Cadenillas and Zapareto

(1999) analyze policy switches that keep the exchange rate in a target zone. However, the theoretical literature does not seem to have investigated in depth exchange rate evolutions that occur after the money supply hits a critical set. Many countries have a floating exchange rate that is occasionally subjected to central bank intervention. Central banks may discourage speculation against their currencies while practicing monetary targeting at the same time. Policy switches at first exit times is one way of modeling this behavior.

The paper is organized as follows. Section 2 extends the discrete time noise trader model of Brock and Hommes (1997,1998). Section 3 presents the exchange rate model. Section 4 presents the theorems critical to proving metastability; section 5 presents the metastability results. Section 6 concludes.

2. The Brock Hommes Model with Time Varying Interest Rate and Trend Chasing

Throughout the paper, the term "bubble" refers to the difference between the fundamental price of the currency and the actual market price. The exchange rate is the domestic price of one unit of foreign currency. At time n it is denoted by y_n. The exchange rate evolves in continuous time and is priced by fundamentalists; the bubble evolves in discrete time. We assume that a subset of traders alter their portfolios at integer times. As they make portfolio shifts they swing between being fundamentalists and speculators. This trading alters the bubble at integer times. The bubble determined at time n is constant over the interval $[n, n+1)$ and affects the exchange rate over that interval. Let $(x_t, t \geq 0)$ be the fundamental exchange rate determined by rational expectations (see section 3) and w_n the bubble at time n whose dynamics are presented below. Then $y_t = x_t + w_n, n \leq t < n+1$.

The original Brock-Hommes model analyzed speculative bubbles in the stock market. Some changes are necessary to adapt it to the foreign exchange market. In particular, Brock and Hommes assumed the interest rate on a risk free bond was constant. Interest parity requires the domestic interest rate equal the foreign interest rate plus expected depreciation of the currency. Assume the foreign money supply is constant. The domestic interest rate cannot be constant if domestic money growth is positive.

Let r be the constant foreign interest rate and $(\mu_s, s \geq 0)$ a càdlàg process that is linked to the bubble. The domestic money supply dynamics in the model are a stochastic differential equation, $k_t^\mu = k_0^\mu + \int_0^t b(s, \mu_s, k_s^\mu)\, ds + \int_0^t \sigma(s)\, dW_s$, where the initial condition k_0^μ can depend on μ. Following Ikeda and Shibata (1995), the expected change in the money supply at time t is $b(t, \mu_t, k_t^\mu)$ provided agents use rational expectations. The actual exchange rate equals the rational expectations exchange rate plus the bubble. Since the bubble is constant on $[n, n+1)$, the expected depreciation at time n is the rate of money growth $b(n, \mu_n, k_n^\mu)$. Consequently, the gross return on the domestic bond from time n to $n+1$ is $R_n = 1 + r + b(n, \mu_n, k_n^\mu)$ for all $n \geq 0$. In Brock and Hommes (1997,1998) the constant gross bond return is denoted by R.

In the model, the exchange rate bubble depends on the percentages of agents who are fundamentalists and noise traders. All agents in the market are mean-variance maximizers. They allocate their wealth to either money or the risk free bond. They can choose between holding either foreign or domestic currency. To apply the Brock-Hommes equations, assume that foreign currency is viewed by agents as an asset and that domestic currency is used for transactions purposes.

The distinction between noise traders and fundamentalists is the expectation of the exchange rate in the next period. For expositional convenience, fundamentalists and noise traders will be referred to as type one and type two respectively. The expectations of type j at time n are denoted by E_{jn}. At each time n, every agent chooses whether to be a noise trader or fundamentalist based on the profitability of each trading type in the previous period.

At each time n the agent will have wealth in domestic currency at time $n+1$ given by

$$W_{n+1} = R_n W_n + (y_{n+1} + d_{n+1} - R_n y_n) h_n \quad (2.1)$$

where W_n is wealth from exchange rate and bond holdings, $d_{n+1} = y_{n+1} r$ and h_n is the number of currency units purchased at time n. The constraint requires explanation. Clearly, $W_n - y_n h_n$ is the amount invested in the bond and this commands a gross return of R_n. Each unit of foreign curerncy earns $1+r$ as a gross return and this equals $y_{n+1}(1+r)h_n$ in domestic currency at time $n+1$.

Assumption 2.1: The conditional variance of returns at time n of type j satisfies $V_{jn}(y_{n+1} + d_{n+1} - R_n y_n) = \gamma^2$ for $j = 1, 2$ where $\gamma > 0$ is a constant.

Remark: Brock and Hommes use this assumption to simplify the problem of solving for the dynamics generated by the investor choice problem. It will not be satisfied when the exchange rate is generated by a stochastic differential money supply. However, in this paper there is not really much loss of generality in making this assumption. The purpose of the paper is to investigate how policy switches can generate fluxes in the bubble. Under assumption 2.1 it is shown in section 5 that there can be bubbles which are constant up to a random time. It is possible to analyze how policy can move the bubble from one positive constant state close to the zero state. If the conditional variance is time dependent using methods in section 5 it is possible to prove that policy can take a fluctuating bubble close to the zero state. Having bubbles constant up to a random time is a convenient way to focus thinking for the results in section 5.

At each time n agents of both types are mean-variance maximizers. Consequently, each agent of type j solves the following problem for h_{jn}, the number of currency units to be held.

$$\max \{E_{jn} W_{n+1} - s/2 V_{jn}(W_{n+1})\} \quad (2.2)$$

where s is the risk aversion assumed to be constant across traders. The solution to the problem is $h_{jn} = E_{jn}(y_{n+1} + d_{n+1} - R_n y_n)/s\gamma^2$.

Assumption 2.2: The fundamental predictor is available at constant cost $C \geq 0$. This represents the cost of learning in markets.

Agents are assumed to change their trading type based on the measure π_{jn}, the weighted sum of realized profits of choosing type j up to time n. Brock and Hommes (1998) show that this structure yields transition probabilities for types of traders q_{jn}, defined by $q_{jn} = \exp(\beta \pi_{j,n-1})/Z_n$ where $Z_n = \sum_{j=1,2} \exp(\beta \pi_{j,n-1})$ is a normalization. The parameter β

measures the intensity to switch predictors. Their derivation is directly applicable to our model.

Let x_n denote the fundamental exchange rate and $\mathcal{F}_n$ the time n information set. Brock and Hommes (1997,1998) assume that all expectations have the form

$$E_{jn}(y_{n+1}) = E(y_{n+1}|\mathcal{F}_n) + g_j(y_{n-1} - x_{n-1}) \quad (2.3)$$

where $E(\cdot|\mathcal{F}_n)$ is the conditional expectation and $g_j \geq 0$ is a parameter called "the trend" of trader type j. Fundamentalists can have no deviation from x_n implying $g_1 = 0$. For convenience denote g_2 by g. The parameter g determines the strength noise traders attach to deviations from the fundamental exchange rate. Clearly, $g > 0$ implies noise traders chase trends because deviations from the fundamental are extrapolated with intensity g. The next assumption generalizes the Brock-Hommes model by making trend chasing a random process that depends on the lagged money supply.

Assumption 2.3: For some right continuous left limit process μ yet to be specified, let k_n^μ be the money supply at time n and suppose that some bounded function f is given. Then $\forall n \geq 1$ trend chasing is time dependent and satisfies $g_n = g + f(k_{n-1}^\mu)$. Noise trader expectations satisfy

$$E_{2n}(y_{n+1}) = E(y_{n+1}|\mathcal{F}_n) + g_n(y_{n-1} - x_{n-1}) \quad (2.4)$$

The parameter g reflects a core amount of trend chasing that occurs independently of the money supply. The term $f(k_{n-1}^\mu)$ in g_n allows changes in the money supply to reduce trend chasing. If f is monotone increasing, raising the money supply increases the tendency to chase trends.

Remark: Although it is only conjecture that monetary policy affects speculation there is some related empirical evidence to suggest that this line of reasoning is worth pursuing. LeBaron (1999) finds that technical trading rules yield significant risk adjusted returns in the foreign exchange market over a time period that includes both heavy and light Federal Reserve intervention. However when intense periods of intervention are deleted from the sample the technical trading rules fail to yield high risk adjusted returns. Also, technical trading rules yield low returns during historical periods of low Federal reserve intervention. Federal Reserve intervention must create patterns that make technical trading profitable. If policy can affect the profitability from noise trading and traders understand this fact, it may affect the propensity to speculate.

The money supply will only be defined for $t \geq 0$ whereas the Brock-Hommes system is defined $\forall n \in Z$, the set of integers. Their paper is concerned with behavior of the bubble as $n \to \infty$. For consistency, to introduce trend chasing lags at all nonnegative times in our model one could define $k_{-1}^\mu = k_0^\mu$. Since k_n^μ will be $\mathcal{F}_n$ measurable by construction the rational exchange rate x_n accounts for changes in the money supply.

Brock and Hommes (1997,1998) incorporate a random dividend into their model. By assuming dividends are independent and identically distributed and by choosing the deviation from the fundamental price as the variable of study, the dynamics in Brock-Hommes (1997,1998) are deterministic. However, the equations governing the evolution of the bubble from their model can be applied to a random fundamental price. Again, this follows because they consider deviations from the fundamental price as the variable of study. The innovation in our model is that the fundamental exchange rate, trend chasing and the interest rate are random.

Definition 2.1: An equilibrium is a sequence $((w_n, m_n))_{n=0}^{\infty}$ where $w_n = y_n - x_n$ and $m_n = q_{1n} - q_{2n}$.

Following the development in Brock and Hommes (1998) it can be shown that $w_{n+1} = \frac{g_n q_{2n}}{R_n} w_n$ where q_{2n} depends on R_n and (w_n, w_{n-1}, w_{n-2}). The following theorem is the key result of Brock and Hommes (1997,1998). It is useful in understanding the fluxes in the bubble presented in section 5.

Theorem 2.1:

1) Let $C \geq 0$ and let $0 < g < R$, then the fundamental state $E_1 = (0, \tanh(-\beta C/2)) \equiv (0, m^e)$ is globally stable.

2) If $g > 2R$ and $C \geq 0$ there are two non-fundamental steady states, E_2 and E_3. E_1 is a steady state but is unstable for $g > 2R$. The non-fundamental steady states are defined by $E_2 = (a^*, m^*)$ and $E_3 = (-a^*, m^*)$ where a^* is the positive solution of $\tanh(\beta/2(1/s\gamma^2(g-1)(R-1)(a^*)^2 - C) = m^*$ and $m^* = 1 - 2R/g$.

3) For $R < g < 2R$ and $C > 0$, there exists β', β^* satisfying $0 < \beta' < \beta^*$ such that for $\beta < \beta'$, E_1 is stable. For $\beta = \beta'$ a pitchfork bifurcation occurs creating the non-fundamental steady states E_2 and E_3. If $\beta' < \beta < \beta^*$ the fundamental steady state is unstable and the non-fundamental states are stable. For $\beta > \beta^*$ all steady states are unstable. At β^* a Hopf bifurcation of the steady states occurs. Periodic or quasi-periodic solutions fluctuate around one of two invariant circles, one above and one below the fundamental steady state.

4) For $R < g < 2R$ and $m^* > m^e$, E_1, E_2 and E_3 are steady states and E_1 is unstable. If $m^* < m^e$ then E_1 is the unique stable steady state.

3. Monetary Policy and the Exchange Rate

In this section, we adapt the model of Flood and Garber (1983); for a detailed treatment the reader is directed to their paper. The Flood-Garber model is a monetary model of the exchange rate. It assumes equilibrium in the domestic and foreign money markets as well as purchasing power parity and interest parity. By convention when referring to the exchange rate we actually mean logarithm of the exchange rate. This is for convenience since the stochastic differential equations we use may assume positive or negative values.

Assumption 3.1: There is a complete probability space $(\Omega, \mathcal{F}, P)$ and a right continuous filtration $(\mathcal{F}_t, t \in R^+)$ such that $\mathcal{F}_0$ contains all P null sets, supporting a Brownian motion $(W_t, t \geq 0)$. For concreteness take $\mathcal{F}_t = \sigma(W_s, 0 \leq s \leq t) \bigvee \mathcal{N}$ where $\mathcal{N}$ is the class of P null sets.

Assumption 3.2: Agents have rational expectations for the fundamental value of the currency ie. they use the conditional expectation operator of probability theory. The conditional expectation of a random variable X at time t is denoted $E(X|\mathcal{F}_t)$.

The model is driven by a stochastic process for monetary policy which incorporates the logarithms of domestic and foreign money supplies, interest rates and incomes. It is usually assumed that single entity called "the government" determines the policy process. Henceforth, the terms government and central bank are used interchangeably. The policy process is denoted by (k_t). Researchers specify a dynamic equation for (k_t) and we will follow this convention. The fundamental exchange rate, x_t, is derived from an equation linking the money supply to the expected exchange rate change. For some constant α, x_t satisfies

$$x_t = \alpha^{-1} \int_t^{\infty} \exp(\frac{t-s}{\alpha}) E(k_s|\mathcal{F}_t)\, ds \quad (3.1)$$

To complete the structure of the model it is assumed that traders choose their type according to the Brock-Hommes dynamics of section 2. Thus, trader types change at integer times only. All traders agree on the fundamental price since all have the same probability measure to describe uncertainty. The fundamental price is calculated at each time $t \in R^+$. The bubble that appears at time n endures over the interval $[n, n+1)$. The exchange rate satisfies $y_t = x_t + w_n, n \leq t < n+1 \quad \forall n$. The fundamental price adjusts to new information continuously, however speculative forces are slow to adjust.

It can be shown that the process $(x_t, t \geq 0)$ has continuous sample paths when (k_t) is given by a stochastic differential equation. This mathematical structure for the bubble implies that the jumps in the exchange rate given by the process $(w_n, n \geq 0)$ are endogenous. While there is a vast literature on asset pricing with jump-diffusion models, cf. León, Solé, Utzet and Vives (2002), Venegez-Martínez (2001), the jumps are an exogenous.

Assumption 3.3: The central bank knows the composition of foreign exchange traders and deviations from fundamentals. Its policy up to a random time yet to be specified is denoted by (k_t^{μ}). It satisfies the following stochastic differential equation (SDE)

$$k_t^{\mu} = k_{\mu_0} + \int_0^t b(s, \mu_s, k_s^{\mu})\, ds + \int_0^t \sigma(s)\, dW_s \quad (3.2)$$

$\mu \equiv (\mu_s)$ is the set of tuples describing discrete time evolution of the bubble defined by $\mu_s = (w_s, m_s)$ where $w_s = w_n, m_s = m_n$ for $n \leq s < n+1$ and k_{μ_0} is the initial condition which depends on μ_0.

The class of stochastic differential equations defined by (3.2) differs from those usually considered in finance since the random process (μ_t) in the function b is endogenous. Conditions for the existence, uniqueness as well as stability properties of this class of equations are discussed in section 4. In section 4 the theorems assume (3.2) governs policy for all $t \geq 0$. The policy change and its relation to (3.2) is discussed in section 5. The initial condition k_{μ_0} is often denoted by k_0 if the bubble is understood. Throughout the exchange rate at time t corresponding to $(k_s^{\mu}, s \geq 0)$ is denoted by x_t^{μ}. Constants are denoted by C, K or L and may vary from line to line. For any dimension d, $|\cdot|$ will denote the Euclidean norm on R^d

4. Stability in the Ucp Topology

Proofs of all the theorems in this section can be found in Gagnon (2007). In Gagnon (2007) they are used to prove bifurcation on the exchange rate. These theorems are needed in the present study to prove metastability. Frequently, no distinction is made between μ and the bubble in the exposition. Throughout, dt will denote Lebesque measure and μ_0^* will denote the vector of inital conditions for the bubble i.e. $\mu_0^* = (\mu_{-1}, \mu_{-2}, \mu_{-3})$.

There are some frequently used notations in this section. Let $\mathcal{M}(R^2)$ be the space of $(\mathcal{F}_t)_{t\geq 0}$ progressively measurable processes, μ, taking values in R^2 such that $\forall T < \infty \quad \sup_{t\in[0,T]} E|\mu_t|^2 < \infty$. For any topological space Y, $\mathcal{B}(Y)$ denotes the Borel sets of Y. Finally, let $D([0,\infty), R^2)$ be the space of right continuous, left limit (càdlàg) functions from $[0,\infty)$ into R^2.

Definition 4.1: Let $b : R^+ \times \Omega \times R^2 \times R^d \to R^d$ and σ be a $d \times d$ matrix with components $\sigma_{i,j} : R^+ \times \Omega \times R^2 \times R^d \to R$. Let the components of $b(s,z,x)$, and $\sigma(s,z,x)$ restricted to $[0,t] \times \Omega \times R^2 \times R^d$ be measurable relative to $\mathcal{B}([0,t]) \times \mathcal{F}_t \times \mathcal{B}(R^2) \times \mathcal{B}(R^d)$ and $\mathcal{B}(R)$ for any t. Let $|\sigma(s,\mu_s,x)|^2 = \sum_{i,j} \sigma_{i,j}^2(s,\mu_s,x)$ and k_{μ_0} be a random d-dimensional vector with $k_{\mu_0}^i \in L^2(\Omega, \mathcal{A}, P) \quad \forall i$. Then a solution to the stochastic differential equation $dk_t^\mu = b(t,\mu_t,k_t^\mu)\, dt + \sigma(t,\mu_t,k_t^\mu)\, dW_t$ with initial condition k_{μ_0} is a continuous, $(\mathcal{F}_t)$ adapted process such that for each $T > 0$:

1) $E\int_0^T |b(s,\mu_s,k_s^\mu)|^2\, ds + E\int_0^T |\sigma(s,\mu_s,k_s^\mu)|^2\, ds < \infty$

2) $k_t^\mu = k_{\mu_0} + \int_0^t b(s,\mu_s,k_s^\mu)\, ds + \int_0^t \sigma(s,\mu_s,k_s^\mu)\, dW_s$ almost everywhere $\forall t \in [0,T]$ given any $T > 0$. This means $k_t^i = k_{\mu_0}^i + \int_0^t b_i(s,\mu_s,k_s^\mu)\, ds + \sum_{j=1}^d \int_0^t \sigma_{i,j}(s,\mu_s,k_s^\mu)\, dW_s^j \quad \forall i = 1,\ldots,d$.

Assumption 4.1: Assume there is a constant $K > 0$ such that for $z \in R^2, s \in R^+$ and $x, y \in R^d$

1) $|b(s,z,x) - b(s,z,y)|^2 + |\sigma(s,z,x) - \sigma(s,z,y)|^2 \leq K|x-y|^2$

2) $|b(s,z,x)|^2 + |\sigma(s,z,x)|^2 \leq K(1 + |x|^2 + |z|^2)$

Theorem 4.1: There exists a unique solution to the SDE defined in (3.2) for μ, a Brock-Hommes equilibrium generated by the model in section 2 with deterministic initial vector μ_0^*. Moreover, $\mu \in \mathcal{M}(R^2)$.

The initial vector of bubbles from the Brock-Hommes equations is deterministic. The theorem also holds for a bubble μ which evolves randomly via the Brock-Hommes equations from random variables μ_i for $i = -1, -2, -3$ provided $\sup_{\omega\in\Omega} |\mu_0^*(\omega)| < \infty$. Notice that under assumption 4.1 any $\mu \in \mathcal{M}(R^2)$ will generate a unique solution to (3.2). When μ is generated by the Brock-Hommes equations existence of (3.2) must be proven interval by interval since μ depends on the past behavior of the SDE and is itself generated inteval by interval.

Theorem 4.2: Suppose $b(s,z_1,z_2,y)$ has partial derivatives in (z_1,z_2,y) which are bounded in (s,z_1,z_2,y). Then there exists a function $C : [0,\infty) \times D([0,\infty),R^2) \times D([0,\infty),R^2) \times R \to R$ such that for $\mu^i \in \mathcal{M}(R^2)$ $i = 1,2$ which have càdlàg sample paths,

$$|k_t^2 - k_t^1| \leq C(t,\mu^1,\mu^2,k_0^1 - k_0^2)$$

By construction a Brock-Hommes equilibrium has càdlàg sample paths. When the lagged money supply affects trend chasing the set of Brock-Hommes bubbles is still a subset of $L(\Omega, D([0,\infty), R^2))$. Theorem 4.2 bounds the growth rate of the money supply sample paths by the sample path growth of the bubbles.

Definition 4.2: Let $L(\Omega, D([0,\infty), R^2)$ be the space of $(\mathcal{F}_t)_{t\geq 0}$ adapted processes in R^2 with càdlàg sample paths. The ucp topology or topology of uniform convergence on compacta for $L(\Omega, D([0,\infty), R^2))$ is the topology defined by $X^n \rightarrow X$ iff $P(\sup_{t\in[0,T]} |X_t^n - X_t| > \delta) \rightarrow 0 \quad \forall \delta > 0$ and all T. Convergence of processes in the ucp topology is denoted $X_n \rightarrow X$ ucp.

Definition 4.3: Let $L_{loc}^p(R^+ \times \Omega, dt \times dP)$ be the set of $\mathcal{B}(R^+) \times \mathcal{F}$ real valued $\mathcal{B}(R)$ measurable functions such that $\forall T > 0, E\int_0^T |f(t,\omega)|^p \, dt < \infty$

The next theorems demonstrate that dynamics of the bubble and its initial conditions determine the money supply dynamics. Since $(x_t^\mu, t \geq 0)$ has continuous sample paths, $(y_t^\mu, t \geq 0) \in L(\Omega, D([0,\infty), R))$.

Theorem 4.3: Let $\mu^n, \mu \in L(\Omega, D([0,\infty), R^2))$, $\quad \mu^n \rightarrow \mu$ ucp. Let $(k^n), (k)$ be the corresponding money supply processes with $k_0^n \rightarrow k_0$ in probability. Also assume $|k_0^n| \leq g \in L^2 \quad \forall n$. Let b be bounded with bounded partial derivatives. Then $k^n \rightarrow k$ ucp. Furthermore if $|\mu_t^n(\omega)| \leq f(t,\omega) \quad \forall n$ for some $f \in L_{loc}^2(R^+ \times \Omega, dt \times dP)$ where $f(\cdot, w)$ is increasing $\forall \omega \in \Omega$, then $x^n \rightarrow x$ and $y^n \rightarrow y$ ucp.

Theorem 4.4: Fix $\delta, \epsilon, T > 0$ and a Brock-Hommes bubble μ^1 such that $\sup_{\omega\in\Omega} |(\mu_0^1)^*(\omega)| < \infty$. Suppose $b \geq 0$ is bounded and that $b(s,z,z',q)$ has first order partial derivatives in (z,z',q) which are bounded in (s,z,z',q). Let b be continuous in (s,z,z',q). Then there exists a $\gamma > 0$ such that if $\mu^2 \in L(\Omega, D([0,\infty), R^2))$ is a Brock-Hommes bubble and $(k_s^1), i = 1,2$ the corresponding money supplies with $|(\mu_0^1)^*(\omega) - (\mu_0^2)^*(\omega)|, |k_0^1(\omega) - k_0^2(\omega)| < \gamma$ for all $\omega \in \Omega$ and $\sup_{\omega\in\Omega} |k_0(\omega)| < \infty$ then

1) $P(\sup_{t\in[0,T]} |\mu_t^1 - \mu_t^2| > \delta) = 0$
2) $P(\sup_{t\in[0,T]} |k_t^1 - k_t^2| > \delta) = 0$
3) $P(\sup_{t\in[0,T]} |x_t^1 - x_t^2| > \delta) < \epsilon$
4) $P(\sup_{t\in[0,T]} |y_t^1 - y_t^2| > \delta) < \epsilon$

5. Metastability of the Dynamical System

Metastability is the phenomenon of being in one equilibrium for a very long time and then abruptly breaking away from that equilibrium and moving to a new equilibrium. It is possible that the system will remain at the new equilibrium for a long time and abruptly switch back to the old equilibrium. However, the time at which the initial or future changes occur is irregular and usually random. Consequently, metastable systems are different from periodic systems.

Since metastability is a concept of sudden switches along a sample path, it is distinct from the bifurcation phenomena often observed in dynamic economic models. Despite its obvious appeal to model changes in equilibria, metastability does not seem to have had a significant impact on economic thinking. Metastable systems have been investigated extensively in the probability and physics literature, see Freidlin and Wentzell (1998), Galves, Olivieri and Vares (1987), Sowers (1992) and Bovier, Eckhoff, Gayrard and Klein (2001).

A customary setup for metastability in a continuous time dynamical system is to assume that a deterministic system is subjected to small random influences. The researcher constructs relations between the deterministic and stochastic systems to show metastability of the stochastic system. This is the approach found in Freidlin and Wentzell (1998), Sowers (1992) as well as Galves, Olivieri and Vares (1987). However, the approach employed here is somewhat different and uses theorem 4.4 to derive metastability. Throughout this section $[\cdot]$ denotes the greatest integer function, μ^i the bubble generated by an initial vector of the Brock-Hommes fixed points (μ^i corresponds to E_i in section 2) and k_t^i will denote the money supply generated by μ^i. By assumption, $\sup_{\omega\in\Omega}|k_0^i(\omega)| < \infty \quad i = 1, 2, 3$.

The mechanism which produces metastability is contained in an assumption about the function f appearing in assumption 2.3. Let $f \in C_c(R)$ the space of continuous, compactly supported functions on R. The money supply is initially defined by (3.2) for μ_0^* in a neighbourhood of a nonzero bubble. The money supply and exchange rate remain close to the nonzero bubble money supply and exchange rate. Standard methods of proof show the money supply leaves $supp(f)$, the support of f, in finite time. At this point policy experiences a structural change and there are no random shocks over a large finite interval. The money supply remains outside $supp(f)$ over this interval and trend chasing falls from $g + f(k_{n-1})$ to g.

At a random time the central bank again implements a monetary policy described by (3.2). The new money supply starts in the neighbourhood guaranteeing stability of the exchange rate and money supply around the zero bubble exchange rate and money supply over a large time interval. However, the money supply remains outside $supp(f)$ implying $g_n = g$. If $\sup_{s,z_1,z_2,y} |g/1 + r + b(s, z_1, z_2, y)| < 1$, the Brock-Hommes equations imply the bubble drifts toward 0. Thus, certain monetary policies produce metastable exchange rates and bubbles. The analysis readily extends to more than one policy switch.

Assumption 5.1: The function $f \geq 0$ in assumption 2.3 satisfies $f \in C_c(R)$, $f(k) = 0$ on U_1 and $f(k) = 1$ on U^i where U^i are the neighbourhoods of $k_0^i \quad i = 2, 3$ necessary for theorem 4.4. Furthermore, assume $R < g + 1 < 2R$ where $R = 1 + r$.

Theorem 5.1: Suppose the Brock-hommes bubble is generated by the model of section 2 with $g_n = g + f(k_{n-1}^\mu)$. Then theorems 4.1-4.4 continue to hold under their particular assumptions.

Proof: Gagnon (2007) only assumes that f is bounded and continuous so the assumptions of the theorems in that paper are satisfied. q.e.d.

Definition 5.1: Let U be an open set of R. Then the first exit time of (k_t^μ) from U is given by $\tau(U) = \inf\{t \geq 0 : k_t^\mu \notin U\}$.

Theorem 5.2: Let k_0^i be the initial condition of (k_t^i), U_i a bounded neighbourhood of k_0^i and $\tau(U_i)$ be the first exit time of (k_t^i) from U_i. Then there exists a $\rho_i > 0$ such that $E\tau(U_i) \leq \exp(\rho_i)$.

Theorem 5.2 is proven by methods found in Freidlin and Wentzell (1998). Theorem 5.2 implies that $P(\tau(U_i) < \infty) = 1$ so that when the system k_s^i starts in U_i it eventually hits ∂U_i, the boundary of U_i, with probability one in finite time.

Lemma 5.1: Let $b(s, \mu^i, z) = 0 \quad \forall z \in R$ for the fixed points μ^i of the deterministic Brock and Hommes model. Then if the initial condition vector corresponds to the fixed point μ^i, $R_n = R \quad \forall n \leq [\tau(U_i)]$ and the money supply k_t^i satisfies $k_t^i = k_0^i + \int_0^t \sigma_s \, dW_s \quad \forall t \leq \tau(U_i), i = 1, 2, 3$. The bubble satisfies $\mu_s^i = \mu^i \quad \forall s \leq \tau(U_i)$.

Proof: We prove the result for $i = 2, 3$; the proof for $i = 1$ is similar. Since $g_0 = g + 1 = g + f(k_{-1}^i)$ and $R_0 = R$ it follows that $\mu_s^i = \mu^i, 0 \leq s < 1$ because μ^i is a fixed point. Thus, $b(s, \mu^i, k_s^i) = 0 \quad \forall s \in [0, 1)$ and $k_t^i = k_0^i + \int_0^t \sigma_s \, dW_s, \quad 0 \leq s < 1$. If $1 < \tau(U_i)$ then $b(0, \mu^i, k_0^i) = 0 \quad R_1 = R$ and $g_1 = g + f(k_0^i) = g + 1$ implying $\mu_s^i = \mu^i, \quad 1 \leq s < 2$. Repeat the argument to yield $k_t^i = k_0^i + \int_0^t \sigma_s \, dW_s, \quad 1 \leq s < 2$. The theorem follows by repeating this argument up to $[\tau(U_i)]$. q.e.d.

Theorem 5.1 implies that if differences between μ_0^* and μ_0^{i*} are small for some $i = 1, 2, 3$ then $k_s^\mu - k_s^i$ remains in a neighbourhood of 0 with overwhelming probability for fixed $T < \infty$. If $E \int_0^T \sigma^2(t) \, dt < \epsilon$, then $P(\sup_{t \in [0, T \bigwedge \tau(U_i)]} |k_t^i - k_0^i| \geq \delta) < 4\epsilon\delta^{-2}$. Hence if the L^2 norm of the noise is small enough $k_t^i \in B(k_0^i, \delta)$ with high probability. Thus after a long period of stability around k_0^i that occurs with high probability the money supply k_t^μ breaks out of $B(k_0^i, 2\delta)$. To fix ideas let the fixed point be μ^2.

Assumption 5.2: Let the function f in assumption 2.3 have $supp(f) \subset B(k_0^2, 2\delta)$.

Throughout this section assume $b(s, \mu_s, z) = b(s, w_s, z)$ for any z. This means money growth depends on the bubble, not differences in proportions of trader types. In this case the bound in theorem 4.3 depends only on w_s^i, w_s^μ and $k_0^i, k_0^\mu, i = 1, 2$. Restrictions on the growth of w_s^i, w_s^μ and hence differences in $(w_n^j)^* \equiv (w_{n-1}^j, w_{n-2}^j, w_{n-3}^j) \quad j = 1, 2, 3, \mu, \quad n \geq 0$ enter the statements and proofs of inequalities in theorem 4.4.

Assumption 5.3: For fixed T, δ, ϵ let $\gamma_2 > 0$ be chosen so that if $(w_0^\mu)^* \in B((w_0^2)^*, \gamma_2)$ and $k_0^\mu \in B(k_0^2, \gamma_2)$ for a Brock-Hommes equilibrium μ then
1) $P(\sup_{t \in [0,T]} |\mu_t - \mu_t^2| \geq \delta) < \epsilon/2$
2) $P(\sup_{t \in [0,T]} |k_t^\mu - k_t^2| \geq \delta) < \epsilon/2$
3) $P(\sup_{t \in [0,T]} |x_t^\mu - x_t^2| \geq \delta) < \epsilon/2$
4) $P(\sup_{t \in [0,T]} |y_t^\mu - y_t^2| \geq \delta) < \epsilon/2$

Assumption 5.4: Let $\sigma : \Omega \times R^+ \to R$ be such that $E \int_0^\infty \sigma(s)^4 \, ds < \infty$. Suppose also that $4\delta^{-2} E \int_0^T \sigma^2(t) \, dt < \epsilon/2$.

Together, assumptions 5.2 and 5.3 imply $P(\sup_{t \in [0, T \bigwedge \tau(U_2)]} |k_t^\mu - k_0^2| \geq 2\delta) < \epsilon$. Thus, when policy before the change is given by (k_t^μ) the money supply remains in the open ball $B(k_0^2, 2\delta)$ with probability greater than $1 - \epsilon$ over the interval $[0, T \bigwedge \tau(U_2)]$. It is necessary to specify the mechanics of the policy change. Let τ be the first exit time from $B(k_0^2, 2\delta)$.

Assumption 5.5: There is a change in monetary policy after time τ. For fixed $\omega \in \Omega$ policy follows (3.2) up to time $\tau(\omega)$. There is a Lipschitz continuous function with linear growth $b_1 : R \to R$ such that at times $\tau(\omega) + t, t \geq 0$ monetary policy is given by the random differential equation

$$k_{\tau(\omega)+t} = k_{\tau(\omega)}^\mu(\omega) + \int_{\tau(\omega)}^{\tau(\omega)+t} b_1(k_s(\omega)) \, ds \quad (5.1)$$

In fact (5.1) is the $(\mathcal{F}_{\tau \bigvee t}, t \geq 0)$ adapted process $k_t = k^{\mu}_{\tau(\omega)}(\omega) + \int_{\tau(\omega)}^{t} b_1(k_s(\omega))\, ds \quad t \geq \tau(\omega), \quad k_t = k^{\mu}_{\tau(\omega)}(\omega), \quad t < \tau.$

Assumption 5.6: Suppose $\forall \omega \in \Omega$ that $k_0^1(\omega)$ is a stable fixed point of the differential equation $k_t'(\omega) = b_1(k_t(\omega)), t \geq \tau(\omega)$. Also let $B(k_0^2(\omega), 2\delta)^C$, the complement of $B(k_0^2(\omega), 2\delta)$, be in the basin of attraction of $k_0^1(\omega)$.

By definition, $B(k_0^2, 2\delta)^C$ being in the basin of attraction of k_0^1 means that solutions of k_t started at $y \subset B(k_0^2, 2\delta)^C$ must converge to k_0^1 as $t \to \infty$. Stability means that given any neighbourhood W of k_0^1 there is a neighbourhood V of k_0^1 such that solutions of k_t started in V remain in W for all t. These assumptions imply that when k_t^{μ} hits $\partial B(k_0^2, 2\delta)$ the money supply experiences a structural change which lead it to enter an arbitrary neighbourhood of k_0^1. If there is no other policy change stability of k_0^1 means the money supply remains near k_0^1 at all future times.

The bubble is still affected by the money supply after the policy switch via the interest rate since $R_{n+1} = 1 + r + b_1(k_n) \quad \forall n+1 > \tau$. The policy switch decreases trend chasing since $g_n = g$ for large $n > \tau$. This holds since $k_t \notin supp(f)$ for large t. If policy experienced no other switch, evolution of the bubble is described by the càdlàg process $(w_t^{\mu}, t \geq 0)$ derived from (3.2) and (5.1).

Assumption 5.7: Replace μ^2 by μ^1 in assumption 5.3. Let $\gamma_1 > 0$ guarantee inequalities (1)-(4) of assumption 5.3 are satisfied for any $(w_0^{\mu})^* \in B(0, \gamma_1)$ and $k_0^{\mu} \in cl(B(k_0^1, \gamma_1))$, the closure of $B(k_0^1, \gamma_1)$. Furthermore, suppose $B(k_0^2, 2\delta) \bigcap cl(B(k_0^1, \gamma_1)) = \emptyset$.

Lemma 5.2: Let $\sup_{z \in R} |g/(R + b_1(z))| < 1$ and $\sup_{0 \leq s \leq \tau, \omega \in \Omega} |w_s^{\mu}(\omega)| < \infty$. Then (w_t^{μ}), the bubble generated by the money supply defined in (3.2) up to τ and by (5.1) after τ, must converge to 0.

Proof: Since $supp(f) \subset B(k_0^2, 2\delta)$ at large times $t \geq \tau \quad f(k_t) = 0$. Without loss of generality we can assume k_t never enters $B(k_0^2, 2\delta)$ for all $t \geq [\tau] + 1$. Thus, $g_n = g$ and $w_n = (g/R + b_1(k_{n-1}))q_{2,n-1}w_{n-1}$. Let $\gamma = \sup_{z \in R} |g/(R + b_1(z))|$. Then $|w_n^{\mu}| \leq \gamma^{n-([\tau]+1)}|w^{\mu}_{[\tau]+1}|$. q.e.d.

There is no loss of generality in assuming $\sup_{0 \leq s \leq \tau, \omega \in \Omega} |w_s^{\mu}(\omega)| < \infty$. We could assume the policy switch happens at $\tau \bigwedge T$. In this case $(w_t^{\mu}, t \leq \tau \bigwedge T)$ is bounded since $(w_t^{\mu}, t \leq T)$ is bounded.

There is also a limit result for the money supply. Let $k_t(y, \eta)$ denote (5.1) with initial condition y started at the deterministic time η. For deterministic dynamical systems it is well known that if a compact set K lies in the basin of attraction of a point k_0^1 and V is a neighbourhood of k_0^1 there exists a constant $M > 0$ such that $\forall y \in K \quad k_t(y, \eta)$ must hit V at a time no larger than $\eta + M$ and remain in $V \quad \forall t \geq \eta + M$. Equation (5.1) is a deterministic system, for fixed $\omega \in \Omega$. Let $M(\omega)$ be the constant for the neighbourhood $B(k_0^1(\omega), \gamma_1)$, compact set $\partial B(k_0^2(\omega), 2\delta)$ and starting time $\tau(\omega)$. Equation (5.1) is random dynamical system since ω can vary thus M must be random. For convenience assume M is a stopping time. Also for convenience delete the superscript μ from the bubble. Define a finite stopping time H by

$$H = \inf\{s \geq \tau : w_{[s]-3} \in B(0, \gamma_1/2)\} \bigvee (\tau + M)$$

Under the assumptions of lemma 5.2 for $t \geq H \quad w_t, w_{[t]-i} \in B(0,\gamma_1), i = 0,1,2,3$ and $k_t \in B(k_0^1, \gamma_1)$. This follows because the absolute value of the bubble is strictly monotone decreasing if it nonzero and $t \geq [t] - i \geq [t] - 3, i = 0,1,2,3$. For the money supply this follows because the system started at τ must enter and remain in $B(k_0^1, \gamma_1) \quad \forall t \geq \tau + M$.

Assumption 5.8: At times $t \geq H$ the central bank pursues the random monetary policy

$$k_t^{\mu} = k_H + \int_H^t b(s, w_s, k_s^{\mu})ds + \int_H^t \sigma(s)\, dW_s \quad (5.2)$$

Therefore, the bank switches to an equation with the same structure as (3.2) but with a random initial starting time. The motivation for the second policy switch is that a central bank will probably have policies without some time dependent randomness only for finite periods of time. A pathwise solution to (5.2) exists by the results found in Protter (1990). However, the random starting time implies it may not be an L^1 random variable at each $t > H$. This would be problematic for the exchange rate equation (3.1) since it requires a finite conditional expectation. Conditional expectations will be finite for random variables in L^1. Theorem 5.4 establishes sufficient conditions for (5.2) to define a process in L^2. The next theorem establishes a representation critical for metasability.

Theorem 5.3: Let $(\xi_s(t, \mu_s^*, x), t \geq s)$ be the solution of (3.2) with initial condition $x \in R$ at time s and initial Brock-Hommes equilibrium vector $\mu_s^* = (\mu_{[s]}, \mu_{[s]-1}, \mu_{[s]-2})$ generated by (3.2) and (5.1). Let $\mu_H^* = (\mu_{[H]}, \mu_{[H]-1}, \mu_{[H]-2})$. Then for $t \geq H, \quad k_t^{\mu} = \xi_H(t, \mu_H^*, k_H)$.

Proof: First, it is necessary to show that $(\mu_t, t \geq 0)$ defined by (3.2) and (5.1) is $(\mathcal{F}_t, t \geq 0)$ adapted. This will ensure that $(\xi_s(t, \mu_s^*, x), t \geq s)$ is well defined since the proof of theorem 4.1 is valid for any initial starting time $s \geq 0$ and $\mathcal{F}_s$ measurable initial vector of bubbles and square integrable initial condition.

Changing notation for clarity, let $(\eta_t, t \geq 0)$ be the bubble generated if (3.2) defines policy $\forall t \geq 0$. Let $(\nu_t, t \geq \tau)$ be the bubble generated by (5.1) started from the $\mathcal{F}_\tau$ measurable bubble η_τ^*. Arguments similar to those in the proof of theorem 4.1 establish (ν_t) is $\mathcal{F}_{\tau \bigvee t}$ adapted. Clearly, $\mu_t = \eta_t 1_{\{t<\tau\}} + \nu_t 1_{\{\tau \leq t\}}$. Right continuity of $(\mathcal{F}_t)$ together with the fact that $\nu_t^{-1}(A) \bigcap \{\tau \leq t\} = \nu_t^{-1}(A) \bigcap \{\tau \bigvee t \leq t\}$ implies

$$\mu_t^{-1}(A) = (\eta_t^{-1}(A) \bigcap \{t < \tau\}) \bigcup (\nu_t^{-1}(A) \bigcap \{\tau \leq t\}) \in \mathcal{F}_t \quad \forall A \in \mathcal{B}(R)$$

There must be a unique solution of (5.2). The vector μ_H^* is necessary to calculate any Brock-Hommes equilibrium path starting at μ_H. Clearly, letting $w_s(\mu_H^*)$ denote the bubble started from the equilibrium μ_H^*,

$$\xi_H(t, \mu_H^*, k_H) =$$

$$k_H + \int_H^t b(s, w_s(\mu_H^*), \xi_H(s, w_s(\mu_H^*), k_H))\, ds + \int_H^t \sigma(s)\, dW_s$$

Clearly, $\xi_H(t, \mu_H^*, k_H)$ is continuous. Consequently, all that remains to be shown in that $(\xi_H(H \bigvee t, \mu_H^*, k_H), t \geq 0)$ is adapted to $(\mathcal{F}_{H \bigvee t}, t \geq 0)$. Let (H_n) be a sequence of stopping times assuming discrete values such that $H_n \downarrow H$. It can be assumed that $H_n = (j+1)/2^n$ if $j/2^n < H \leq (j+1)/2^n$. If T_n, T are any stopping times $T_n \downarrow T$ then $\bigcap_{n=1}^{\infty} \mathcal{F}_{T_n} = \mathcal{F}_T$. Hence if X is $\mathcal{F}_{T_n}$ measurable $\forall n$ it must be $\mathcal{F}_T$ measurable. Since $H_{n+1} \leq H_n \quad \mathcal{F}_{H_{n+1} \bigvee t} \subset \mathcal{F}_{H_n \bigvee t}$. The proof will be complete if $\xi_{H_n}(H_n \bigvee t, \mu^*_{H_n}, k_{H_n})$ is $\mathcal{F}_{H_n \bigvee t}$ measurable. For then $\xi_{H_m}(H_m \bigvee t, \mu^*_{H_m}, k_{H_m})$ is $\mathcal{F}_{H_n \bigvee t}$ measurable $\forall m \geq n$ and $\xi_{H_m}(H_m \bigvee t, \mu^*_{H_m}, k_{H_m}) \to \xi_H(H \bigvee t, \mu^*_H, k_H)$ as $m \to \infty$. To avoid interruptions to the flow of the proof, the result $\xi_{H_m}(H_m \bigvee t, \mu^*_{H_m}, k_{H_m}) \to \xi_H(H \bigvee t, \mu^*_H, k_H)$ will be proved after measurability of $\xi_{H_n}(H_n \bigvee t, \mu^*_{H_n}, k_{H_n})$ is established.

Consider $\xi_{H_n}(H_n \bigvee t, \mu^*_{H_n}, k_{H_n})$; for notational simplcity denote it by $\xi_n(t)$. For notational convenience the bubble is dropped from the function ξ and let $k_{(j+1)/2^n} = k^j$ where k_u is the money supply from (5.1).

$$\xi_n(t)^{-1}(A) =$$

$$\{k_{H_n} \in A; t \leq H_n\} \bigcup_{j=0}^{\infty} \{\xi_{(j+1)/2^n}(t, k^j) \in A; j/2^n < H \leq (j+1)/2^n; H_n < t\}$$

The sets indexed by j in the set defined above are nonempty iff $(j+1)/2^n < t$. For such $j \quad k^j$ is $\mathcal{F}_{\tau \bigvee t}$ measurable. Moreover $\xi_s(u, \cdot, \cdot)$ is $\mathcal{F}_u \times \mathcal{B}(R)$ measurable for $u \geq s$. Define $\phi : \Omega \to \Omega \times R$ by $\phi(\omega) = (\omega, k^j(\omega))$. Clearly, ϕ is measurable relative to $\mathcal{F}_{\tau \bigvee t}$ and $\mathcal{F}_t \times \mathcal{B}(R)$. Furthermore $\xi_{(j+1)/2^n}(t, k^j) = \xi_{(j+1)/2^n}(t, \cdot, \cdot) \circ \phi$ implying $\xi_{(j+1)/2^n}(t, k^j)$ is $\mathcal{F}_{\tau \bigvee t}$ measurable. Thus, for any $A \in \mathcal{B}(R)$

$$\{\xi_{(j+1)/2^n}(t, k^j) \in A, \tau < t\} = \{\xi_{(j+1)/2^n}(t, k^j) \in A, \tau \bigvee t \leq t\} - \{\tau = t\} \in \mathcal{F}_t$$

Thus, since $H > \tau$

$$\{\xi_{(j+1)/2^n}(t, k^j) \in A; j/2^n < H \leq (j+1)/2^n; H_n < t\} =$$

$$\{\xi_{(j+1)/2^n}(t, k^j) \in A, \tau < t\} \bigcap \{j/2^n < H \leq (j+1)/2^n; H_n < t\} \in \mathcal{F}_t \quad (5.3)$$

It is only necessary to show for $s > t$ that $\xi_n(t)^{-1}(A) \bigcap \{H_n < s\} \in \mathcal{F}_s$. Clearly, (5.3) implies

$$\{\xi_{(j+1)/2^n}(t, k^j) \in A; j/2^n < H \leq (j+1)/2^n; H_n < t\} \bigcap \{H_n < s\} \in \mathcal{F}_s$$

Since H is also a $(\mathcal{F}_{\tau \bigvee t}, t \geq 0)$ stopping time, H_n is a $(\mathcal{F}_{\tau \bigvee t}, t \geq 0)$ stopping time. Moreover, H_n assumes countably many values and k_{H_n} is measurable relative to the stopping time σ-field for H_n generated by $(\mathcal{F}_{\tau \bigvee t})$. Let $\{s_j, j = 1, \ldots, m\}$ be the values H_n assumes which are less than s. Then,

$$\{k_{H_n} \in A; t \leq H_n\} \bigcap \{H_n < s\} = \{k_{H_n} \in A; \tau \bigvee t \leq H_n\} \bigcap \{H_n < s\}$$

$$= \bigcup_{j=1}^{m} \{k_{H_n} \in A; H_n = s_j; \tau < s; \tau \bigvee t \leq s_j\} \in \mathcal{F}_s$$

Consequently, $\xi_n(t)^{-1}(A) \in \mathcal{F}_{H_n \bigvee t}$.

For $s < t$ let $w_t(z), w_s(z)$ be the bubbles at time z given the bubbles starting at times t and s respectively. The bubbles at times t, s are $w_{[t]}$ and $w_{[s]}$ respectively since bubbles are only determined at integer times. It can be assumed the bubbles are determined by the Brock-Hommes system beginning at a time less than s since to prove convergence of the processes bubbles are partially determined by (5.1) after time τ. This implies $w_t(z)$ is actually evolving from $w_{[s]}$.

To show convergence repeat a calculation similar to the one used in proving theorem 4.2. Let $R_{st} = |\int_s^t \sigma(u)\, dW_u|$. Then for $s < t$

$$|\xi_t(u, x) - \xi_s(u, y) \leq |x - y| + L \int_s^t |w_s(z)|\, dz + L(t - s) + R_{st}$$

$$L \int_t^u |\xi_t(z, x) - \xi_s(z, y)| + |w_t(z) - w_s(z)|\, dz + L \int_s^t |\xi_s(z, y)|\, dz$$

Applying Gronwall's inequality

$$|\xi_t(u, x) - \xi_s(u, y)| \leq (1 + \exp(L(u - t)))[|x - y| + L \int_s^t |w_s(z)|\, dz + L(t - s)] +$$

$$(1 + \exp(L(u - t)))[L \int_t^u |w_t(z) - w_s(z)|\, dz + L \int_s^t |\xi_s(z, y)|\, dz + R_{st}]$$

As $t \rightarrow s$ $[t] \rightarrow [s]$. Since $[t]$ and $[s]$ are integers $[t] = [s]$ for $|t - s| < \delta$ for some $\delta > 0$. Thus, $w_{[t]} = w_{[s]}$ when $|t - s|$ is small enough. Applying the same argument found in theorem 4.4 there exists a γ independent of s but depending on $T, \epsilon > 0$ such that if the vectors of bubbles $(w^i_{[s]})^*, i = 1, 2$ satisfy $|(w^1_{[s]})^* - (w^2_{[s]})^*| < \gamma$ then $\sup_{t \in [[s],[s]+T]} |w^1_t - w^2_t| < \epsilon$. This fact is also used in theorem 5.5. It implies when $[t] = [s]$ $\sup_{z \in [t,u]} |w_t(z) - w_s(z)| < \epsilon$ since $w^*_{[t]} = w^*_{[s]}$ due to the common ancestory of the bubbles. Of course in the special case that $[t] = [s]$, then $w_t(z) = w_s(z)$ $\forall z \geq t$. Continuity of the stochastic integral implies $R_{st} \rightarrow 0$ as $t \rightarrow s$. If in addition $x \rightarrow y$ it is clear from the inequality above that $\xi_t(u, x) \rightarrow \xi_s(u, y)$.

Applying this to the original problem, if $t \leq H$ $\xi_{H_m}(H_m \bigvee t, \mu^*_{H_m}, k_{H_m}) = k_{H_m}$ and $\xi_H(H \bigvee t, \mu^*_H, k_H) = k_H$. Convergence follows from continuity of (k_t) defined in (5.1). If $t > H$ then $t > H_m$ $\forall m > N$ for some N. Clearly taking $s = H$ $t_m = H_m$, $x_m = k_{H_m}$ and $y = k_H$ the proof above implies $\xi_{H_m}(t, \mu^*_{H_m}, k_{H_m}) \rightarrow \xi_H(t, \mu^*_H, k_H)$ as $m \rightarrow \infty$ q.e.d.

Theorem 5.4: Let $k_H \in L^2$ then $k^\mu_t \in L^2$ where k^μ_t is defined in (5.2).

Proof: To prove square integrability observe that since b is bounded

$$\int_H^t b(s, w_s, k^\mu_s) ds \leq C(t - H) \leq Ct$$

for some constant C when $t > H$. Let $H_n = H \bigwedge n$. To show $\int_H^{H \bigvee t} \sigma(s)\, dW_s \in L^2$ it is sufficient to prove $\sup_{n \geq 1} E(\int_{H_n}^{H_n \bigvee t} \sigma(s)\, dW_s)^4 < \infty$. If this bound is satisfied

$\{|\int_{H_n}^{H_n \bigvee t} \sigma(s)dW_s|^2\}_{n=1}^{\infty}$ is uniformly integrable and continuity of $(\int_0^t \sigma(s)\, dW_s, t \geq 0)$ implies

$$\int_{H_n}^{H_n \bigvee t} \sigma(s)dW_s \rightarrow \int_{H}^{H \bigvee t} \sigma(s)\, dW_s \quad (5.4)$$

Thus, $\int_H^{H \bigvee t} \sigma(s)\, dW_s \in L^2$ and convegence in (5.4) can also be taken in L^2.

Clearly, $(H_n \bigvee t) - H_n \leq t$. By the Burkholder-Davis-Gundy inequality $\exists$ a constant C_2 such that $E(\int_{H_n}^{H_n \bigvee t} \sigma(s)\, dW_s)^4 \leq C_2 E(\int_{H_n}^{H_n \bigvee t} \sigma(s)^2\, ds)^2 \leq$

$$E(H_n \bigvee t - H_n) \int_{H_n}^{H_n \bigvee t} \sigma(s)^4\, ds \leq tE \int_0^{\infty} \sigma(s)^4\, ds \quad \text{q.e.d.}$$

With the two policy changes the equilibrium exchange rates and money supply are still denoted by $x_t^{\mu}, y_t^{\mu}, k_t^{\mu}$ for initial Brock-Hommes bubble μ_0^*. Theorem 5.5 is the precise statement of metastability.

Theorem 5.5: With probability greater than $1 - \epsilon$ the following dynamical behavior is observed provided $\gamma_i, i = 1, 2$ in assumptions 5.3 and 5.7 are appropriately chosen. For solution processes $(\mu_t), (k_t^{\mu})$ with initial conditions $(\mu_0)^*, k_0$ started in $B((\mu_0^2)^*, \gamma_2)$ and $B(k_0^2, \gamma_2)$ respectively, $k_t^{\mu}, x_t^{\mu}, y_t^{\mu}$ remain within δ of k_t^2, x_t^2, y_t^2 respectively over the interval $[0, T \bigwedge \tau]$. For $t \in [H, H + T]$ $k_t^{\mu}, x_t^{\mu}, y_t^{\mu}$ remain within δ of $k_t^1(H), x_t^1(H), y_t^1(H)$ respectively where $k_t^1(H), x_t^1(H), y_t^1(H)$ are the money supply and exchange rates corresponding to the zero bubble started at time H with initial condition k_0^1.

Proof: It suffices to show

$$P(\{\sup_{t \in [0, T \bigwedge \tau]} |x_t^{\mu} - x_t^2| > \delta\} \bigcup \{\sup_{t \in [H, H+T]} |x_t^{\mu} - x_t^1| > \delta\}) < \epsilon$$

$$\text{Clearly,} \quad P(\{\sup_{t \in [0, T \bigwedge \tau]} |x_t^{\mu} - x_t^2| > \delta\} \bigcup \{\sup_{t \in [H, H+T]} |x_t^{\mu} - x_t^1| > \delta\}) \leq$$

$$P\{\sup_{t \in [0, T \bigwedge \tau]} |x_t^{\mu} - x_t^2| > \delta\} + P\{\sup_{t \in [H, H+T]} |x_t^{\mu} - x_t^1| > \delta\}$$

$$\leq \epsilon/2 + P\{\sup_{t \in [H, H+T]} |x_t^{\mu} - x_t^1| > \delta\}$$

Let $1_{\{H<t\}}$ be the indicator of the set $\{H < t\} \in \mathcal{F}_t$. For $t > H$

$$x_t = \int_t^{\infty} \exp(t-s) E(k_s^{\mu}|\mathcal{F}_t)\, ds = \int_t^{\infty} \exp(t-s) 1_{\{H<t\}} E(k_s^{\mu}|\mathcal{F}_t)\, ds =$$

$$\int_t^{\infty} \exp(t-s) E(\xi_H(s, \mu_H^*, k_H)|\mathcal{F}_t)\, ds =$$

$$\int_t^{\infty} \exp(t-s) E(\xi_H(H \bigvee s, \mu_H^*, k_H)|\mathcal{F}_t)\, ds$$

In the proof of theorem 4.4 the Brock-Hommes equilibria can be started at any time S and inequalities (1)-(4) will hold over the interval $[S, S+T]$. The SDE will have the structure of (5.2) but the conclusions of theorem 4.4 can be derived in the same way as Gagnon (2007).

The parameter $\gamma = \gamma(T, \delta)$ is independent of S. This includes times S that are random and given by a stopping time. Thus, γ_1 in assumption 5.7 implies inequalities (1)-(4) hold over $[H, H+T]$. Clearly, $\xi_H(H \bigvee s, \mu_H^*, k_H)$ is a money supply that satisfies the conditions of assumption 5.7. Consequently, $P\{\sup_{t\in[H,H+T]} |x_t^\mu - x_t^1| > \delta\} < \epsilon/2$ q.e.d.

Theorem 5.6: Suppose $\sup_{0\leq s\leq \tau, \omega\in\Omega} |\mu_s(\omega)| < \infty$ for the bubble with initial condition μ_0^*. Let $|g/(1+r+b(s,z_1,z_2))| < 1 \quad \forall(s,z_1,z_2)$ and $|(g+f(z))/(1+r+b_1(z))| < 1 \quad \forall z \in R$. Under the assumptions of theorem 5.5 for large T and arbitrary η, w_n remains close to w^2 over $[0, \tau(U_2)]$ and $w_n \in B(0,\eta)$ for large n close to $H+T$, with probability greater than $1-\epsilon$.

Proof: Let the bubble begin near w^2 and the money supply near k_0^2. For large T, $T \geq \tau(U_2)$ with high probability since $\tau(U_2) < \infty$ almost surely. By appropriate choice of γ_2 assumption 5.3 implies the money supply remains in $B(k_0^2, 2\delta)$ and the bubble remains close to w^2 over $[0, \tau(U_2)]$ with overwhelming probability. After the money supply leaves $B(k_0^2, 2\delta)$, conditional on its point of exit, there is overwheming probability that it remains close to k_t^1. If $E\sup_{t\in[H,H+T]} |\int_H^t \sigma(s)\, dW_s|$ is suitably small, the money supply lingers in $B(k_0^1, 2\delta)$ with high probability implying $f(k_n) = 0, H < n < H+T$ for large enough n. Hence $g_n = g$ and the bubble satisfies $w_{n+1} = g/(1+r+b(n,\mu_n,k_n^\mu))q_{2,n}w_n$. Since $|(g+f(z))/(1+r+b_1(z))| < 1 \quad \forall z \in R$ the bubbles must be uniformly bounded over finite random intervals in the model with policy switches. Hence, $w_t \in B(0,\eta)$ at large times. q.e.d.

6. Conclusions

The model demonstrates that carefully constructed random monetary policies can practically eliminate speculative bubbles. Future research could address equilibria which result when agents have learning devices other than rational or adaptively rational expectations. There is also great need to investigate stochastic processes which are not Gaussian or Poisson in nature. The mathematical finance literature has explored asset pricing with processes which do not have independent increments, see Rogers (1997) as well as Stottinen (2001). Financial market fluctuations with speculators should be investigated under a fractional Brownian motion assumption for prices or policies.

References

Arnold, L., 1998. *Random Dynamical Systems.* Springer, New York, NY.

Brock, W., Lakonishok, J., LeBaron, B., 1992. Simple technical trading rules and the property of stock returns. *Journal of Finance* **47**, 1731-1764.

Brock, W., Hommes, C., 1998. Heterogeneous beliefs and routes to chaos in a simple asset pricing model. *Journal of Economic Dynamics and Control* **22**, 1235-1274.

Brock, W., Hommes, C., 1997. Models of complexity in economics and finance. In *System Dynamics in Economic and Financial Models*, C. Hey et al. (Eds.), Wiley, New York, pp. 1-34.

Bovier, A., Eckhoff, M., Gayrard, V., Klein, M., 2001. Metastability in stochastic dynamics of disordered mean field model. *Probability Theory and Related Fields* **119**, 99-161.

Cadenillas, A., Zapareto, F., 1999. Optimal central bank intervention in the foreign exchange market. *Journal of Economic Theory* **87**, 218-242.

De Long, J., Shleifer, A., Summers, L., Waldman, R., 1990. Noise trader risk in financial markets. *Journal of Political Economy* **98**, 703-738.

De Grauwe, P., Grimaldi, M. 2005. Heterogeneity of agents, transactions costs and the exchange rate. *Journal of Economic Dynamics and Control* **29**, 691-719.

Flood, R., Garber, P., 1983. A model of stochastic process switching. *Econometrica* **51**, 537-551.

Froot, K., Obstfeld, M., 1991. Stochastic process switching: some simple examples. *Econometrica* **59**, 241-250.

Freidlin, M., Wentzell, A., 1998. *Random Perturbations of Dynamical Systems*. Springer, New York, NY.

Galves, A., Olivieri, E., Vares, M., 1987. Metastability for a class of dynamical systems subject to small random perturbations. *Annals of Probability* **15**, 1288-1305.

Gagnon, G., 2004. Exchange rate fluctuations in an economy with noise traders. *Journal of Macroeconomics* **26**, 45-63.

Gagnon, G., 2007. Stability and bifurcation of a two scale system in evolutionary finance. submitted to *Journal of Evolutionary Economics*.

León, J., Solé, J., Utzet, F., Vivres, J., 2002. On Levy processes, Mallaivin calculus and market jumps. *Finance and Stochastics* **6,** 197-225.

Ikeda, S., Shibata, A., 1995. Fundamentals, uncertainty, bubbles and exchange rate dynamics. *Journal of International Economics* **38**, 199-223.

Kabanov, Y., Pergamenshchikov, S., 2003. *Two Scale Stochastic Systems*. Springer. New York, NY.

LeBaron, B., 1999. Technical trading rule profitability and foreign exchange market intervention. *Journal of International Economics* **49**, 125-143.

Mundaca, G., Øksendal, B., 1998. Optimal stochastic intervention with application to the exchange rate. *Journal of Mathematical Economics* **29**, 225-243.

Protter, P., 1990. *Stochastic Integration and Differential Equations: A New Approach.* Springer, New York, NY.

Rogers, L.C.G., 1997. Arbitrage with fractional Brownian motion. *Mathematical Finance* **7**, 95-105.

Sottinen, T., 2001. Fractional Brownian motion, random walks and binary market models. *Finance and Stochastics* **5**, 343-355.

Sowers, R., 1992. Large deviations for a reaction-diffusion equation with non-Gaussian perturbations. *Annals of Probability* **20**, 504-537.

Venegas-Martínez, F., 2001. Temporary Stabilization: A stochastic analysis. *Journal of Economic Dynamics and Control* **25**, 1429-1449.

In: Monetary Growth: Trends, Impacts and Policies
Editors: W.N. Squires et al, pp. 129-150
ISBN 978-1-60692-305-4

Short Communication E

The Effects of Inflation Variability and the Inflation Level on Default Risk *

Marcelo Sánchez †
European Central Bank, Kaiserstrasse, Germany

Abstract

This paper studies the effects of inflation variability and the inflation level on the default risk of the private sector. Two alternative measures of default risk premia are used, one derived from bond market data and the other consisting of bank lending spreads. I find evidence of a robust positive effect of the inflation level on default risk. This positive impact appears to be considerably higher when default risk premia are measured on the basis of bond returns data. In contrast, the evidence about the effect of inflation variability on default risk is mixed. Inflation variability appears to raise my bank-based measure default risk when the former variable is defined as the standard error over a one-year horizon, but fails to do so when defined over a two-year horizon. Moreover, inflation variability does not seem to significantly affect default risk when the latter is defined in terms of bond-based alternative measure. Other results appear to depend on the definition of default risk used. For the bank-based measure, the default risk is found to be very persistent and rise with higher realisations of money supply growth. In the case of the bond-based measure, the default risk is particularly affected by external variables, in particular going down as a result of higher world interest rates.

1. Introduction

There is a large literature on the effects of inflation on financial variables such as the level of financial activity and asset returns. Concerning the latter, Choi *et al.* (1996), Boyd *et al.* (1996), Barnes *et al.* (1999) and Sánchez (2000) present regressions supporting a negative correlation between inflation and real asset returns for a number of countries. With regard

*I acknowledge comments received from Maurice Obstfeld and David Romer. I also benefited from discussions with Roger Craine, Brad DeLong, Dwight Jaffee and James Wilcox. Views expressed do not necessarily reflect those of the European Central Bank. The usual disclaimer applies.

†E-mail address: marcelo.sanchez@ecb.int. Tel.: +49 69 1344 6531; fax: +49 69 1344 7602. Corresponding author. European Central Bank. Kaiserstrasse 29. D-60311. Frankfurt am Main. Germany.

to the nexus between inflation and financial activity, Boyd *et al.* (2001) find substantial evidence that financial market development is negatively correlated with inflation.[1] The present paper extends this literature by examining the effect of the *variability* of inflation on the financial system alongside that of the *level* of inflation. Furthermore, it focuses on a different financial variable, namely, the default risk of the private sector.

Ideally, the default risk premium is measured as the difference between the return on corporate bonds and the return on government bonds. Unfortunately, while government bond indices are widely available it is not possible to obtain data on corporate bond indices for many countries. Therefore, my first measure of default risk is based on data on corporate bond returns for some countries combined with complementary information on returns on some alternative indices (such as mortgage, convertible and general bond indices) that are available for other countries. A series of this measure can be constructed for bonds with an intermediate length, that is, average maturity of about four years. Such relatively long horizon is a desirable property of the data since it allows to adequately assess the effect –if any– of inflation variability on the default risk. An alternative, short-run, measure of default risk is also employed. It is obtained by taking the difference between lending and deposit rates in the banking sector.

There are several channels through which inflation uncertainty can affect default risk. An obvious link involves a negative relationship between inflation variability and real activity. Therefore, higher inflation uncertainty makes it more likely that firms will have trouble paying back their debt. An alternative link is given by the fact that the financial sector of the economy is partly characterized by nominal contracts, such as bank deposit and loans. In particular, whenever yields on bank loans are set in nominal terms inflation uncertainty is responsible for the variability of the borrowing real interest rate. More concretely, the actual real burden given by the interest rate charged on the loans will depend positively on the difference between expected and actual inflation. Therefore, unexpected disinflation will make it more likely that borrowers default on their loans, while higher than expected inflation will make it less likely. Under higher inflation uncertainty risk-averse investors will demand a larger default risk premium on borrowers' liabilities (such as corporate bonds).

The regression results presented here provide mixed evidence in favor of a significant positive effect of inflation variability on default risk. The former variable fails to be significant in the case of the bond-based default risk measure. Using banking data, inflation volatility is found to have a significantly positive effect on default risk when it is measured over a one-year horizon. It does not enter significantly, though, when inflation variability is measured over a two-year period.

In order to evaluate these contrasting results it is crucial to compare the relative importance of inflation variability under the two definitions of default risk. The main difference between the two is the maturity of the financial instruments involved. One would expect that the longer the period over which default risk premia are measured, the higher the importance of inflation variability. Therefore, the lack of significance of inflation variability in the bond-based regressions is far more conclusive than the significance of that variable in the regressions using banking data.

In contrast with the afore-mentioned mixed results concerning inflation variability, the

[1] Other relevant papers in this area are Rousseau and Wachtel (2002), Andrés *et al.* (2004) and McCaig and Stengos (2005).

present study finds strong evidence of a significant positive effect of the level of inflation on default risk. The positive coefficient was found to be considerably lower in the case of the bank-based definition of default risk. Given the characteristics of the data employed, one plausible interpretation of this result is that inflation has a stronger effect in the medium term than in the short run. Furthermore, the analysis shows that the previous results on the effects of the level and variability of inflation do not depend on the strength of the American disinflation experience of the early eighties. At most, this experience is characterized by a stronger effect of the level of inflation on default risk premia than that present in the rest of the sample. Finally, the effects of the remaining explanatory variables (such as the lagged dependent variable, money growth and foreign variables) were found to be not robust to the definition of default risk employed.

The remainder of this paper proceeds as follows. Section 2 describes the data employed. Section 3 discusses the methodology used. Section 4 presents my findings when I assess the effect of inflation variability on default risk. Finally, section 5 briefly concludes.

2. The Data

The object of the present analysis is to explain the behavior of default risk premia of the private sector. Information on bond returns and bank interest rates, which is available in nominal terms, is used to calculate two alternative measures of the default risk of the private sector.[2]

The ideal measure of default risk premium is the difference between the return on corporate bonds and the return on government bonds. Government bond indices are widely available. However, it is not possible to obtain data on corporate bond indices for many countries. Therefore, my first measure of default risk is based on data on corporate bond returns for 6 countries. I combine this information with complementary data on returns on some alternative indices (such as mortgage, convertible and general bond indices) that are available for other 11 countries.[3] A series of this measure can be constructed for bonds with an intermediate length, that is, average maturity of about four years. I also employ an alternative, short-run, measure of default risk, which is calculated as the difference between lending and deposit rates in the banking sector.

The first measure has the advantage that at least 6 countries fit the ideal measure of default risk premium. It is based on bond indices data and is intermediate-term in nature. Such relatively long horizon is a desirable property of the data since it allows to adequately assess the effect –if any– of inflation variability on the default risk better than the second, short-run, measure. Among the drawbacks of the first measure I should mention that data on the remaining 11 countries deviate to some extent from the ideal measure. Although dummy variables will be used in the estimation process to control for these deviations, it goes without saying that the average quality of the data is far from perfect. The bank-based measure of default risk is considerably more homogeneous. However, some degree

[2] A description of the data on bond returns can be found in Appendix A, while the list of countries and periods for which bank interest rates are available appears in Appendix B.

[3] As explained in the next section, the methodological approach I follow is to employ all the information available on bond returns, using dummy variables to control for deviations with respect to the "ideal" measure of default risk premia.

of heterogeneity is also present, particularly due to a good deal of cross-country variation in the maturity of bank loans (whose interest rates are used to define the variable in question).[4] Finally, with only one exception, the countries represented in the bond-based measure are advanced economies. As will become clearer after the description of the different variables, one of the advantages of the second measure is that it is available for many countries which are at very different stages of development.

I use quarterly data on the variables listed below for up to 132 observation units,[5] depending on the variable in question.

Default risk premia are the dependent variables in the regression results reported in section 4. The two alternative definitions of default risk premium employed in this study are discussed in the next section.

Many RHS variables are defined as rates of change. In the case of some variables (CPI, international commodity prices and output), the quarterly rates of change are calculated from monthly average indices. This means that the rates of change used here are calculated between the middle of the last month of a given quarter and the middle of the last month of the next quarter. In the remaining case of money supply growth, quarterly rates of change are computed between the end of two periods.

In all cases of rate-of-change variables,[6] which are the relevant two periods between which they are computed depends on two considerations. First, the end of the last period must be such that by then agents get to know the value of the variable in question. That is, the variable must be in the information set of agents. Second, the period over which the rates of change are calculated need not coincide with the measurement period which is always a quarter. The former period is a quarter when I analyze the behavior of bank-based default risk measures, while it is a 16-quarter (4-year) period in the case of bond-based default risk premia.

Among the RHS variables that are not rates of change, there are series for world interest rates. As indicated below, world interest rates are measured as the ones prevailing at the end of the period. Finally, the set of explanatory variables include different measures of inflation variability and some dummy variables, all of which are discussed in the next section.

Nominal returns on corporate bonds and other related bonds (pb_t)*:* They are rates of change in different types of bond indices for a total of 17 countries. The source of information is Datastream and Appendix A describes the nature of bond indices used for each country.

The data include corporate bond indices for 6 countries, mortgage bond indices for 3 countries and convertible bond indices for 5 countries. For the remaining 5 countries, I use general bond indices which encompass a universe of both private and government bonds. For 11 out of these 17 countries, a bond return index is available. For the remaining 6 countries, the rate of return is based on either a bond price index (2 countries) or calculated as a redemption yield (4 countries). Finally, for 8 out of the 17 countries the source permits to

[4]Footnote 11 below gives some details on the countries which were excluded from the sample because of the irregular behavior of the bank-based series.

[5]The use of the expression "observation units" instead of "countries" has to do with the fact that the series for bank lending and deposit interest rates are discontinuous in the case of 15 countries, for each of which data are divided into two separate observation units. All other series are continuous, and thus in the analysis of the bond-based measure of default risk, the expression "observation units" is synonymous with "countries."

[6]A similar consideration is in place in the case of the computation of inflation variability (see next section).

characterize bonds as of intermediate length. For the remaining 9 countries no information related to bond average maturities is provided.

Nominal goverment bond returns (gb_t)*:* They are rates of change in indices of goverment bond returns for 17 countries. Again, the source of information is Datastream and Appendix A contains a description of the goverment bond indices used for each country. The way the rate of return is measured matches the way it is calculated in the case of bonds issued by firms. Therefore, as was described in the previous paragraph, the rate of return on government bonds is based on a return or a price index, or else measured as a redemption yield, depending on the country in question. Finally, the government bonds represented in the indices were selected to be of intermediate maturity on average.[7]

Bank lending and deposit rates $(l_{t+1}$ *and* $i_{t+1})$*:* These are short-run measures of lending and borrowing interest rates originated in the banking system. The former is a prime lending rate (IFS line 60p), while the deposit rate is the nominal rate offered by banks to resident customers for demand, time or savings deposits (IFS line 60l). Moreover, both rates are measured at the end of the period and I assume that they prevail for a quarter.

Inflation (π_t)*:* For the inflation rate I use the quarterly rate of change in each country's CPI, expressed as a percentage. The CPI data are from IFS line 64.

Money supply growth: Two measures of the money supply are available from IFS. First, there is an $M1$ measure including currency and demand deposits ("money," IFS line 34). This is the preferred measure since it is more homogeneous across countries. The corresponding growth rate is denoted by μ_t. Second, a broader measure ("quasi-money," IFS line 35) including time deposits and savings will be used complementarily.[8]

Rate of change in commodity prices: I employ the rate of change in the indices of the international prices of food (P_{1t}), crude oil (P_{2t}), metals (P_{3t}) and agricultural raw materials (P_{4t}). Data on these indices are from IFS lines 176ex, 176aa, 176ay and 176bx, respectively.

World interest rates (r^*_{jt})*:* These are London Interbank Offer real rates on US deposits. The subscript j equals 3, 6 or 12, depending on whether the term to maturity of deposits is 3 months, 6 months or 12 months, respectively. Data on interest rates are from IFS lines 60ldd, 60lde and 60ldf, respectively. In order to capture the idea that changes in world interest rates can have different effects on borrower and lender countries, I construct a dummy variable, DEV_{it} for developed countries ($DEV_{it} = 1$ if country i is developed, 0 otherwise) which I use as a proxy for lender countries. I then define $r^{*DEV}_{jit} \equiv DEV_{it} * r^*_{jt}$ to be equal to the world interest rate r^*_{jt} if country i is developed, 0 otherwise. Similarly, $r^{*NDEV}_{jit} \equiv (1 - DEV_{it}) * r^*_{jt}$ is defined to be equal to the world interest rate r^*_{jt} if country i is developing, 0 otherwise.

Real growth (g_t)*:* This is the rate of change in an industrial production index (IFS line 66).

[7]For some of the same 9 countries for which no information on average maturity was provided in the case of pb_t, however, no information on the average length of government bonds was provided either.

[8]In this paper, however, I only report regression results using the first measure since the inclusion of the "quasi-money" alternative did not yield significantly different results.

3. The Methodology

In this paper I run regressions of the default risk premium of firms on past information. As was explained in the last section, information on bond returns and bank interest rates is used to calculate two alternative measures of the default risk of the private sector. Past information is represented by some measure of inflation variability, the level of inflation, money growth, real growth and some variables that capture the influence of external factors (such as commodity prices and the world interest rate). Additional RHS variables are seasonals and, in the case of the bond-based default risk premium regressions, some dummy variables related to deviations from the "ideal" measure of the dependent variable.

The general estimation procedure is given by cross-country panel data regressions. Using inference analysis, the only two specifications of the model that were found to be relevant are the fixed effects and random effects models. As with the analysis of the second chapter, the Tables below report the Hausman test statistic for the difference between the fixed effects and random effects estimates, along with its p-value.

In the remainder of this section, I describe how the dependent and explanatory variables are constructed and defined. The next section reports the regression results.

3.1. Bond-Based Default Risk Premia

In this case the default risk premium is defined as the difference between the return on corporate (and related) bonds, pb_t, and the return on government bonds, gb_t, for several countries over time. I denote this definition by $dr_t^I \equiv pb_t - gb_t$, where I refers to the "intermediate" maturity of the bonds here considered.

Bond yields are calculated as rates of return between the end of the previous quarter and the end of the current one. Therefore, the bond-based measure of default risk is also computed on a quarterly basis. The period over which the RHS variables are measured is also a quarter. As was mentioned before, in the case of some RHS variables (such as rates of change and inflation variability) this measurement period does not coincide with the period over which they are calculated. More precisely, since the benchmark bond has an intermediate maturity, the RHS variables are calculated over a period of four years. The other important feature of explanatory variables concerning timing is that they must be part of the information set of agents. In this regard, I assume that values of variables up to the end of the quarter previous to the current one are known to agents. The regressions below will assess how much of the current quarter's default risk premium can be explained in terms of past information, and in particular, whether inflation variability has a positive impact on that premium.

Many explanatory variables are rates of change. Taking into account the comments in the last paragraph, a typical such rate-of-change variable measures the proportional change during a period of four years (16 quarters) up to the quarter previous to the current one.[9]

[9]This definition of inflation variability as a standard deviation for overlapping periods is similar to the ones used in empirical studies on the relationship between inflation and growth. The only difference is that the measurement period here is one quarter, while in that literature the relevant period is one year. For instance, Barro (1995) defines inflation variability as the standard deviation of the inflation rate around its decadal mean, and Fischer (1993) works with a time series estimate calculated as the standard deviation of the inflation rate around its mean for overlapping (say, decadal) periods.

Among the RHS that are not rates of change one finds inflation variability, world interest rates and dummy variables. With regard to inflation variability, two alternative measures are considered. The difference between the two relates to alternative assumptions about whether agents are aware of changes in the price level during the last month of the quarter or not. Since neither alternative is *a priori* superior, rather than choosing one I will consider both in turn. Taking all this into account, the two measures of inflation variability here considered are as follows:

$\sigma^I_{1,t}$ is defined to be the standard deviation of quarterly CPI inflation over the last two four-year periods up to the month previous to the end of period t;

$\sigma^I_{2,t}$ is defined to be the standard deviation of quarterly CPI inflation over the last two four-year periods up to the end of period t;

where I stands for "intermediate."

Seven dummy variables are used to control for potential measurement errors in the dependent variables. This problem arises because, for many countries, available data deviate from the "ideal" return index on a corporate bond of intermediate maturity. The list and description of such dummy variables is as follows:

D_1 is defined to be equal to 1 for countries for which information on a bond price index –rather than a return index– is used (namely, Austria and Italy), and equal to 0 otherwise;

D_2 is defined to be equal to 1 for countries for which information on bond redemption yield –rather than a return index– is employed (namely, Belgium, Luxembourg, Canada and Korea), and equal to 0 otherwise;[10]

D_3 is defined to be equal to 1 for countries for which information on mortgage bond indices –rather than on corporate bond indices– is employed (namely, Germany and Sweden), and equal to 0 otherwise;

D_4 is defined to be equal to 1 for one country (namely, Netherlands) for which information on bonds issued by financial institutions –rather than on corporate bonds– is employed, and equal to 0 otherwise;

D_5 is defined to be equal to 1 for countries for which information on convertible bond indices –rather than on corporate bond indices– is employed (namely, United Kingdom, France and Japan), and equal to 0 otherwise;

D_6 is defined to be equal to 1 for countries for which information on general bond indices –rather than on corporate bond indices– is employed (namely, Austria, Belgium, Italy, Luxembourg and Switzerland), and equal to 0 otherwise;

D_7 is defined to be equal to 1 for countries for which no information on average bond maturity is available, and equal to 0 otherwise.

Since dummy variable D_4 is defined to be equal to 1 for only one country, any coefficients associated with dummy variables could not be estimated by fixed effects. This, and the fact that D_4 turned out to be not significant in any of the regressions estimated by an alternative technique (such as pooled regression or random effects), reasonably led me to the exclusion of D_4 from the results reported in the next section.

[10]The principle used in calculating a redemption yield is to consider the amount of money paid for the bond (price including accrued interest and expenses) and relate this to the future dividend and capital payments, either or both of which may be paid net of tax. It is a "net present value" calculation, equating the amount of money paid for the bond to the discounted income and capital payments, the yield being the discount rate which makes the two equivalent to each other.

3.2. Bank-Based Default Risk Premia

In this case the default risk premium is defined as the difference between the bank lending and deposit rates for several countries over time.[11] I denote this definition by $dr_t^S \equiv l_{t+1} - i_{t+1}$, where S refers to the "short-run" nature of the loans and deposits that are used by the data source. Some clarification is needed with regard to the notation used in this case. The subscript of the default risk premium, dr_t^S, refers to the fact that the raw data are reported as end-of-the-period (t) interest rates. The latter, however, are indexed by $t + 1$ because they correspond to deposits and loans between periods t and $t + 1$.

It is crucial to make sure that the RHS variables are actually known at t, and thus are elements of the information set of agents. Many of the RHS variables are rates of change which are in general calculated over the quarter elapsed between (the end or the middle of) the last month in quarter $t - 1$ and (the end or the middle of) the last month in quarter t.[12] Among the RHS that are not rates of change one finds world interest rates and dummy variables. The former will be measured between the middle of the last month in quarter $t - 1$ and the middle of the last month in quarter t.

Among the RHS variables that are also a rate of change, the only exception to the general rule regarding timing described in the preceding paragraph is given by an alternative definition for the level of inflation. Inflation between (the middle of the last month in) quarter $t-1$ and (the middle of the last month in) quarter t will be used. This is a reasonable definition under the assumption that agents get to know the behavior of the general level of prices up to (the middle of the last month in) period t. However, one may believe that, as of (the middle of the last month in) period t, agents have trouble figuring out the inflation rate during the last monthly period because the last public information on CPI inflation refers to the middle of previous month. Under that assumption, it would be more reasonable to define the latest quarterly inflation rate in the information set of agents to be that between the month previous to the end of quarter $t-1$ and the month previous to the end of quarter t. For completeness, I consider the two alternative definitions of inflation. I denote the former simply as the already defined π_t and the latter as π_t^{LU}, where LU stands for "last (monthly inflation rate) unknown."

Four alternative measures of inflation variability are considered. This number is the result of taking into consideration two different aspects of the definition of the variable

[11]A total of 20 observation units were dropped from the sample consisting of 132 observation units. The main reason behind these drops is that, for at least a fair number of quarters, the end-of-period interest rate differential between the lending and deposit rates was negative (Switzerland, Bolivia, Brazil, El Salvador, Mexico, Panama, Uruguay, Venezuela, The Bahamas, Netherlands Antilles –second period–, Cyprus –first period–, Nepal, Philippines –first period–, Zambia –second period–, Salomon Islands, Samoa and Kyrgyz Republic). In the case of two observation units (Paraguay and Cyprus –second period–) such differential was found to be inadmissibly high and positive in certain quarters. Either of these two anomalies is indicative of some limitations of the data here employed. One possible explanation is that in some of these countries the authorities seem to have control over lending and deposit rates (as indicated by the constancy of rates over long periods of time). Moreover, the source of information sometimes fails to report the maturity of either deposits or loans. In case there were significant maturity differences between the loans and deposits for which the interest rates are reported, this would constitute an additional explanation for the irregular behavior of the series.

[12]Whether the end or the middle of the last month in a given quarter is the relevant moment in time depends on the given variable. The definitions of the different regressors employed here were already discussed in the previous section.

in question. The first feature has to do with the point raised in the previous paragraph concerning two alternative assumptions about whether agents are aware of changes in the price level during the last month of the quarter or not. The second feature is the number of quarters over which the variability of inflation is calculated. Taking both of these issues into account, the four measures of inflation variability here considered are as follows:

$\sigma^S_{1,t}$ is defined to be the standard deviation of quarterly CPI inflation over the last year up to the month previous to the end of period t;

$\sigma^S_{2,t}$ is defined to be the standard deviation of quarterly CPI inflation over the last year up to the end of period t;

$\sigma^S_{3,t}$ is defined to be the standard deviation of quarterly CPI inflation over the last two years up to the month previous to the end of period t;

$\sigma^S_{4,t}$ is defined to be the standard deviation of quarterly CPI inflation over the last two years up to the end of period t.

In all cases, the superscript S stands, again, for "short-run," given the fact that inflation variability refers to quarterly indices.

4. Results

In this section I present the panel data regressions of the default risk premium of firms on past information. The latter is represented by some measure of inflation variability, the level of inflation, money growth, real growth and some variables that capture the influence of external factors (such as commodity prices and the world interest rate). Additional RHS variables are seasonals and, in the case of the bond-based default risk premium regressions, some dummy variables related to deviations from the "ideal" measure of the dependent variable.

As was said before, with regard to the specific estimation technique employed in each case, the Hausman test statistic for the difference between fixed effects and random effects will be used to identify which of these two methods must be used.

4.1. Bond-Based Default Risk Premia

Table 1 shows the results obtained from running a regression of the bond-based measure of the default risk premium, dr^I_t, on past information. The latter is represented by the two alternative measures of inflation variability, and the levels of inflation, money supply growth, production growth, international commodity prices and world interest rates.[13]

Table 1 presents two different regression results, which correspond to the inclusion of two different measures of inflation variability. The first column corresponds to the case when inflation variability $\sigma^I_{1,t-1}$ is measured over the last two four-year periods up to the quarter previous to the current one. The second column reports regression results obtained using the alternative definition, $\sigma^I_{2,t-1}$, which is the standard deviation of inflation over the last three four-year periods up to the quarter previous to the current one.[14]

[13]Lagged values of the dependent variable were also considered. The corresponding results are not reported here because these variables failed to be significant and their presence involves a considerable loss of degrees of freedom.

[14]The inflation variability measures, which require the availability of inflation data for periods of eight to

Table 1. Panel Data Regressions(#)

Dependent variable: Default risk premium on bonds (dr^I_t)

	(1)	(2)
$\sigma^I_{1,t-1}$	0.435	
	(0.836)	
$\sigma^I_{2,t-1}$		0.265
		(0.598)
π_{t-1}	0.763	0.589
	(4.255)	(3.190)
μ_{t-1}	0.0002	0.0002
	(0.034)	(0.040)
g_{t-1}	-0.028	-0.026
	(-1.836)	(-1.693)
$P_{1,t-1}$	0.019	0.012
	(1.899)	(1.296)
$P_{2,t-1}$	0.001	0.001
	(0.295)	(0.360)
$P_{3,t-1}$	0.004	0.006
	(0.830)	(1.187)
$P_{4,t-1}$	-0.015	-0.012
	(-2.223)	(-1.856)
$i^*_{3,t-1}$	-0.190	-0.189
	(-2.388)	(-2.031)
D_1	3.451	3.538
	(3.838)	(3.894)
D_2	1.822	1.891
	(3.034)	(3.113)
D_3	0.817	0.868
	(1.422)	(1.491)
D_5	0.675	0.689
	(1.089)	(1.098)
D_6	-0.743	-0.791
	(-1.061)	(-1.118)
D_7	0.549	0.575
	(1.124)	(1.162)
Hausman χ^2	13.57	14.00
p-value	0.19	0.08
Technique	random effects	random effects
R^2	0.245	0.235
Regression *F*	13.94	13.10
p-value	0.00	0.00
No. obs.	556	540
No. units	15	15

(#)Estimated coefficients of the seasonals are not reported. t-statistics for the parameters are in parenthesis. Hausman X^2 refers to the test statistic for correlated effects (random effects is the null hypothesis).

---

twelve years, cannot be constructed for Slovak Republic. Furthermore, money supply data are not available for Switzerland. Although there is information on quasi-money for this country, I prefer to report results using the narrower measure of money supply growth. Therefore, in the case of regressions of dr^I_t on past information, the sample actually employed includes 15 countries out of the 17 for which data on bond-based default risk

Table 2. Panel Data Regressions(#)

Dependent variable: Default risk premium on bonds (dr^I_t)	(1)	(2)
$\sigma^I_{1,t-1}$	0.446 (0.858)	
$\sigma^I_{2,t-1}$		0.341 (0.742)
$DESINF_{t-1}*\sigma^I_{1,t-1}$	-1.292 (-0.609)	
$DESINF_{t-1}*\sigma^I_{2,t-1}$		-8.999 (-1.165)
π_{t-1}	0.676 (3.688)	0.575 (3.114)
$DESINF_{t-1}*\pi_{t-1}$	0.982 (2.360)	3.006 (1.657)
μ_{t-1}	0.0004 (0.065)	0.0002 (0.036)
g_{t-1}	-0.027 (-1.659)	-0.026 (-1.687)
$P_{1,t-1}$	0.016 (1.617)	0.012 (1.210)
$P_{2,t-1}$	-0.001 (-0.461)	0.001 (0.423)
$P_{3,t-1}$	0.005 (1.059)	0.007 (1.324)
$P_{4,t-1}$	-0.016 (-2.309)	-0.013 (-1.906)
$i^*_{3,t-1}$	-0.213 (-2.327)	-0.211 (-2.092)
D_1	3.518 (3.718)	3.556 (3.912)
D_2	1.858 (2.938)	1.904 (3.132)
D_3	0.843 (1.392)	0.880 (1.510)
D_5	0.659 (1.010)	0.696 (1.109)
D_6	-0.754 (-1.025)	-0.799 (-1.128)
D_7	0.593 (1.152)	0.572 (1.156)
Hausman χ^2 *p*-value	14.01 0.08	13.89 0.08
Technique	random effects	random effects
R^2 Regression *F* *p*-value	0.244 8.62 0.00	0.239 8.15 0.00
No. obs. No. units	556 15	540 15

(#)Estimated coefficients of the seasonals are not reported. t-statistics for the parameters are in parenthesis. Hausman X^2 refers to the test statistic for correlated effects (random effects is the null hypothesis).

premia are available.

Table 3. Panel Data Regressions(#)

Dependent variable: Default risk premium on bank loans (dr^s_t)				
	(1)	(2)	(3)	(4)
dr^s_{t-1}	0.782 (97.357)	0.798 (98.973)	0.782 (99.837)	0.795 (100.465)
$\sigma^s_{1,t-1}$	0.019 (3.472)			
$\sigma^s_{2,t-1}$			0.221 (4.335)	
$\sigma^s_{3,t-1}$				0.002 (0.451)
$\sigma^s_{4,t-1}$				0.002 (0.501)
π^{LU}_{t-1}	0.029 (3.660)		0.029 (3.756)	
π_{t-1}		0.040 (5.008)		0.039 (4.866)
μ_{t-1}	0.034 (6.035)	0.035 (6.020)	0.034 (6.052)	0.034 (5.991)
$P_{1,t-1}$	-0.022 (-0.944)	-0.022 (-0.890)	-0.021 (-0.927)	-0.022 (-0.911)
$P_{2,t-1}$	0.003 (0.356)	0.002 (0.253)	0.003 (0.376)	0.002 (0.276)
$P_{3,t-1}$	0.017 (0.944)	0.017 (0.909)	0.017 (0.947)	0.017 (0.889)
$P_{4,t-1}$	-0.015 (-0.535)	-0.800 (-0.277)	-0.015 (-0.562)	-0.009 (-0.299)
$i^*_{3,t-1}$	0.048 (0.559)	0.046 (0.515)	0.044 (0.518)	0.040 (0.458)
Hausman χ^2 p-value	1.91 0.00	1.93 0.00	1.92 0.00	1.91 0.03
Technique	fixed effects	fixed effects	fixed effects	fixed effects
R^2 Regression F p-value	0.759 1452.97 0.00	0.611 757.86 0.00	0.759 1461.91 0.00	0.618 783.50 0.00
No. obs. No. units	5093 116	4836 114	5116 116	4866 114

(#)Estimated coefficients of the seasonals are not reported. t-statistics for the parameters are in parenthesis. Hausman X^2 refers to the test statistic for correlated effects (random effects is the null hypothesis).

The regression results presented in the two columns are very similar. Past information explains about a quarter of the variation in the default risk premium. In both cases, the inflation variability coefficient in question exhibits a positive sign, but the variable fails to be significant. The inflation rate coefficient is positive and significant, while money supply growth does not enter significantly. Real growth has a negative effect on default risk, but the variable does not seem to be quite significant.

Out of the external variables two appear to have a significant effect. World interest rates have a negative effect on default risk, which makes sense since most of the countries represented here are net creditors. The negative effect of agricultural raw materials is much harder to interpret.

With regard to the dummies D_1 through D_7, the ones that appear to be significant are the first two only, which capture measurement errors associated with the use of bond price and redemption yield data rather than information on return indices. This seems to imply that the feature that represents a more dangerous potential measurement error of bond returns is the way you measure yields themselves, rather than the types and the maturity of bonds included in the index.

Given that the sample size is relatively small, it makes sense to analyze whether the results on the impact of the level and variability of inflation are driven by a very strong within-sample experience. One episode that has attracted the attention of many specialists is that of the sharp disinflation process in the US during the early eighties. I thus start by defining a dummy variable, $DESINF_t$, which is equal to 1 from 1980 to 1984 for the US only and is equal to 0 otherwise. I the interact this dummy variable with both the inflation variability measures and the level of inflation.

The results can be found in Table 2. As with Table 1, one observes two different regression results, which correspond to the inclusion of two different measures of inflation variability. The first column of Table 2 corresponds to the case when inflation variability $\sigma^I_{1,t-1}$ is measured over the last two four-year periods up to the quarter previous to the current one. The second column reports regression results obtained using the alternative definition, $\sigma^I_{2,t-1}$, which is the standard deviation of inflation over the last three four-year periods up to the quarter previous to the current one. The only difference with respect to Table 1 is the inclusion of the variables interacted with $DESINF$.

With regard to the first column of Table 2, the interaction variable $DESINF_{t-1} * \sigma^I_{1,t-1}$ does not enter significantly, which means that during the American disinflation process inflation variability did not have an effect significantly different from the rest of the sample. Since inflation variability is not significant either, I conclude that the latter variable has no effect on default risk for any country. Instead, the interaction variable $DESINF_{t-1} * \pi_{t-1}$ does enter significantly with a positive coefficient. This, together with the significantly positive impact of the level of inflation itself, implies that, during the period of American disinflation under study, inflation had a stronger effect on default risk premia than that present in the rest of the sample.

The results just described are not completely robust. On the one hand, the second column of Table 2, which involves an alternative definition of inflation variability, shows that the interaction variable $DESINF_{t-1} * \sigma^I_{1,t-1}$ does not enter significantly. The same result was found in the first column of Table 2. On the other hand, however, the second column of Table 2 also shows that the interaction variable $DESINF_{t-1} * \pi_{t-1}$ no longer enters significantly (although it still exhibits a positive coefficient). This, together with the significantly positive impact of the level of inflation, means that the American disinflation process of the early eighties was characterized by a effect of inflation on default risk premia that was not significantly different from that present in the rest of the sample.

All the other results in Table 2 are essentially the same as in Table 1. Therefore, I conclude that the results obtained in Table 1 do not depend on the strength of the American experience of sharp disinflation during the early eighties. At most, this experience is characterized by a stronger effect of the level of inflation on default risk premia than that present in the remainder of the sample.

In sum, the level of inflation seems to play a more important role than inflation variability in determining the behavior of default risk. The higher the initial level of a country's inflation, the higher the default risk of the private sector. This conclusion does not depend on the strength of the American experience of sharp disinflation during the early eighties. At most, this experience is characterized by a stronger effect of the level of inflation on default risk premia than that present in the remainder of the sample. Finally, external variables (such as the world interest and the price of agricultural raw materials) also seem to impact default risk premia.

4.2. Bank-Based Default Risk Premia

Table 3 shows the results obtained from running regressions of the bank-based default risk premia on past information. The latter is represented by the four alternative measures of inflation variability described in subsection 3.2., and the levels of inflation, money supply growth, international commodity prices and world interest rates. This time, I report coefficients for the first lag of the dependent variable.[15]

While the bond-based measure of default risk is of intermediate length, the one constructed using banking data is of a short-run nature. The other important difference is that, while Korea is the only developing country represented in the dr_t^I regressions (after Slovak Republic is dropped as explained in footnote 14), the regressions discussed in this subsection include a wide variety of both advanced and developing countries.

The first two columns of Table 3 present two different regression results, which correspond to the inclusion of two different measures of inflation variability (out of the four that were described in subsection 3.2.). The measure used in the first column is $\sigma_{1,t}^S$ and the one employed in the second column is $\sigma_{3,t}^S$. These two measures are defined to be the standard deviation of quarterly CPI inflation over one-year periods. The difference between them is that the former is calculated up to the month previous to the end of period t, while the latter is computed up to the end of period t.

The regression in the first column of Table 3 exhibits a somewhat better performance than the regression in the second column. The reason for this is that inflation variability has a positive and significant coefficient in the first case, while this variable does not enter significantly in the second case. One possible explanation for this seemingly striking result is that policymakers adopt stabilization programs in order to reduce inflation volatility in the short run. Thus, the higher inflation variability over the last year the more likely that the government will try to reduce it over the current year.

The remaining regression results presented in the first two columns of Table 3 are similar. In both cases, the first lag of the dependent variable has a positive and significant coefficient. The somewhat high value of this coefficient indicates the existence of a considerable degree of short-run inertia in the default risk of firms. In both cases, past levels of the inflation rate and money supply growth have a positive and significant effect. Inflation was

[15]Further lags were considered but the corresponding results are not reported here because these variables failed to be significant and their presence involves a loss of degrees of freedom.

found to be significant using bond-based data (see Table 1), but in that case the coefficient was much larger than here. The rest of the variables do not seem to be significant.

The last two columns of Table 3 report two different regression results, which correspond to the inclusion of the two remaining measures of inflation variability. The measure used in the first column is $\sigma^S_{2,t}$ and the one employed in the second column is $\sigma^S_{4,t}$. These two measures are defined to be the standard deviation of quarterly CPI inflation over two-year periods. The difference between them is that the former is calculated up to the month previous to the end of period t, while the latter is computed up to the end of period t.

The regression results in the two columns of Table 3 are very similar, column by column, to those just described in the case of Table 2. The regression in the first column of Table 3, again, shows a somewhat better performance than the regression in the second column due to the significance of inflation variability. In both columns, the first lag of the dependent variable has a positive and significant coefficient, revealing a considerable degree of short-run inertia in default risk premia. In both columns also, past levels of the inflation rate and money supply growth have a positive and significant effect. Again, the rest of the variables do not seem to be significant.

In sum, this time inflation variability is found to have a positive effect on default risk (at a one-year horizon, though not at a two-year one). As with the case of bond-based default risk premia, the higher the level of inflation the higher default risk premia. This effect is considerably smaller than in the case of the bond-based measure of default risk. Given the characteristics of the data employed, one plausible interpretation of this result is that inflation has a stronger effect in the medium term than in the short run. This time money supply growth, another nominal variable, has a positive impact on default risk of the private sector. Finally, it was possible to detect a considerable degree of short-run inertia in the behavior of default risk premia.

5. Conclusion

This paper examines the effects of inflation variability and the inflation level on the default risk of the private sector. Two alternative measures of default risk premia are used. The first is constructed using information on the bond market and the second one is based on banking data. Both data sets, but especially the one based on bond market information, are subject to certain limitations. Because of this, the results of the present chapter should be used with care.

The regression results provide mixed evidence in favor of a significant positive effect of inflation variability on default risk. The former variable fails to be significant in the case of the bond-based default risk measure. Using banking data, inflation volatility is found to have a significantly positive effect on default risk when it is measured over a one-year horizon. It does not enter significantly, though, when inflation variability is measured over a two-year period.

In order to evaluate these contrasting results it is crucial to compare the relative importance of inflation variability under the two definitions of default risk. Moreover, the quality of the data employed in each case must also be considered. With regard to the former aspect, the main difference between the two is the maturity of the financial instruments involved. One would expect that the longer the period over which default risk premia are measured, the higher the importance of inflation variability. Therefore, in terms of this first aspect, the lack of significance of inflation variability in the bond-based regressions is, in principle, more conclusive than the significance of that variable in the regressions using banking data. However, it is a fact that the the bond-based data set exhibits considerably more limitations than that of the bank-based data set. This means that the results obtained using latter data set (and in particular the significance of inflation variablity) are more reliable than those derived from the former data set (including the non significance of inflation variability). Taking into consideration the two aspects of the problem at hand, it is not clear which of the two results on the significance of inflation variablity mentioned before is more conclusive.

This study does find strong evidence of a significant positive effect of the level of inflation on default risk. The positive coefficient was found to be considerably lower in the case of the bank-based definition of default risk. Given the characteristics of the data employed, one plausible interpretation of this result is that inflation has a stronger effect in the medium term than in the short run.

It must be borne in mind that in the case of the bond-based data set the sample size is relatively small. Therefore, I analyzed whether the results on the impact of the level and variability of inflation were driven by the sharp disinflation process in the US during the early eighties. This is an episode of considerable importance, which has attracted the attention of many specialists. The analysis showed that the previous results on the effects of the level and variability of inflation do not depend on the strength of the American disinflation experience. At most, this experience is characterized by a stronger effect of the level of inflation on default risk premia than that present in the rest of the sample.

Other results worth reporting concern the degree of persistence of default risk and the effect of the controlling variables used in the analysis. These additional results appear to depend on the definition of default risk used. For the bank-based measure, the default risk is found to be very persistent and rise with higher realisations of money supply growth. In the case of the bond-based measure, the default risk is particularly affected by external variables, in particular going down as a result of higher world interest rates.

Appendix A. Bond Returns: Description of the Data

In all cases the data on bond yields described below were obtained from *Datastream*. In many cases, government bond indices are calculated by *Datastream* itself.[16] In the case of the remaining government bond indices and all non-government bond indices, the data provided by *Datastream* originates in a different source, which is indicated for each individual country below.[17]

United States: I use Lehman Brothers return index data on intermediate (1-10 year maturity) corporate bonds (Grade AA). Moreover, I employ Datastream return index data on government bonds of 3-5 year maturity. The quarterly period for which the default risk premium can be calculated is 80:1-99:1.

[16] In that case, I choose the index for all bonds traded (both liquid and illiquid) in a given maturity range.

[17] In many cases, Shilling (1996) helped me identify the most adequate index for the purpose of the present study.

United Kingdom: I use Warburg Dillon Read return index data on convertible bonds. Moreover, I employ Datastream return index data on all government bonds. The quarterly period for which the default risk premium can be calculated is 94:1-99:1.

Austria: I use price index data on all fixed rate bonds which are calculated by Oesterreichische Kontrollbank Aktiengesellschaft (OKB). Moreover, I employ OKB price index data on all government bond issues. The quarterly period for which the default risk premium can be calculated is 88:1-99:1.

Belgium: I use redemption yield data on Dewaay bonds of 2-6 year maturity. Moreover, I employ Datastream redemption yield data on government bonds of 3-5 year maturity. The quarterly period for which the default risk premium can be calculated is 87:4-99:1.

France: I use return index data on the Exane convertible bond index. Moreover, I employ Datastream return index data on all government bonds. The quarterly period for which the default risk premium can be calculated is 91:3-99:1.

Germany: I use return index data on a mortgage market index, the PEX Deutscher Pfandbrief Index for bonds of 4 year maturity. Moreover, I employ Datastream return index data on government bonds of 3-5 year maturity. The quarterly period for which the default risk premium can be calculated is 87:4-99:1.

Italy: I use price index data on the Lordo index. Moreover, I employ Datastream return index data on all government bonds. The quarterly period for which the default risk premium can be calculated is 88:4-99:1.

Luxembourg: I use LUF redemption yield data on medium-term bonds. Moreover, I employ Datastream return index data on all government bonds. The quarterly period for which the default risk premium can be calculated is 93:2-99:1.

Netherlands: I use Amsterdam ANP/CBS return index data on bonds issued by financial institutions. Moreover, I employ Amsterdam ANP/CBS return index data on government bonds of 3-5 year maturity. The quarterly period for which the default risk premium can be calculated is 89:1-99:1.

Sweden: I use OM Benchmarks return index data on mortgage bonds of intermediate maturity. Moreover, I employ Datastream return index data on government bonds of 3-5 year maturity. The quarterly period for which the default risk premium can be calculated is 96:1-99:1.

Switzerland: I use Pictet return index data on industrial and miscelaneous bonds. Moreover, I employ Datastream return index data on all government bonds. The quarterly period for which the default risk premium can be calculated is 83:4-99:1.

Canada: I use Scotia McLeod return index data on mid-term corporate bonds. Moreover, I employ Datastream return index data on government bonds of 3-5 year maturity. The quarterly period for which the default risk premium can be calculated is 84:4-99:1.

Japan: I use Warburg Dillon Read return index data on convertible bonds. Moreover, I employ Datastream return index data on all government bonds. The quarterly period for which the default risk premium can be calculated is 94:1-99:1.

Australia: I use Warburg Dillon Read return index data on intermediate (0-5 year maturity) corporate bonds. Moreover, I employ Datastream return index data on government bonds of 3-5 year maturity. The quarterly period for which the default risk premium can be calculated is 89:3-99:1.

New Zealand: I use Warburg Dillon Read return index data on intermediate (0-5 year maturity) corporate bonds. Moreover, I employ Warburg Dillon Read return index data on government bonds of 3-5 year maturity. The quarterly period for which the default risk premium can be calculated is 96:1-99:1.

South *Korea:* I use redemption yield data on corporate bonds of 3-year maturity (not bank-guaranteed). Moreover, I employ redemption yield data on monetary stabilization bonds of 1-year maturity. The quarterly period for which the default risk premium can be calculated is 92:2-99:1.

Slovak Republic: I use return index data on SDX corporate bond issues provided by Bratislava SE & ING Bank. Moreover, I employ return index data on SDX government bond issues provided by the same source. Data on duration of either type of bonds permits to conclude that the average maturity is about intermediate. The quarterly period for which the default risk premium can be calculated is 96:4-99:1.

Appendix B. Banking Data: List of Countries

The quarterly periods that accompany the names of the countries are those for which the IMF's International Financial Statistics permits to construct a series for the default risk premium $dr^S{}_t$[18]

United States	63:1-98:4
United Kingdom	57:1-99:1
Austria	80:3-99:1
Belgium	78:3-99:1
Denmark	80:2-90:1
France	66:1-86:1
	86:2-99:1
Germany	77:5-99:1
Italy	83:1-99:1
Luxembourg	85:2-98:3
Netherlands	80:4-99:1
Sweden *	62:1-89:2
Switzerland	81:1-99:1
Canada	71:1-99:1
Japan	57:1-99:1
Finland	85:1-98:1
Greece	60:4-99:1
Iceland	83:1-92:4
	95:1-98:1

[18]The symbol $*$ means that the country was not considered in the regressions due to the lack of data on the rate of change of the money supply.

Appendix B. Continued

Ireland	97:1-99:1
Malta	77:1-98:3
Spain	82:1-98:3
Turkey	78:4-98:3
South Africa	77:4-99:1
Bolivia	87:1-99:1
Brazil	82:4-99:1
Chile	77:1-99:1
Colombia	86:1-98:2
Costa Rica	82:1-99:1
Ecuador	83:1-99:1
El Salvador	83:1-99:1
Guatemala	78:1-99:1
Haiti	96:4-99:1
Honduras	85:1-99:1
Mexico	81:4-99:1
Nicaragua	88:1-97:2
Panama	96:4-99:1
Paraguay	89:4-98:4
Peru	88:1-99:1
Uruguay	76:3-99:1
Venezuela	84:1-99:1
Bahamas	85:1-98:4
Aruba	86:1-98:3
Barbados	80:4-98:3
Dominica	81:4-98:3
Grenada	83:4-98:3
Guyana	94:1-99:1
Jamaica	78:4-98:3
Netherlands Antilles	84:1-91:3
	92:3-99:1
St. Kitts and Nevis	80:4-98:3
St. Lucia	81:4-94:3
St. Vincent & Grenadines	82:4-88:3
	92:1-99:1
Trinidad & Tobago	88:4-95:1
	96:1-98:3
Bahrain	75:3-90:3
Cyprus	70:4-74:3
	74:4-96:4

Appendix B. Continued

Israel	83:4-99:1
Jordan	80:1-90:2
	91:3-96:4
Kuwait	80:1-90:2
	91:3-96:4
Saudi Arabia	97:1-98:4
Egypt	76:1-98:2
Bangladesh	76:1-98:2
Cambodia	94:4-99:1
Sri Lanka	78:1-99:1
Hong Kong	94:1-99:1
Indonesia	74:2-86:1
	86:2-98:4
South Korea	70:1-98:4
Lao People's Democratic Republic	93:2-96:4
Malaysia	79:1-99:1
Nepal	75:2-90:3
Philippines	76:2-80:2
	81:4-98:4
Singapore	77:1-99:1
Thailand	77:1-99:1
Angola	95:1-98:4
Botswana	80:1-99:1
Burundi	85:1-89:2
Cameroon	79:1-98:1
Cape Verde	92:1-99:1
Central African Republic	81:1-98:3
Congo Republic	79:1-97:2
Equatorial Guinea	86:1-94:3
Ethiopia	85:4-98:2
Gambia	84:4-98:4
Ghana	91:1-97:4
Guinea-Bissau	88:1-98:1
Cte d'Ivoire	70:1-93:3
Kenya	68:1-91:2
	94:4-99:1
Madagascar	90:4-98:3
Malawi	80:1-97:2
Mali	87:3-93:3

Appendix B. Continued

Mauritania	85:3-93:1
Mauritius	80:2-99:1
Morocco	78:3-89:3
Niger	70:1-93:3
Nigeria	70:1-79:1
	79:2-97:4
Zimbabwe	80:1-98:2
Seychelles	81:1-88:4
Senegal	70:1-93:3
Sierra Leone	86:4-98:3
Swaziland	73:4-99:1
Tanzania	95:1-99:1
Tunisia	87:3-89:4
Uganda	81:2-98:1
Burkina Faso	82:3-93:3
Zambia	85:1-91:2
	93:1-98:1
Solomon Islands	81:1-98:1
Fiji	74:1-98:4
Samoa	82:4-98:4
Tonga	90:1-98:4
Armenia	95:2-98:4
Albania	92:1-97:4
Kyrgyz Republic	96:1-98:4
Bulgaria	91:1-96:4
Moldova	96:2-98:3
Czech Republic	94:1-99:1
Slovak Republic	94:1-98:4
Estonia	93:1-99:1
Latvia	93:3-99:1
Hungary *	76:1-98:2
Lithuania	93:1-99:1
Croatia	93:1-98:4
Slovenia	92:1-99:1
Macedonia	94:1-97:2
Poland	89:4-99:1
Belarus	95:3-99:1
Russian Federation	95:1-99:1
Ukraine	93:1-98:3

References

Andrés, J., I. Hernando and D. López-Salido (2004): "The Role of the Financial System in the Growth–Inflation Link: the OECD Experience," *European Journal of Political Economy* **20**, 941-61.

Barnes, M., J. Boyd and B. Smith (1999): "Inflation and Asset Returns," *European Economic Review* **43**, 737-54.

Barro, R. (1995): "Inflation and Economic Growth," *Bank of England Quarterly Bulletin*, May.

Boyd, J., R. Levine and B. Smith (2001): "Inflation and Financial Market Performance," *Journal of Monetary Economics* **47**, 221-48.

Choi, S., B. Smith and J. Boyd (1996): "Inflation, Financial Markets, and Capital Formation," *Federal Reserve Bank of St. Louis Review* **78**, 9-30.

Fischer, S. (1993): "The Role of Macroeconomic Factors in Growth," *Journal of Monetary Economics* **32**, 485-512.

McCaig, B. and T. Stengos (2005): "Financial Intermediation and Growth: Some Robustness Results," *Economics Letters* **88**, 306-12.

Rousseau, P. and P. Wachtel (2002): "Inflation Thresholds and the Finance–Growth Nexus," *Journal of International Money and Finance* **21**, 777-93.

Sánchez, M. (2000): "Determinants of the Real Rate of Return: Evidence from Cross-Country Panel Data," in M. Sánchez: *The Effects of Inflation on Financial and Real Activity*, Ph.D. Thesis, University of California at Berkeley, chapter 2.

Shilling, H. (1996): *The International Guide To Securities Market Indices*, Chicago: Fitzroy Dearborn Publishers.

In: Monetary Growth: Trends, Impacts and Policies
Editors: W.N. Squires et al, pp. 151-159
ISBN 978-1-60692-305-4

Short Communication F

Technical Analysis as a Method of Risk Management

Gregor Dorfleitner*
Department of Finance, University of Regensburg
93040 Regensburg, Germany
Christian Klein†
Department Finance and Accounting (510c)
University of Hohenheim, 70593 Stuttgart, Germany
Dennis Kundisch‡
Department of Information Systems and Financial Engineering
University of Augsburg, 86135 Augsburg, Germany

Abstract

While the academic world is still discussing if charting works or if it is more or less something like "Voodoo finance", the practical orientated world has been using technical analysis for decades. One argument of practitioners is that technical analysis is useful to "disciplinate" the trader and consequently is a method of risk reduction. We discuss this argument theoretically and empirically and show that it is not always right.

Key Words: Technical Analysis, Risk Management

1. Motivation

Technical Analysis (TA) can be defined as the analysis of historical stock quotes with the aim of predicting future stock quotes. There has been a lot of empirical work on the performance and the prediction power of TA, with both negative[1] and positive[2] findings. Empirical research on TA trading rules is problematic, since scientists face quite a few methodical

*E-mail address: gregor.dorfleitner@wiwi.uni-regensburg.de
†E-mail address: cklein@uni-hohenheim.de
‡E-mail address: dennis.kundisch@wiwi.uni-augsburg.de
[1]See e.g. Hofmann (1973) or Dorfleitner and Klein (2002).
[2]See e.g. Pruitt and White (1988), Brock et al. (1992) or Lo et al. (2000).

problems.[3] From a theoretical point of view it is impossible to earn above-average returns with the help of TA, if the efficient market hypothesis is taken for granted.[4] Although the academic finance has still not found an argumentation why TA should work, charting is widespread in industry practice.[5] Two reasons for the enormous popularity of TA in the practical finance world are the simple handling in comparison to "fundamental" methods and a reputation to have at least a litte forecasting power. A newer argument stated by trading professionals is that TA is mainly an instrument which helps to reduce risk. Practitioners point out that TA helps to "disciplinate" an investor by forcing him to leave the market from time to time, when a corresponding signal appears. With the end of the dotcom bubble the demand for effective risk management systems has grown, especially for private investors. In this context, TA seems to play a more and more important role as an instrument for risk management. As an example, one of the largest German direct brokers offers a service tool based on TA, which analyses the investment risks of every stock held in the portfolio.

In this paper we discuss the question, whether TA is an useful instrument for risk management, or to be more precise for risk reduction. We show that using TA for investment decisions can have a bad effect on the volatility of an investment.

2. The Model

In this paper, we define risk as the standard deviation of returns.[6] We focus on a certain security or stock index (from now on referred to as "share") with prices K_t at times $t = 0, 1, \ldots, n$. The return R_t (belonging to the period $[t-1, t]$) is defined as:

$$R_t = \frac{K_t - K_{t-1}}{K_{t-1}} = \frac{K_t}{K_{t-1}} - 1 \quad \text{for } t = 1, \ldots, n\,. \tag{1}$$

One period may be a day or a week. The returns are random variables which we analyze ex post. Thus the distribution of the random variables is not relevant in our context.

As a benchmark for the trading strategies considered below we chose the buy-and-hold strategy (B&H). An investor who buys the share at time 0 and holds it until time n enjoys the overall return

$$R = \prod_{t=1}^{n} (R_t + 1) - 1\,. \tag{2}$$

The (estimated) volatility of his investment is the standard deviation of the returns:

$$\hat{\sigma} = \sqrt{\frac{n \sum_{t=1}^{n} R_t^2 - \left(\sum_{t=1}^{n} R_t\right)^2}{n(n-1)}}\,. \tag{3}$$

[3] In most cases historical data are used. Ball et al. (1995) show that this may lead to an "upward bias". Researchers working with historical data sometime face the reproach of missing objectivity. See for example Jegadeesh (2000) or Dorfleitner and Klein (2002).

[4] See e.g. Schmidt (1976) or Malkiel (1996).

[5] Cf. Bankhofer and Hilbert (1999) or Tayler and Allen (1992). Both papers find a high acceptance (about 90%) of TA by practitioners.

[6] This is the standard approach for many practical applications such as performance analysis of mutual funds. See e.g. Fischer (2001).

Formula (3) measures the risk of the B&H investment.[7] We assume that an investor uses TA for his investment decisions. His intention is to achieve a lower volatility value than he would have obtained with the B&H strategy. Using TA means that he receives a signal at the beginning of every single period. For simplicity we assume only three kinds of signals:

- A "buy" signal: Induces the investor to buy the share. If he already owns the share, he does nothing.
- A "sell" signal: Induces the investor to sell the share. If he is not invested, he does nothing.
- A "hold" signal (or no signal): The investor does not do anything in any case.

During the time of the investment he may leave and re-enter the market several times. After n periods the investment is over. We denote the returns induced by a certain trading strategy by $\tilde{R}_1, \ldots, \tilde{R}_n$. Formulae (2) and (3) can be applied analogously to calculate the overall return and the volatility of the strategy. In the following we consider three different types of strategies where we derive the returns $\tilde{R}_1, \ldots, \tilde{R}_n$ from the B&H returns $R_1, \ldots, R_n$. The following analysis is based on two simplifying assumptions: 1. We assume a riskless interest rate of zero. Otherwise the investor could face the risk of changing interest-rates while being not invested. 2. We do not consider transaction costs.

2.1. Reinvestment Strategy

Using the reinvestment strategy means, that every time the share is (re-) bought the cumulated amount of money is invested. For $t = 1, \ldots, n$ the returns $\tilde{R}_t$ of each single period t are:

$$\tilde{R}_t = \begin{cases} R_t, & \text{if invested} \\ 0, & \text{if not invested.} \end{cases}$$

As long as the investor is in the market, the value of his investment changes with the price of the share. During the time he is out of the market, the value of his investment does not change. The latter fact may lead to the conjecture that the volatility of the reinvestment strategy is generally lower than the one of B&H. This is not true, as the following example shows:[8]

Be

$$R_t = a \qquad \text{with } a \neq 0, \qquad t = 1, \ldots, n. \tag{4}$$

Then the returns of the investment are

$$\tilde{R}_t = \begin{cases} a, & \text{if invested} \\ 0, & \text{if not invested} \end{cases} \qquad t = 1, \ldots, n. \tag{5}$$

[7] Note that the volatility refers to the time span of one single period.

[8] This numerical example is also used by Dorfleitner and Klein (2004).

Obviously the $\hat{\sigma}$ value of the B&H strategy is 0 and the estimated volatility of the reinvestment strategy is:

$$\tilde{\sigma} = \sqrt{\frac{m(n-m)}{n(n-1)}a^2}$$

where m is the number of periods in which the investor is in the market. This example proofs that the case $\hat{\sigma} < \tilde{\sigma}$ is possible. Here, the impact of the investment strategy on the volatility is negative.

2.2. Rebalancing

Another possible investment strategy is to invest a fixed amount of money every time the share is (re)bought.

The calculation of the periodical returns during the investment process is not as easy as in formula (1), because now the cash account is not necessarily equal to zero while the investor is in the market. It is easier to calculate the returns in a recursive way. The periodical returns are now:

$$\tilde{R}_1 = \begin{cases} R_1, & \text{if invested} \\ 0, & \text{if not invested} \end{cases} \tag{6}$$

and for $t > 1$:

$$\tilde{R}_t = \begin{cases} \frac{\prod_{i=s+1}^{t}(R_i+1)+\prod_{i=1}^{s}(\tilde{R}_i+1)-1}{\prod_{i=s+1}^{t-1}(R_i+1)+\prod_{i=1}^{s}(\tilde{R}_i+1)-1} - 1, & \text{if invested long at time } s < t \\ 0, & \text{if not invested.} \end{cases} \tag{7}$$

If the investor has only been long for one single period, i.e. if $s = t - 1$, the return simplifies to:

$$\tilde{R}_t = \frac{R_t}{\prod_{i=1}^{t-1}\left(\tilde{R}_i + 1\right)} . \tag{8}$$

Table 1 shows an example for the calculation of the periodical returns with rebalancing. In this case the risk of the investment strategy is higher than the risk of the B&H strategy.

2.3. Short Strategy

In the last two subsections we assumed that the investor would leave the market (or not enter it) if he received a sell signal. A different scenario is possible, if the investor has the possibility to go short: If he believes in the quality of the signals (which he does, of course, otherwise he would not use TA) going short is rational in the case of a sell signal. Table 2 contains one possible strategy, where the actions are dependent on the signal and the current state of the investment process (short, long or not invested).

Table 1. Investment with Rebalancing

Period	Price Share	Return B&H	Invested	Cash	Share	Saldo	Return Strategy
1	100		Yes		100,00	100,00	
					140,00		
2	140	0,40	No	140,00		140,00	0,40
				140,00			
3	135	-0,04	Yes	40,00	100,00	140,00	0,00
				40,00	37,04		
4	50	-0,63	No	77,04		77,04	-0,45
				77,04			
5	55	0,10	Yes	-22,96	100,00	77,04	0,00
				-22,96	190,91		
6	105	0,91	No	167,95		167,95	1,18
$\hat{\sigma}$		**0,57**					**0,61**

Table 2. A possible short strategy

signal \ state	short	not invested	long
buy	get not invested	go long	stay long
hold	stay short	stay uninvested	stay long
sell	stay short	get short	get not invested

There are several possible ways to implement the option of going short. We assume that there exists a futures market for the share. Going short here means that we build up a short position in the futures contract and simultaneously invest an amount of cash equal to the share price.[9] The returns for a short strategy (based on the reinvestment strategy) of each single period are now ($t = 1, \ldots, n$):

$$\tilde{R}_t = \begin{cases} R_t, & \text{if invested long} \\ \frac{2-\frac{K_t}{K_s}}{2-\frac{K_{t-1}}{K_s}} - 1 = \frac{2-\prod_{i=s+1}^{t}(R_i+1)}{2-\prod_{i=s+1}^{t-1}(R_i+1)} - 1, & \text{if invested short since } s < t \\ 0, & \text{if not invested.} \end{cases} \tag{9}$$

The case study in section 3. includes an example, where the estimated $\tilde{\sigma}$ value of the short strategy is higher than the corresponding value of the B&H strategy.

[9]The "amount of cash" is necessary to calculate a return. Otherwise, with an investment of 0, the return would go to $\pm\infty$.

3. Case Study

In this section, we apply the issues discussed above on the findings of Dorfleitner and Klein (2002). The paper investigates the quality of forecasts based on TA. To avoid the reproach of missing objectivity, data stemming from a widely known and accepted stock-investment magazine are used. The empirical survey includes weekly data of the Dow Jones Industrial Average (USA) and the Nikkei 225 (Japan) ranging from August 1995 to August 2001. Every week we have a short-termed (s-t) and a medium-termed (m-t) forecast for the Dow Jones and the Nikkei index. In addition to the investigation of the prediction power, several investment strategies based on the forecasts are analysed. The first four strategies (strategies I to IV in Table 3) reproduce the rational reaction of an investor on TA signals. The next four strategies (strategies V to VIII) use the signals as a contra indicator, i.e. the investor interprets a sell signal as a buy signal and vice versa. Strategies I to VIII are reinvestment strategies as defined above. Finally four short strategies (strategies IX to XII) are considered. Table 3 shows the estimated $\tilde{\sigma}$ values of the different strategies. In five cases the volatility of the strategies is higher than the volatility of the B&H strategy. All of these cases are based on a short strategy on the Dow Jones Index.

Table 3. Estimated $\tilde{\sigma}$ values of different investment strategies

investment strategy		Nikkei		Dow Jones	
		s-t	m-t	s-t	m-t
B&H		**0,0293**		**0,0237**	
rational	**I**	0,0232	0,0272	0,0133	0,0174
	II	0,0204	0,0205	0,0162	0,0158
	III	0,0051	0,0163	0,0075	0,0101
	IV	0,0282	0,0278	0,0227	0,0227
contra indicator	**V**	0,0171	0,0106	0,0197	0,0162
	VI	0,0210	0,0208	0,0174	0,0178
	VII	0,0072	0,0090	0,0069	0,0069
	VIII	0,0288	0,0242	0,0225	0,0215
short strategy	**IX**	0,0235	0,0278	**0,0428**	**0,0299**
	X	0,0253	0,0263	0,0211	0,0222
	XI	0,0261	0,0291	**0,0447**	**0,0320**
	XII	0,0280	0,0271	0,0237	**0,0239**

Figure 1 shows the cumulated returns of two investment cases on the Dow Jones Index between 07/1995 and 08/2001 on a weekly basis. The first investment is the B&H strategy, the second investment is short strategy IX. The total return of the B&H strategy is much better, but this is not the focus of this paper. Our point of interest is the estimated volatility of these strategies. The Figures 2 and 3 show the returns of both strategies on a weekly basis. Between week 177 and 243 the investor leaves the market and the weekly return of his investment is zero during this time. Between week 58 and 175 he is short and the magnitude of the returns of his investment is much higher than the corresponding magnitude of the B&H strategy. Here, this effect is so strong that the estimated $\tilde{\sigma}$ value is higher than the corresponding value of the B&H strategy. Following the TA-based strategy to invest in the Dow Jones here has a negative impact on the volatility of the investment.

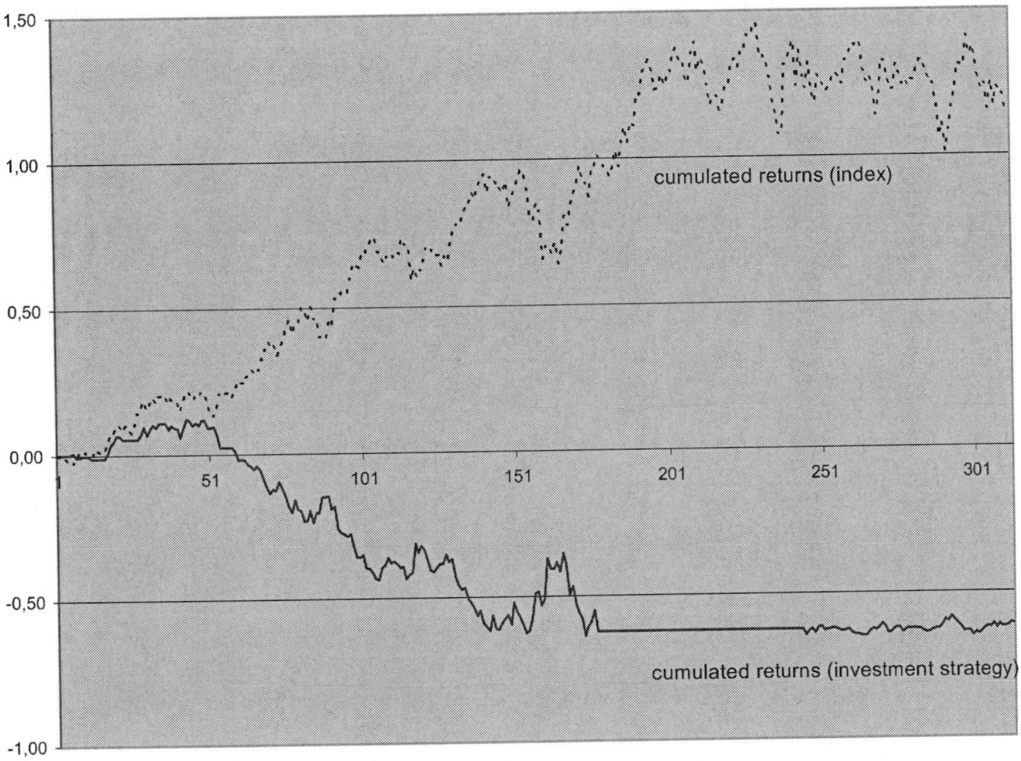

Figure 1. Cumulated returns Dow Jones and short strategy.

4. Conclusion

We examined three different types of investment strategies that one can follow when leaving and re-entering the market on the base of TA trading signals. We focused on the risk dimension of the investment measured by the volatility of periodical returns. It could be shown by counter examples that each of the investment strategies can lead to a higher volatility compared to the B&H investment. Our case study also showed, that this effect can occur, but mostly it did not do so, i.e. TA was successfull at risk reduction. We did not take the expected return dimension into account. In the case study this dimension is also not apt to clearly justify the use of TA.

Summarizing, we state that TA as a method of risk management is at least dangerous, since it can damage the performance of the investment whereas the risk reduction effect is not granted.

In this paper we focused on investment strategies based on technical analysis. Most of our findings also hold for any other investment strategy which forces the investor to leave and re-enter the market from time to time (e.g. fundamental analysis).

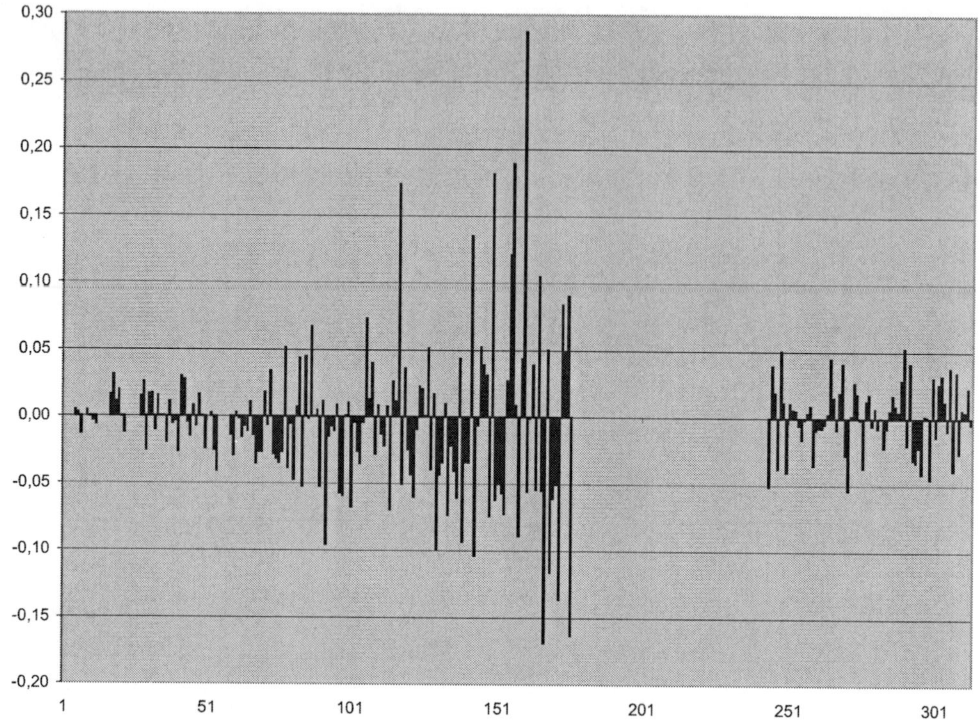

Figure 2. Weekly returns of a short strategy.

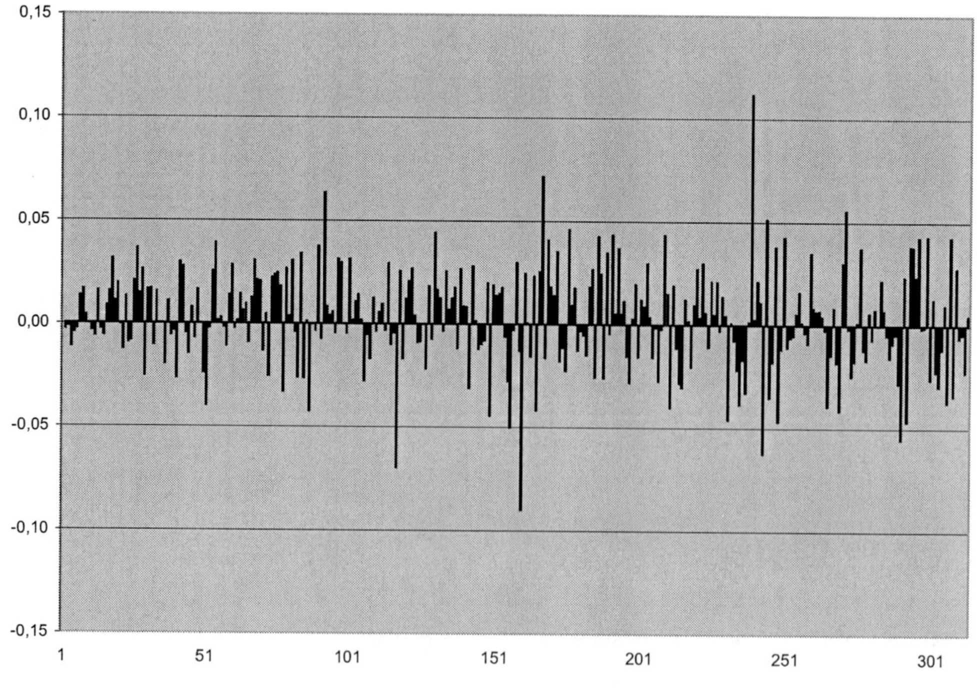

Figure 3. Weekly returns of the index (= B&H strategy).

References

Ball, R., Kothari, S.P. and Wasley, C.E. (1995): Can we implement Research on Stock Trading Rules? *Journal of Portfolio Management* **21**, 54 – 63

Bankhofer, U. and Hilbert, A. (1999): Eine empirische Studie zur Anwendung mathematischer Methoden in der Versicherungspraxis. *Zeitschrift für das gesamte Versicherungswesen*, 611 – 644

Brock, W., Lakonishok, J. and Lebaron, B. (1992): Simple Technical Trading Rules and the Stochastic Properties of Stock Returns. *Journal of Finance* **47**, 1731 – 1764

Dorfleitner, G. and Klein, C. (2002): Kursprognose mit Hilfe der Technischen Analyse – Eine empirische Untersuchung. *Financial Markets and Portfolio Management* **16**, 497 – 521

Dorfleitner, G. and Klein, C. (2004): Renditen und Volatilitt bei Ein-/Ausstiegsstrategien, *WiSt* **33**, 582 – 590

Fischer, B.R. (2001): *Performanceanalyse in der Praxis – Performancemaße, Attributionsanalyse, DVFA-Performance Presentation Standards, 2nd Edition*. Oldenbourg, München/Wien.

Hofmann, H.W. (1973): *Empirische Untersuchung verschiedener Anlagestrategien der Technischen Analyse anhand von 100 deutschen Standardaktien über einen Zeitraum von fünf Jahren (1967-1972) und Vergleich mit einer durch Simulation ermittelten Zufallsauswahl bzw. einer Kauf- und Halte-Strategie*. Dissertation at the Ludwigs-Maximilians-Universität München.

Jegadeesh, N. (2000): Foundations of Technical Analysis - Discussion. *Journal of Finance* **55**, No. 4, 1765 – 1770

Lo, A.W., Mamaysky, H. and Wang, J. (2000): Foundations of Technical Analysis: Computational Algorithms, Statistical Inference, and Empirical Implementation. *Journal of Finance* **55**, 1705 – 1765

Malkiel, B. (1996): *A Random Walk Down Wallstreet: Including a Life-Cycle Guide to Personal Investing*, **6th** Edition. W. W. Norton & Company, New York.

Pruitt, S. and White, R. (1988): The CRISMA trading system: Who says technical analysis can't beat the market? *Journal of Portfolio Management* **14**, 55 – 58

Schmidt, R.H. (1976): *Aktienkursprognose*. Gabler, Wiesbaden.

Tyler, M. and Allen, H. (1992): The use of technical analysis in the foreign exchange market. *Journal of International Money and Finance* **11**, 304 – 314

In: Monetary Growth: Trends, Impacts and Policies
Editors: W.N. Squires et al, pp. 161-170
ISBN 978-1-60692-305-4

Short Communication G

MONETARY CONTRACTIONS AND CUMULATIVE DEPRESSIONS: A MONETARY OPTIMIZING MODEL

Hiroyuki Yoshida*
College of Economics, Nihon University
1-3-2 Misaki-cho, Chiyoda-ku, Tokyo 101-8360, Japan

Abstract

In this chapter we argue the possibility of cumulative depressions by using a monetary optimizing model. For our purpose we develop the money-in-the-utility-function approach. We assume the rigidity of the price level in the commodity market, and hence adopt a quantity adjustment mechanism, where the quantity of output moves infinitely fast to clear the commodity market. In addition, we presuppose that policy makers follow a constant growth rule for the nominal money supply.

Within the particular model, we show that deflationary monetary policy causes a cumulative depression, which appears as a perfect foresight equilibrium path. On this path the consumption level approaches zero eventually. Equally important, we draw attention to the result of inflationary monetary. In this case, policy makers avoid completely the emergence of deep depressions. Namely, inflationary monetary policy is a successful tool for eliminating the cumulative depressions that may arise under deflationary monetary policy.

Finally, we discuss the effectiveness of fiscal policy. While an independent use of fiscal policy cannot rule out the cumulative depressions, a combination of fiscal and monetary policies stimulates economic activity. In this sense, fiscal policy is effective in achieving and maintaining the efficiency of the economy.

1. Introduction

The study of the economic depression is an important topic in macroeconomics, since it has huge negative impacts on the economy and destroys the livelihood of millions of people. For example, the Great Depression in the United States was a severe and extreme event in the late 1920s and the early 1930s: the unemployment rate jumped from 3.2 percent in 1929

*E-mail address: yoshida.hiroyuki@nihon-u.ac.jp.

to 24.9 percent in 1933. Over the same period, GNP fell by nearly 30 percent in the United States. Such economic downturns were observed in most of the major industrial countries such as France, Germany, Japan, and the United Kingdom. These countries experienced a significant depression at almost the same time.

As stated by Temin (1976), there are two main explanations of the Great Depression: the monetary view and the spending view.[1] The monetary view has argued that the Great Depression was caused by monetary contraction, which was the consequence of the misguided monetary policy and the continuous crises in the financial system. In fact, the nominal money stock, $M1$, declined by approximately 25 percent from 1229 to 1933. On account of this fact, Friedman and Schwartz (1963) and Hamilton (1987) suggested that a more accommodative monetary policy could have reduced the severity of the Great Depression. On the other hand, the spending view emphasized that the Great Depression was caused by the decreases in various sorts of autonomous expenditures. This view was mainly expressed by Keynesian economists. Temin proposed a variant of the spending view and argued that the autonomous decline in consumption spending in 1930 played an important role in depressing and worsening the economic performance of the United States.

However, these two views are not mutually exclusive, but rather complementary. The interaction between monetary and real factors contributed to the occurrence, severity, and persistence of the Great Depression. Several efforts have been devoted to investigating a relationship between the Great Crash of 1929 and the collapse of consumption spending in 1930. Mishkin (1978) argued that a deterioration in the household balance sheet led to a sharp decline in the purchase of durable goods. Romer (1990) presented the uncertainty hypothesis: the stock market crash amplified temporary uncertainty about the level of future income, and caused the drop in spending on consumer durables. Added to these, Olney (1999) showed that the large drop in consumption spending on both durables and nondurables resulted from the combination of high consumer indebtedness and severe debt default penalties. They all emphasized the importance of the consumption collapse generated by the stock market crash in the early stage of the Great Depression.

The purpose of the present chapter is to investigate the possibility of cumulative depressions within the purely theoretical framework including both real and monetary factors. For our purpose, we shall employ the money-in-the-utility-function, or MIUF, approach: see, for example, Sidrauski (1967), Brock (1974, 1975), Obstfeld and Rogoff (1983), Gray (1984), and Obstfeld (1984). In particular, we shall extend the Gray (1984) model to allow for the principle of effective demand. The Gray model deals with the dynamics of real balances as a central variable, while consumption remains at an exogenous level of real income. The last matter evidently embodies the conception of the supply-constrained equilibrium. In contrast, the notion of demand-determined equilibrium is introduced in our structure. In other words, we shall place effective demand on the center of the stage and construct a differential equation concerning consumption. Such an attempt will carry Keynesian features into the model.

Our model is in the tradition of disequilibrium theory. The issues of Böhm (1978), Honkapohja (1980), Honkapohja and Ito (1982), Picard (1983), and Flaschel (1999) are re-

[1]This classification is not the only one existing. Gordon and Wilcox (1981) distinguished four views, which were labeled "hard-line monetarism," "soft-line monetarism," "soft-line nonmonetarism," and "hard-line nonmonetarism."

lated to our analysis; they studied dynamic disequilibrium models with money. It is true that these prior publications have made a large contribution to Keynesian macroeconomics, but they have never built up intertemporal optimization models, which have become dominant in dynamic macroeconomics over the past decade or so.[2] Accordingly, we aim to examine a model of infinitely lived households that maximize their lifetime utility with perfect foresight. From this viewpoint, a new Keynesian foundation is laid in this chapter.

There is one other thing that is important in this chapter. It is well known that the assumption of the non-separable utility function between consumption and money yields the indeterminacy of equilibrium. A typical example is Obstfeld (1984). It has a positive steady state point, which is asymptotically stable in terms of dynamical systems. However, our result is different from that of the above model; the indeterminacy of perfect foresight paths occurs also in our model even if the utility function is additively separable. Our system has two stationary points: a low-consumption point and a high-consumption point. Although the latter is a determinate stationary point, the former displays the indeterminacy of equilibrium.

This chapter is organized as follows. Section 2 lays out the basic economic structure and describes the individual and aggregate workings of economic variables. To establish a relationship between the behavior of agents and the state of the economy we shall adopt the fiction of the representative agent in our analysis. Section 3 analyzes the dynamics of perfect foresight paths and discusses the effects of monetary and fiscal policy. Section 4 summarizes our results.

2. The Model

We consider an economy of infinitely lived, utility maximizing agents with perfect foresight. There are in the economy a single consumption good and money; the latter is the unit of account and the only storable good, while the former is perishable. The economy consists of consumers, firms, and the government. Every agent acts as a price taker; in this sense we study a Walrasian economy. However, we shall take a departure from the Walrasian environment: the firm is subject to the quantity constraint on its output sales. Detailed account is presented below.

The Firm

The firm produces its output operating the capital stock, k. For simplicity, we abstract from the accumulation and depreciation of capital; the amount of capital is fixed throughout time. Thus, our analysis is restricted to the medium-run dynamics. The firm has the efficient level of production, y_e, which is attained when the capital stock is fully utilized;

$$y_e = \sigma k, \tag{1}$$

where σ is the efficient output-capital ratio, which is constant.

[2] Bénassy (1993, Chapter IV) is, however, an exceptional study, which investigates an intertemporal model. Our analysis is different from that of Bénassy in two respects. First, our model surely employs Pontryagin's maximum principle, setting up the current value Hamiltonian. Second, we consider explicitly the cost of holding money (in other words, the rate of inflation in our framework) by using the MIUF approach.

However, there is no guarantee that consumption demand, $c_d(t)$, always equals to the efficient output in the Keynesian system. The firm controls the utilization rate of capital stock, u, according to the state of economy. The production function is expressed as

$$y_s(t) = u(t)\sigma k, \tag{2}$$

where y_s denotes actual output. It will be apparent that $u = 1$ means the efficient production activity. If consumption demand exceeds the efficient output, the firm produces the corresponding level of demand by increasing the utilization rate of capital stock, and in opposite case the firm meets effective demand by decreasing the rate of utilization. We assume that this adjustment process is so rapid that $y_s(t) = c_d(t)$ is always realized at each moment in time. That is, the production level is determined by the level of aggregate demand through the perfect quantity adjustment process; this situation reflects the principle of effective demand.

Furthermore, it is assumed that the firm can change the level of output with no additional costs.[3] Thus the profit obtained by the firm is simply equal to y_s. This means that the above quantity adjustment process ensures the maximization of profit under the quantity constraint on current sales. The firm in our model pays out the whole profits as dividends, d, to the owner, i.e., the consumer;

$$d(t) = y_s(t). \tag{3}$$

In the economic circumstances we consider, the firm holds some excess capacity and faces the quantity constraint on production activity. This is our fundamental cognition. In such situations, as mentioned above, it may be safely assumed that output is costless to produce. However, this assumption would be far from realities, in that it permits an unlimited amount of output without additional inputs. Thus, we need to incorporate a supplementary hypothesis. That is, we shall pay attention to the existence of physical maximum limitation on the productive facilities. Let $\bar{y}$ be the capacity level of output, which satisfies the following relation, $y_e < \bar{y}$.

The Consumer

The representative consumer maximizes the following welfare function:

$$\int_0^\infty \left\{ \frac{{c_d}^{1-\gamma}}{1-\gamma} + v(m_d) \right\} \exp(-\rho t) dt, \gamma > 0, \tag{4}$$

where c_d denotes the demand for the consumption good, m is the demand for real money balances, and $\rho (> 0)$ is the subjective discount factor.[4] The function $v(m)$ is increasing and concave, and has the usual smoothness properties. Note that the instantaneous utility function is additively separable between consumption and real balances.

The flow budget constraint is given in nominal terms by

$$\dot{M}_d = pd - pc_d + p\tau, \tag{5}$$

[3] A similar discussion on the production structure can be found in Calvo (1983).

[4] Here and henceforth time arguments are suppressed when no ambiguity results.

where p is the price level, d is dividends in real terms, τ is real lump-sum transfers (lump-sum taxes, if negative), and M_d is the demand for nominal money balances ($M_d = pm_d$). Since we intend to focus our attention on the analysis of the inflationary or deflationary situation later, it is convenient to employ the flow budget constraint in real terms. Using $m_d = M_d/p$ and (5), the budget constraint can be rewritten as

$$\dot{m}_d = d - c_d - \pi m_d + \tau, \tag{6}$$

where π denotes the rate of inflation.[5]

The agent chooses the sequences for consumption and real balances so as to maximize (4) subject to the flow budget constraint (6), taking as given the initial money holdings and the sequences: $\{d(t)\}_{t=0}^{\infty}$, $\{\tau(t)\}_{t=0}^{\infty}$, and $\{\pi(t)\}_{t=0}^{\infty}$. The above maximization problem is solved by defining the current value Hamiltonian

$$H = \frac{{c_d}^{1-\gamma}}{1-\gamma} + v(m_d) + \lambda(d - c_d - \pi m_d + \tau), \tag{7}$$

where λ represents the costate variable associated with the budget constraint. The following equations must be satisfied by optimal c and m paths:

$${c_d}^{-\gamma} = \lambda, \tag{8}$$

$$\dot{\lambda} = \rho\lambda - (v'(m_d) - \lambda\pi), \tag{9}$$

and the associated transversality condition is

$$\lim_{t\to\infty} \lambda m_d e^{-\rho t} = 0. \tag{10}$$

The Government

We treat the fiscal and monetary authority as a single ruling entity, referring to it as "government" simply. It is assumed that the government maintains a constant growth rate of nominal money supply, M_s,

$$\frac{\dot{M}_s}{M_s} = \theta. \tag{11}$$

The value of θ could be negative, but we make a restriction that $\theta > -\rho$. The government budget constraint is described by

$$\tau = \theta m_s, \tag{12}$$

where m_s denotes the real money supply ($m_s = M_s/p$).[6] Equation (12) implies that monetary expansion (contraction) occurs through the lump-sum transfers (taxes).

3. Analysis of the Dynamics

Thus far, we have set out and displayed the framework to be analyzed. We now turn to consider a perfect foresight equilibrium in detail.

[5] By definition, $\dot{p}/p = \pi$.

[6] In a later of this chapter we shall extend the model to include government expenditures.

Perfect Foresight Equilibrium

The commodity market clearing requires

$$c_d = y_s. \tag{13}$$

As mentioned above, this condition is not accomplished by flexible price adjustment but by perfect quantity adjustment. It should be, therefore, noted that the price level is not determined, but the rate of utilization is settled through the commodity market equilibrium. In addition, this condition implies the money market equilibrium by means of Walras's Law;

$$m_d = m_s. \tag{14}$$

Henceforth we shall focus on equilibrium quantities and simply drop the subscript on real balances; $m_d = m_s = m$.

Our concern is to consider perfect foresight equilibrium paths. Let $\{p(t)\}_{t=0}^{\infty}$ be a sequence of non-negative price level. The perfect foresight equilibrium relative to $\{p(t)\}_{t=0}^{\infty}$ is defined as a situation in which (i) the planned demands for output and money equal to the corresponding supplies and (ii) all expected variables are correctly realized.

The Dynamics

Now we proceed to study the dynamic characteristics in our model. As stated above, $p(t)$ takes an auxiliary position in that it does not contribute to clearing the commodity market. For analytical purpose, we shall adopt the following assumption:

Assumption 1

$$\pi(t) = \theta \quad \text{for all } t > 0.$$

This assumption reflects the quantity theory of money, which states that changes in the money supply cause proportional changes in the price level. To put it another way, the government has the ability to control the inflation rate through monetary targeting.

From the above consideration, we can obtain the following differential equation, which describes the perfect foresight equilibrium paths:

$$\dot{c} = \left[v'(m)c^{\gamma} - \theta - \rho\right] c/\gamma \; (:= F(c)), \tag{15}$$

where c is the market clearing level of consumption.[7] What needs to be emphasized at this point is that m is fixed over time by Assumption 1. There exist two steady state points: a positive stationary point is given by

$$c_* = \left[\frac{\rho + \theta}{v'(m)}\right]^{1/\gamma}, \tag{16}$$

[7] We assume the global existence and uniqueness of solutions. For further details of this topic, see Perko (1996, pp.186-187).

and a zero stationary point, $c_{**} = 0$. We can easily verify that $F'(c_*) = \theta + \rho > 0$ and $F'(c_{**}) = -(\theta + \rho)/\gamma < 0$. Since the positive stationary point is unique and $F(0) = 0$, it follows that $\dot{c}$ is negative on the interval $(0, c_*)$ and $\dot{c}$ is positive to the right of c_*. The phase diagram is depicted in Figure 1.

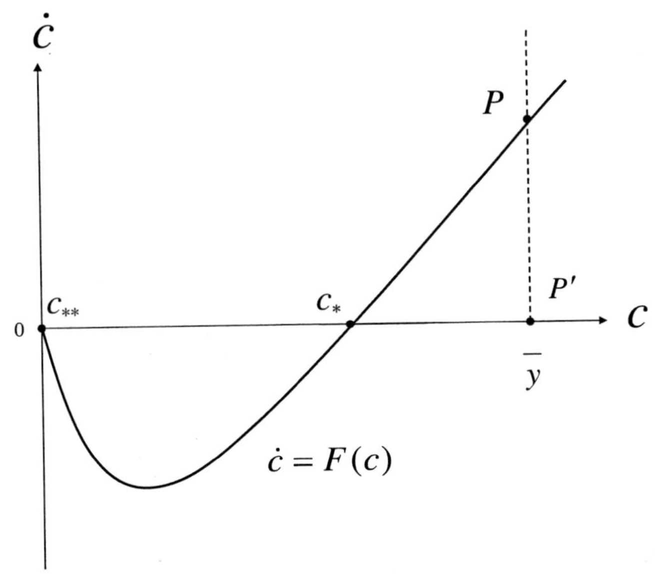

Figure 1. Phase diagram.

It seems reasonable to investigate the consumption paths through three categories: the steady state path, cumulative depression paths, and cumulative prosperity paths. In the first place, consider the steady state path of consumption, $c(t) = c_*$ for all t. We can be certain that this path is an admissible path, since it satisfies both the Euler and transversality conditions.

In the second place, we turn to cumulative depression paths, along which consumption eventually decreases to zero. Using (8), (9), and the market clearing conditions, we obtain

$$\frac{\dot{\lambda}}{\lambda} + \frac{\dot{m}}{m} - \rho = -v'(m)c^{\gamma} + \theta. \tag{17}$$

This equation implies that cumulative depression paths ($\lim_{t\to+\infty} c(t) = 0$) satisfy the transversality condition given in (10) so long as $\theta < 0$. Accordingly they are admissible paths if $\theta < 0$. By contrast, when $\theta > 0$, we must eliminate them as perfect foresight paths on the ground that they violate (10).

Finally, consider cumulative prosperity paths, where consumption is monotonically and indefinitely increasing ($\lim_{t\to+\infty} c(t) = +\infty$). If $c(0) > c_*$, then the economy experiences cumulative prosperities and the consumption Euler equation (15) generates a sequence of $c(t)$ such that $c(T) = \bar{y}$ at some finite point in time T. However, when the sequence reaches point P, the economy cannot increase consumption any more and has to move to point P' with a discontinuous jump. This behavior violates the Euler equation. Thus, cumulative prosperity paths can be ruled out as perfect foresight paths.

To sum up, monetary expansion ($\theta > 0$) guarantees the uniqueness of perfect foresight path, while monetary contraction ($\theta < 0$) yields cumulative depressions with persistent deflation. It should be noted that our model generates the indeterminacy of equilibrium paths when $\theta < 0$, although cumulative prosperity paths are ruled out as perfect foresight paths. There exists a continuum of perfect foresight equilibria indexed by initial consumption, $c(0)$, satisfying $0 < c(0) < c_*$. All equilibrium paths starting within the above interval converge to the zero consumption point. If agents take a pessimistic view of the future, then the result is what agents have expected; the economy actually goes through continuous and permanent deteriorations. Such phenomena are termed "self-fulfilling prophecies" in the framework of perfect foresight.[8]

4. Policy Implications

We shall inquire into policy implications. The effects of monetary and fiscal policy are analyzed in turn. Judging from the above, there is no doubt that the expansive monetary policy is effective in the sense that it can eliminate cumulative depressions and restore determinacy. In addition, the importance of the effect of monetary policy on the real sector cannot be overemphasized. Taking the derivative of (16), we can obtain

$$\frac{dc_*}{d\theta} = \frac{1}{\gamma v'(m)} \left[\frac{\rho + \theta}{v'(m)}\right]^{(1/\gamma)-1} > 0. \tag{18}$$

This result implies that a monetary expansion leads to a rise in consumption. The consumer decide to increase consumption, since the inflationary pressure increases the cost of holding money.

We turn next to fiscal policy. Consider a situation that the government balances its budget at each point in time and a source of revenue is the lump-sum taxes. Although the consumption dynamics (15) remains unaltered, the government budget constraint becomes

$$\tau + g = \theta m_s, \tag{19}$$

where g denotes government purchases in real terms. Similarly, the level of economic activity, or the commodity market equilibrium changes to

$$y_s = c_d + g. \tag{20}$$

We are now ready to consider the multiplier effect of government spending by restricting our analysis to the stationary state. This restriction is justified by the execution of expansive monetary policy. From (16), the increase in government spending causes no change in consumption; $dc_*/dg = 0$. There are two main reasons for this result. One is that the increase in taxes through lump-sum taxation is exactly compensated with the increase in dividends, which is due to the increase in effective demand. The other is that the commodity market equilibrium is realized by highly flexible quantity adjustments. We can therefore confirm the *balanced budget multiplier* result; $dy_s/dg = 1$. This means that the change in aggregate demand is equal to the change in government spending.

[8]Extensive discussions are given in Farmer (1996).

Taking the above result into consideration, one remark should be made concerning the achievement of production efficiency. In general, the efficient level of output is not always equal to effective demand in our model, for example, $c_* < y_e$. In this case, the economy suffers social losses from the inefficient production. Thus policymakers would be requested to perform government spending at all times; strictly speaking, $g(t) = y_e - c_*$ for all t. In this respect, fiscal policy is also necessary and effective in improving social welfare.

It should be concluded, from what has been said above, that we need a policy mix, which is the combination of expansive monetary policy to ensure the determinacy of equilibrium and discretionary fiscal policy to realize the efficiency of production.

5. Concluding Remarks

In this chapter, we have constructed an effective demand model in the MIUF framework. Two features are worth noting in our model. The first one is the occurrence of cumulative depressions under monetary contractions ($\theta < 0$), which mean lump-sum taxation. On cumulative depression paths, the level of economic activity gradually decreases to naught, and hence these circumstances make persistent reductions in dividends paid out to the consumer. If agents expect that the economy as a whole will follow the path converging to zero consumption, the expectation of lower economic activity makes it optimal for any individual agent to make pessimistic decisions that are consistent, in aggregate, with the anticipated path.

The second one concerns the indeterminacy of equilibrium paths. This is caused by a multiplicity of equilibrium paths. To explain the problem of indeterminacy, we need the animal spirits explanation, which is preferred in recent literature and connected with Keynes's idea: see, for example, Farmer (1996). The animal spirits of economic agents select one from among multiple paths.

Finally, we considered policy implications. The expansive monetary policy ($\theta > 0$) can eliminate cumulative depressions by inducing inflation. In addition, it enables the economy to establish the determinacy of equilibrium. We must draw further attention to the fact that the level of effective demand does not always correspond with that of efficient output($c_* \neq y_e$) in our framework. In this case, policymakers would be requested to perform government spending. We therefore conclude that fiscal policy is also effective.

References

[1] Bénassy, J.-P. (1993). Nonclearing markets: Microeconomic concepts and macroeconomic applications. *Journal of Economic Literature*, **31**, 732–761.

[2] Böhm, V. (1978). Disequilibrium dynamics in a simple macroeconomic model. *Journal of Economic Theory*, **17**, 179–199.

[3] Brock, W. A. (1974). Money and growth: The case of long run perfect foresight. *International Economic Review*, **15**, 750–777.

[4] Brock, W. A. (1975). A simple perfect foresight monetary model. *Journal of Monetary Economics*, **1**, 133–150.

[5] Calvo, G. A. (1983). Staggered prices in a utility-maximizing framework. *Journal of Monetary Economics*, **12**, 383–398.

[6] Farmer, R. E. A. (1996). *The Macroeconomics of Self-Fulfilling Prophecies*. Cambridge, MA: MIT Press.

[7] Flaschel, P. (1999). On the dominance of the Keynesian regime in disequilibrium growth theory: a Note. *Journal of Economics*, **70**, 79–89.

[8] Friedman, M. and Schwartz, A. J. (1963). Monetary History of the United States, 1867-1960. Princeton: Princeton University Press

[9] Gordon, R. J. and Wilcox, J. A. (1981). Monetarist Interpretations of the Great Depression: An Evaluation and Critique. In K. Brunner (Ed.), *The Great Depression Revisited* (pp. 49–107). Boston: Martinus Nijhoff Publishing.

[10] Gray, J.A. (1984). Dynamic instability in rational expectations models: An attempt to clarify. *International Economic Review*, **25**, 93–122.

[11] Hamilton, J. D. (1987). Monetary factors in the Great Depression. *Journal of Monetary Economics*, **19**, 145–169.

[12] Honkapohja, S. and Ito, T. (1982). Disequilibrium dynamics with monetarist price expectations. *Economics Letters*, **9**, 69–75.

[13] Mishkin, F. S. (1978). The Household Balance Sheet and the Great Depression. *The Journal of Economic History*, **38**, 918–937.

[14] Obstfeld, M. (1984). Multiple Stable Equilibria in an Optimizing Perfect-Foresight Model. *Econometrica*, **52**, 223–228.

[15] Obstfeld, M. and Rogoff, K. (1983). Speculative Hyperinflations in Maximizing Models: Can We Rule Them Out? *Journal of Political Economy* **91**, 675–687.

[16] Olney, M. L. (1999). Avoiding Default: The Role of Credit in the Consumption Collapse of 1930. *The Quarterly Journal of Economics*, **114**, 319–335.

[17] Perko, L. (1996). *Differential Equations and Dynamical Systems* (Second edition). New York: Springer-Verlag.

[18] Picard, P. (1983). Inflation and Growth in a Disequilibrium Macroeconomic Model. *Journal of Economic Theory*, **30**, 266–295.

[19] Romer, C. D. (1990). The Great Crash and the Onset of the Great Depression. *Quarterly Journal of Economics*, **105**, 597–624

[20] Sidrauski, M. (1967). Rational Choice and Patterns of Growth in a Monetary Economy. *American Economic Review*, **57**, 534–544.

[21] Temin, P. (1976). Did Monetary Forces Cause the Great Depression? W W Norton: New York

INDEX

A

B

C

H

I

J

K

L

M

N

O

P

Q

R

S

T

U

V

W

Y

Z